Anabaptism
and
Mission

Anabaptism and Mission

Edited by
Wilbert R. Shenk

Institute of Mennonite Studies (IMS)
Missionary Studies, No. 10

HERALD PRESS
Scottdale, Pennsylvania
Kitchener, Ontario
1984

Library of Congress Cataloging in Publication Data
Main entry under title:

Anabaptism and mission.

    (Missionary studies; no. 10)
    Bibliography: p.
    Includes index.
    1. Anabaptists—Missions—Addresses, essays, lectures.
I. Shenk, Wilbert R.   II. Series.
BV2498.A53   1984   266´.43   84-12863
ISBN 0-8361-3367-6 (pbk.)

Contents

Introduction

The justification for this volume rests on three considerations. First, we offer this collection of essays as an alternative "reading" of mission. Virtually all mission history and theology has been presented from the viewpoint of the dominant ecclesiastical traditions. We believe fresh perspectives can be opened up through an alternative approach. Second, we are committed to encouraging conversation among the various Christian traditions. This represents a modest contribution to that larger discussion. Third, the missiological literature from a believers' church stance is not plentiful. This, therefore, is an attempt to identify this limited body of literature in the hope it will encourage further development.

This collection must be set within a wider scholarly context. It is frequently remarked that only in the twentieth century have scholars begun to take seriously the Radical Reformation of the sixteenth century. Anabaptist studies have gained a place in the fields of church history and historical theology over the past two generations.

This movement of "recovery" among scholars received important impetus from Harold S. Bender in his attempt to define the essence of "The Anabaptist Vision" in his 1943 presidential address to the American Society of Church History. Despite the brilliance of Bender's statement, it did not address the missionary nature of the church. By contrast, Franklin H. Littell has argued persuasively that obedience to the Great Commission was definitive for Anabaptists in the sixteenth century. It is as if in the twentieth century the agenda for debate has been set by the

mainline scholars, whereas in the sixteenth century it was the
Radical Reformers who insisted on a broader agenda, including
the mission of the church to the world. Current theology has
largely treated mission as an addendum; the sixteenth-century
Radical Reformers viewed mission as constitutive.

To complete the "recovery" begun by the previous generation we must recover an ecclesiology that takes its apostolic
character seriously. This is required, of course, not only out of historical faithfulness, but biblically and theologically as well.

Thus far three doctoral dissertations have appeared which
treat aspects of Anabaptist understandings of mission: Wolfgang
Schäufele, *Das missionarische Bewusstsein und Wirken der
Täufer*, Neukirchern-Vluyn: Neukirchener Verlag des
Erziehungsvereins GmbH, 1966. Georg Gottfried Gerner, *Der Ge-
brauch der Heiligen Schrift in der oberdeutschen Täuferbe-
wegung*, Heidelberg: University of Heidelberg, 1973. Ray C.
Gingerich, *The Mission Impulse of Early Swiss and South
German-Austrian Anabaptism*, Nashville, Tenn.: Vanderbilt
University, 1980. In addition, mention has already been made of
the significant part the theme plays in the writings of Franklin H.
Littell, especially his *The Origins of Sectarian Protestantism; a
Study of the Anabaptist View of the Church* (New York:
Macmillan and Co., 1964, reprint of *The Anabaptist View of the
Church, an Introduction to Sectarian Protestantism*, Philadelphia:
American Society of Church History, 1952). David A. Thiessen
presented a Master's thesis, *The Church in Mission: Factors That
Contributed to the Sixteenth-Century Anabaptists Being a
Missionary People*, to Regent College, Vancouver, British
Columbia, in 1979.

This collection is long on the cognitive and short on the narrative. Some of the stories of Anabaptist evangelization and missionary expeditions are known but have not been assembled into a
coherent whole. Hans Kasdorf's tabulation hints at the incidents
that make up that chapter. Wolfgang Schäufele's study builds
directly on another body of experience. Work is needed in this
area.

The essays which comprise this volume present a variety of perspectives. But there are certain lineages running through them. In his essay David Shank pays tribute to the crucial influence which Franklin Littell's essay, with which this volume opens, had on his own faith pilgrimage. Harold Bender's "vision" statement has directly influenced the mission thinking of both Hans Kasdorf and Takashi Yamada. The entire volume is bound together by these and other common influences and convictions.

Some of the essays have been published, but others are appearing here in print for the first time. Some retain a somewhat tentative, exploratory character, reflecting the time and occasion in which they originated. They are presented here as stimulus to students who wish to work further in this relatively underworked field.

The missiological task today is to recover some clarity about the mission of the church in our generation. This book is based on the conviction that the Radical Reformers of the sixteenth century had insight into the nature of the church and its mission to the world which will throw needed light on our questions today.

—Wilbert R. Shenk
Elkhart, Indiana

Anabaptism
and
Mission

"You must consider this a sure, eternal, unchanging, and a permanent principle of divine truth in order to fulfill all righteousness, namely: First, to preach the holy gospel of Jesus Christ. Second, to hear eagerly and to understand. Third, heartily to believe this Gospel and to bring forth fruit."

  —Menno Simons, *Complete Writings*, p. 241.

o o o

"And as the king of kings excludes no one, nor does he condemn anyone, but commands his servants to go as his messengers and teach all people, heathen, tribes, languages, and nations as it was done in the times of the apostles. Christ has given himself for all people, for each human being, and has paid therefore for the sins of all, and has taken them away and destroyed them and established eternal salvation. And now, the time has come that the word of God should be proclaimed among all nations as a testimony. . . . That is the service of the true apostle, that he goes out from the covenant of the highest God—to teach all nations and proclaim the good news unto them and to bring the greeting of peace from the mouth of the groom that is the holy gospel of the crucified Christ, the word of eternal life, who has paid for all sins."

  —Melchior Hofmann, *Die Ordonnantie Godts (The Ordinance of God)*.

o o o

"Firstly, Christ said, go forth into the whole world, preach the Gospel to every creature. Secondly, he said, whoever believes, thirdly—and is baptized, the same shall be saved. This order must be maintained if a true Christianity is to be prepared and though the whole world rage against it. Where it isn't maintained there is also no Christian community of God, but of the devil, and thereby of the whole world and all false Christians who alter it in their topsy-turvy order, and fight perversely."

  —Hans Hut (cited in F. H. Littell, *The Origins of Sectarian Protestantism,* p. 111).

o o o

"It is clear that the missionary response was for the Anabaptists the primary alternative to the methods of the magisterial reformers and that the believers' church was an attractive alternative to the *corpus Christianum.* Not coercion but persuasion, not primary emphasis on reforming society but on establishing a new society, not individualistic or sacramental salvation but personal experience and corporate faith were their alternatives."

  —C. J. Dyck (in J. C. Brauer, *The Impact of the Church Upon Its Culture,* University of Chicago Press, 1968, p. 220).

1

The Anabaptist Theology of Mission

Franklin H. Littell

Within the lifetime of many of us the far places of the earth have come within the instant range of a single voice. We may not take an easy comfort in the fact, for sometimes the voice is that of a subtly insidious or openly demanding anti-Christian ideology. Nevertheless, the fact remains with its enormous consequence for good or evil. If the children of darkness seem often more alert to use the instant communication and ready personal association which are provided, let us learn our lessons quickly. Technical progress has compressed the entire globe into a small and intensely explosive unit. The most successful engagement of the War of 1812, from an American standpoint, was fought four months after the signing of the peace treaty; at the end of World War II, a single explosion in the air above a Japanese city had immediate repercussions from the quiet farms of Iowa to the little Tartar villages of the Crimea. We live in an apocalyptic age when a premonition of things to come weighs heavily upon all who think and feel.

Franklin H. Littell, Marion Station, Pennsylvania, is professor of Religion at Temple University (1969-). He was Professor of History of Christianity at Chicago Theological Seminary (1962-69). His most recent publications include The Macmillan Atlas History of Christianity *(Macmillan, 1976); he edited* Religious Liberty in the Crossfire of Creeds *(Ecumenical Press, 1978). This chapter is from a paper read at the Annual Meeting of the American Society of Church History, New York, December 30, 1946. It is reprinted from* The Mennonite Quarterly Review, *Vol. 21, No. 1, 1947.*

In our awareness of imminent catastrophe—a consciousness shared with contemporaries of many faiths, and none—we must not forget another great eschatological fact which assumes its true proportion only in terms of the biblical worldview: *that in our own time Christianity has become the first global religion.* There have been several religions of universal prospect, but only in Christianity do we see the fulfillment of that time of which the prophets dreamed, when people of all races and tongues, all nations and stations and colors, are gathering about the hill of the Lord. The great vision of the fifty-sixth chapter of Isaiah and the promise of our Lord in the twelfth chapter of John are being fulfilled in this day of destiny: "I, when I am lifted up from the earth, will draw all [people] to myself" (Jn. 12:32).

The tremendous meaning of this present fact should enlighten our historical reviews and enliven our hope for time to come. Neither is this general background remote from our study of a special movement, for the Anabaptists were deeply conscious of the race in history between the end of time and fulfillment of God's promise to his people.

There is a more immediate reason for providing such a backdrop to a study of the "evangelical Täufer"[1] and their theology of missions. As Dr. Latourette so clearly portrayed it in his presidential address in 1945, the world expansion of our faith is coming to be more and more a function of the "left wing" of Protestantism. And the map of Christianity shows markedly the signs of a faith less bound by national and racial lines than Christendom of the sixteenth century, both Roman Catholic and Protestant.

> Protestantism is becoming more weighted on the left wing, radical phases of the movement, more ecumenical and less regional, more inclusive and less a sectarian division, and more varied and yet finding a comprehensive unity which permits and even encourages diversity.

> From the radical wing come a majority of the missionaries who are propagating Christianity in other lands. This means that the worldwide Protestantism of the decades ahead is probably to de-

part further from the Christianity of pre-Reformation days than has that of Western Europe and the British Isles. Presumably, the trend will be augmented as the "younger churches" in non-Occidental countries mount in strength.[2]

The greatest century of Christian expansion, 1815-1914, was precisely that time when the lay believer in the congregation, rather than the political economic lord, became the prototype and carrying power of the movement. Rather than continuing to consider that the Christian drama came to an end with the Reformation and that "subsequent events have been akin to curtain calls," whereby "both the scholar and reader are led to the conclusion that in the last four centuries Christianity has been a waning force," we are advised to reorient our thinking in line with the facts.[3]

The way in which the Great Century has authenticated the faith and testimony of the free churches is clearly indicated in the record. The latest full figures of money and personnel going to the field from the various agencies are conclusive tribute to a church life with mobility.[4] We are free to conclude that the maintenance and implementation of a missionary worldview are more a mark of the voluntary religious associations than of the ancient geographical centers of "Christian civilization,"[5] where congregational life is rendered less mobile by intimate collaboration with political and social centers of power. When we come to this point, it is pertinent to remember that Reformation Europe once had its chance to embrace a pattern of free religious association and rejected it.[6] Anabaptism was suppressed in a welter of blood by Roman Catholic and Protestant authorities, among whom the restraint of Adam of Dietrichstein and Philipp of Hesse, who wanted to convert the radicals rather than kill them, provides only slight relief. Both Rome and dominant Protestantism were committed to the medieval parish pattern,[7] and determined to suppress the independent congregational and freely conceived evangel of the party of the Restitution.

The doctrine of classical Protestantism in regard to compulsion must be rather quickly summarized. The concept of the church, in the words of Dr. Bates, "comprehended the entire population of a parish or of a territory, implied infant baptism and coordination with the state system, and tended either toward a rigid absolutism of doctrine and authority . . . or toward a latitudinarian dilution."[8]

It was a continuation of the use of coercion as a method of evanglization, a method in high standing in the church from the beginning of the fourth century until the emergence of the modern idea of Religious Liberty. "Consider coercion as a method of evangelization, for, as a matter of fact, it has had a large place in the history of Christianity. The church has depended upon the support of secular forces for the defense and extension of the faith throughout most of its history. Under Constantine the church made an alliance with political power which has never been completely dissolved."[9]

The Anabaptist quarrel with the Reformers was basically a conflict of concepts of the church. It was not, as Social Democrats have claimed, primarily a matter of class alignment and economic interest.[10] Neither was the conflict due to Anabaptist prophetism, revolutionary violence, and social disorder, except for certain marginal groups which the Täufer[11] repudiated vigorously and completely.[12]

If this review of issues seems too sharply "participative," we may be reminded that the problems are still with us. Karl Holl, in stating a few years ago the traditional Lutheran position in regard to the relation of church and state, concluded: "Therein our German interpretation is sharply different from the sect-influenced English-American. For us cohesion in the State, the furthering and deepening of the national community, count for more than the free movement of individuals."[13]

In the theology of missions itself we have Gustav Warneck's correlative conclusions: although the object of the Christian evangel was originally the whole world.

> In the relationships of today there is, however, an obvious limitation to missionary territory, namely that only that nation is the object of a proper mission where the dominant part of mankind is yet

conformed outside salvation in Christ, and among whom the
Christian Church must first be planted.

> . . . But where the Christian territory embraces already a world be-
> ing Christianized, where there is a School of Christ with an or-
> ganized ministry—also whether the mission has to have its own
> missionary or not—there is no longer a missionary object.[14]

The Anabaptist church polity and theology of missions
assumed a proper significance against this background. They
developed their apologetic and practice in opposition to what they
regarded an unbaptized conformity of the church to national and
political destinies. Their congregations were, as they said, "cut
loose from the world." At a time when dominant Protestantism
was willing to commit 300 little states to a territorial determina-
tion of religion (Augsburg, 1555—"*cuius regio, eius religio*") the
Anabaptists were sending their missioners where they could get a
hearing, for "The earth is the Lord's, and the fulness thereof . . ."
(Ps. 24:1),[15] and no land should be forbidden to the proclamation
of the gospel. Krakau, Aachen, Stockholm, and probably Venice
and Salonica, would appear on our map of the movement. Wan-
derings and exile, for individuals and whole families, fill the annals of the movement. And in their defeat they triumphed; they
confessed themselves strangers and pilgrims upon the earth. They
elaborated a theology of martyrdom.[16] They developed what we
might call a "concept of mobility" in analyzing their doctrines of
the church and its world mission.

The Anabaptists and the Great Commission

We have referred to the Anabaptists as the Party of the Restitution to distinguish them from the Reformers. This reference is not
for mere convenience: *Their commanding theme was, in fact, the
Restitution of the Early Church.*[17] They looked back to the church
before Constantine, and especially to the church at Jerusalem
(Acts 2, 4, 5), as the Golden Age of Christian history. They were
fascinated by the Eusebian history of the power and triumph of
the early church[18]; the growth and victory against incredible odds
made a mysterious record, a sign of the secret workings of God.

But more mysterious still was the fact that in the very hour of her apparent triumph and well-being the church fell into disgrace. The inspired church of the martyrs became the persecuting imperial hierarchy, while the true faith went out into the wilderness. "So after Constantine (it was) above all the communities of heretics which took over and furthered the traditions of the true and precisely for that reason persecuted community of Christ." [19]

The Anabaptists rejected the classical periodization of Christian history. The dark condition of the church was that time from "the Fall" to their own "Restitution" of New Testament doctrine and ordinances. [20] Their criticisms of the imperial Roman religion are their criticisms of the Reformers: Church and state were amalgamated, empty formalism and spiritual slackness prevailed, infants were baptized into Christianity before their understanding was mature enough to give the association any content. Luther and Zwingli were condemned as "half-way men," because they did not introduce a thoroughgoing reformation of church life.

The little group of radicals which broke from Ulrich Zwingli in the fall of 1524 represented a studied effort to restore in full the New Testament life of the early church. [21] It was Zwingli's intention to bring the whole land over to Protestantism, with the visible church order subject to a Christian magistracy. [22] Conrad Grebel and his associates found the Reformer's continual deference to the Great Council extremely distasteful, and they broke away to gather a congregation disciplined only according to the New Testament.

No words of the Master were given more serious attention by his Anabaptist followers than his final command:

> Go ye therefore, and teach all the nations, baptizing them in the name of the Father, and of the Son, and of the Holy Ghost: teaching them to observe all things whatsoever I have commanded you: and, lo, I am with you alway, even unto the end of the world (Mt. 28:19-20).

> Go ye into all the world, and preach the gospel to every creature. He that believeth and is baptized shall be saved; but he that believeth not shall be damned" (Mk. 16:15-16).

These words seemed to point up his whole teaching in a glorious program comprehending the world. The pilgrim, familiar figure of the Middle Ages, was transformed in the fiery experience of the Anabaptists into an effective evangelist and martyr. His wandering footsteps and shedding of blood came to be a determined if not always systematic testimony to the influences of lay missioners who counted no cost too dear to them who would walk in the steps of the Crucified.

In right faith the Great Commission is fundamental to individual confession and to a true ordering of the community of believers. *The Master meant it to apply to all believers at all times.* The proof-text appears repeatedly in Anabaptist sermons and apologetic writings. The large body of court testimonies and confessions of faith recently made available indicate its central significance, and the various series of questions prepared by the authorities for use in court indicate that they expected it to be of prime importance.[23] "Our faith stands on nothing other than the command of Christ (Mat. 28, Marc. 16). For Christ didn't say to his disciples: Go forth and celebrate the Mass, but go forth and preach the Gospel."[24]

The very order of the words convey his intent: "*Firstly*, Christ said, go forth into the whole world, preach the Gospel to every creature. *Secondly*, he said, whosoever believes, *thirdly*— and is baptized, the same shall be saved. This order must be maintained if a true Christianity is to be erected. . . ."[25] The evangel comes first, then faith, and finally baptism; a failure to respect this scriptural sequence indicates a lack of respect for the mind of Christ for his disciples: "Go forth into the whole world and preach the Gospel; whosoever believes and is baptized the same shall be saved; for the preaching of God's word shall go before and not after the baptism, etc."[26]

Baptism of those in whom faith is stirred by the preaching of the gospel is the logical culmination of the mandate which begins, "Go forth. . . ."

Although the polemic of the party of the Reformers was aimed usually at weak spots in the radicals' armor, the authorities

were evidently well aware of the Anabaptist missionary worldview. Justus Menius knew their emphasis and repeated it before
attempting refutation: they teach that "no one shall be baptized
before he learns and believes because Christ said at the last of
Matthew go forth, teach all peoples, and baptize them. *Item*, the
last of Mark: Whosoever believes and is baptized the same shall
be saved. But children cannot be taught anything/therefore they
also cannot believe/ therefore man shall also not baptize them."[27]

Menius denies flatly that the Great Commission was
intended for Christians after the time of the apostles.

> ... the Apostles not only ordered themselves but also through
> their disciples and in their writings, teachings, and examples left
> after them how it should be done with the calling of the Servants
> of the Gospel in the church; namely that the Servant of the Gospel
> does not travel here and there in the land in one church today and
> another tomorrow, preaching one thing in one and another in the
> other. But one servant serves with true industry his assigned
> church and remains with it, leaving other churches to peace and
> tranquility. Thereby each church has its own constituted servant
> and avoids and excludes strange, unlicensed landcombers. . . .[28]

Heinrich Bullinger was also bitterly critical of those who
subverted the social order by leaving their callings to wander in
the land.[29] The Reformers could not understand the apparent in-
stability of one who . . . had a wife and four children, no home
place and was the citizen of no city,[30] for they were concerned to
carry over from medieval civilization those relationships which
made for a stable society. But to the religious radical, driven by
persecution and the Lord's Commission, these were "worldly
concerns." We can hear him say to the authorities of church and
state who tried to hold him fast in his "natural" responsibilities: "I
no longer live but Christ in me and the world crucified in me."[31]

A missionary community

Although believer's baptism (*Spättaufe, Erwachsenentaufe*) was
not the heart of the argument, still it became a ready mark of
those who stood firm in the faith at the cost of persecution.
"Standing still" was a sign of cowardice, in the opinion of the

chief leaders of the Anabaptist movement.[32] The Great Commission was the stock argument for the use of the sign. The Article on Baptism in the Five Articles (c.1547), a Confession of Faith and second most important document of the Hutterians, found its cornerstone in Matthew 28 and Mark 16.[33] Hans Hut, foremost missioner of the South German Brethren, used a standard formula as he baptized hundreds: He told them to obey the commandments, preach the gospel, and baptize others in the Great Commission.[34] "The word which stands in Mark 16 had moved him to preach, namely, that preaching was first, afterwards faith, and thirdly baptism. And man must let the word of the Lord stand. (He is) not to do anything apart from it, (and) also shall depart neither to the right nor to the left, according to the last of Matthew that one shall first teach and afterwards baptize."[35]

The evidence from other groups and leaders is of a kind. The freely spoken evangel was the moving force in a complete reworking of the Old Man, whose crucifixion and rebirth in faith were sealed by the sign. Only those of mature judgment, passed through a crucial and transforming adult experience, could rightly be let through the door into a responsible covenantal relation to God and his fellows, for the strenuous life of a Christian wanderer and martyr is no child's play (*kein kinderspiel!*).[36]

The Anabaptist missionary impulse was crippled by persecution among the South Germans and Swiss and by prosperity among the Dutch Mennonites. Only two or three of the famous Martyr Synod which met in Hans Denck's house in Augsburg, August 20, 1527, lived to see the fifth year of the movement. (This meeting could as well be termed a "Missionary Synod" as "Martyr Synod," for the outstanding leaders of that wing of the movement were all there and divided the land for systematic cultivation.)[37] But among the Hutterites, where some provisional peace was enjoyed for a season, a highly ordered and well-supported missionary work was maintained. Their rich epistolary literature, in which we see again the faith and style of communication of the early church, has been analyzed by Dr. Robert Friedmann. He has listed about four hundred epistles and similar

writings, composed by seventy-five to eighty writers. "Of these
writers, about half (that is forty) were martyrs, having been executed by fire or sword. Most of them were ministers of the word
(*Diener des Wortes*) or missionaries (*Sendboten*)."[38]

, The richest period of all was the so-called Golden Era under
the Elder (*Vorsteher*) Peter Walpot, 1565 to 1578, just before the
Jesuit reaction scattered the faithful in Moravia and drove a small
remnant to a new frontier home. Some of the writings are naively
winsome, and all indicate a lay faith of very high order.

*The Anabaptists looked for the triumph of the true faith by
the Pauline missions-method*, and they knew the ground of their
opposition to the establishment. The brother, Veith Uhrmacher,
many years in a Salzburg dungeon "for the sake of God's truth,"
reported his conversation with Roman Catholic priests who came
to convert him. They said, "Saint Peter says, 'be willing to give account.' Upon which I said, 'What shall I say? You are prosecutor
and judge all in one person. What you cannot decide, constables
and hangmen have to carry out in your place. You tell it to the
prince, the prince tells it to the judge, the judge tells it to the
constable, and the constable tells it to the hangman. He then
finishes up the case. He is your high priest, he helps you to win
the field!' "[39]

The proof that the so-called Christians (*vermainten Christen*)
were not truly Christian was in their use of compulsion in matters
of faith.[40] The true Christian is fighting a different battle with different weapons from those of the world. "The angel with the
sword in the mouth indicates that for us Christians also the sword
does not belong in the hand, but in the mouth—namely, the
sword of the Spirit."[41]

The martyr church is able to establish its place in history in
terms of its suffering.[42] It is the wolf which drives others: the
sheep is a poor defenseless beast. The Bible, which tells of the
Good Shepherd, frequently calls his flock "the sheep." "By sheep
Christians alone were meant. A sheep is a meek, weaponless, submissive beast, that has no other defence for itself than to run as
long as it can and may. And it resembles the governance of the

sword not at all, as little as a sheep resembles a wolf or lion."[43]

The Anabaptists made much of the struggle and suffering in Hebrews 11:33-38, and the analogy between baptism and death ("blood-baptism"), in restoring the eschatology and martyr theology of the early church. "And there are three that bear witness in earth, the spirit, and the water and the blood: and these three agree in one" (1 Jn. 5:8).[44] Martyrdom was their carrying power, their triumph beyond obvious defeat, their final long pilgrimage free from the world and its particularisms.

Accepted by the common people but savagely persecuted by the authorities, driven to death and exile by the enemies of the Restitution of New Testament church life, the Anabaptists did not lose their faith that the Master was gathering his people from the far corners of the earth and that in his own good time God would give them the kingdom.

2

The Anabaptist Understanding of the Good News

Cornelius J. Dyck

Sixteenth-century Anabaptism was part of a larger movement of protest outside classical Protestantism. In 1941 Roland H. Bainton called this larger movement the *left wing* of the Reformation, with Luther the center and Roman Catholicism the *right wing*. He listed the emphasis of the left wing as a strong ethical concern, primitivism—a desire to return to the patterns of the early church, a heightened sense of eschatology, anti-intellectualism, and complete separation of church and government.[1]

In the Menno Simons Lectures of 1954, Franklin H. Littell gave fresh currency to the term *free church* as most appropriate for this movement which, alongside the parish system of medieval Catholicism and the territorial system of the Reformers, was a voluntary gathering of convinced believers free from cultural, political, or social coercion. Among the marks of the free church he listed voluntaryism, religious liberty, consensus, spiritual resistance to evil, missionary concern, and discipline and binding community.[2] His discussion of the free church heritage helped im-

Cornelius J. Dyck in professor of Anabaptist and Sixteenth Century Studies at Associated Mennonite Biblical Seminaries, Elkhart, Indiana. This chapter is the text of an address presented to the First Asia Mennonite Conference at Dhamtari, M.P., India, in October 1971, when he was executive secretary of Mennonite World Conference.

measurably in relating implications from the sixteenth- to-twentieth-century issues and concerns.

More recently Donald F. Durnbaugh brought together in book form a growing discussion of the term *believers' church,* which he characterizes as "the covenanted and disciplined community of those walking in the way of Jesus Christ. Where two or three such are gathered, willing also to be scattered in the work of their Lord, there is the believing people."[3] This is not intended as a polemical term, as though all others were unbelievers, but as a description of the uniqueness of the movement. A parallel usage, for example, would be the Reformed church which would not argue that all others are unreformed, or the Orthodox church that all others are unorthodox. Believers' church is a broader term than Anabaptism, also including movements such as the Waldensians of the twelfth century and the Disciples of Christ of the twentieth century. Durnbaugh summarizes its characteristics in five chapters with the following titles: "Discipleship and Apostolicity," "Mission and Evangelism," "Church and State," "Mutual Aid and Service," and "Sectarian and Ecumenical."

In 1967 a study conference was held in Louisville, Kentucky, on the theme *The Concept of the Believers' Church.* The proceedings were published.[4] In chapter 12, "A People in the World: Theological Interpretation," John H. Yoder lists the following as marks by which to test the faithfulness of the church of Jesus Christ: a sense of mission, holy living, brotherly love, witness, and the cross.[5]

All of these writings are in essential agreement on the marks of the faithful church, though supplementing each other on various details. Sixteenth-century Anabaptism was a diverse and heterogeneous movement, with many charismatic and independent leaders and radical congregationalism. We think, for example, of the various hermeneutical emphases from Melchior Hofmann's Spirit versus letter, to Hans Denck's inner versus outer Word, to Pilgram Marpeck's Old Testament-as-promise and New Testament-as-fulfillment approach of the Swiss Brethren, and the hermeneutical circle or reading the Bible together in the con-

gregation approach of the Brethren. But the preceding interpretations of the genius of Anabaptism *viz.* free church, *viz.* believers'
church do provide a background norm against which we can discuss their understanding of the good news. Yet we must recognize
that it is a long step from the sixteenth century to the present,
from translating a great vision into reality, past or present.
Perhaps the term *believers' church* can help span these 450 years
of history more readily than the more historically conditioned
term *Anabaptist*.

The possibility of holiness

Sixteenth-century Anabaptist witness often began at the point of
personal morality. To follow Christ meant to adopt a disciplined,
almost ascetic style of life. Public and private morality was no
more corrupt than it is today, but secularism had not yet
developed as the great catch-all for the irreligious; everybody was
in the church. In Germany, Luther's emphasis on salvation by
faith instead of works had lifted the controls of the medieval
penance system. Private conscience and civil law were to take its
place under the gospel. "The Word will do it," he believed. But
the Word was interpreted as teaching the impossibility of escape
from sin, making grace people's only option. And so, half jokingly,
Luther once said, "sin bravely" in order that grace may abound.
Medieval work-righteousness was to be abolished forever.

The biggest obstacle to holiness, however, was the
Reformers' acceptance of the medieval social structure which
made church and state coterminous. Neither Luther nor Zwingli
could bring themselves to the founding of a church of believers
only, though both considered it. In his *German Mass* of 1526, for
example, Luther wrote: "They who seriously want to be Christians and want to confess the Gospel in word and deed, these
ought to inscribe their names in a book and assemble in a house
by themselves for purposes of prayer, the reading of Scripture, the
administration of baptism, the reception of the sacrament and to
engage in other Christian activities . . . but I neither can or may
as yet set up such a congregation; for I do not as yet have the

people for it. If, however, the time comes that I must do it, so that I cannot with a good conscience refrain from it then I am ready to do my part."[6]

At another point he wrote: "When they [the Anabaptists] look at us and see the offensive defects with which Satan distorts our churches then they deny that we are a Church and they are unable to lift themselves over this.... Whatever remains of sin this verily offends these spiritual Donatists ... but it does not offend God, seeing that for the sake of faith in Christ He excuses it and forgives."[7]

Martin Bucer, the Strassburg Reformer who was much more open to Anabaptism than Luther, wrote: "Their [the Anabaptists] most pointed argument is always this that we keep house so badly; with this argument they lead astray many people. God help us, so that one day we may be able to take this argument away from them, yes from our own conscience and from the Lord our God."[8] And at another time he said: "The magistrates are rather coarse and carnal men, and the preachers are very neglectful; many of them frequently get drunk. Since the Lords and the council-men are that kind of people ... they drive the poor people away with their wild way of life [mit irem überbolderen]. The plain man cannot bring himself to recognize the Church of Christ among such wild persons, and to distinguish correctly between doctrine and life."[9]

To hear Menno indict the established state church in the following words, then, is no surprise: "Oh, how lamentably is the fair vineyard desolated and how sadly are its branches withered, its walls broken down! The destroying foxes have taken over, the clouds are dry and give rain no longer; there is none to prune or dung it.... O merciful, gracious Father, how long will this great misery continue? Our rulers are like devouring lions and bears.... They who pastor us deceive us. And those who pose as pastors are thieves and murderers of our souls.... Our house is left unto us desolate. For that which was once the church and kingdom of Christ is now, alas, the church and kingdom of Antichrist."[10]

The Anabaptist emphasis on the possibility of holiness must be understood against this background. They did not proclaim a set of dogmas to be believed, but addressed themselves to the immediate life situation with simple and terrible relevancy. Their understanding of the possibility of holiness centered in a new understanding of sin and of grace. Let us look at these briefly.

The nature of sin

The Anabaptists believed in the fall of humankind and in the historical reality of original sin. They did not believe in Augustinian total depravity. The cause of the fall is in the will, not the flesh. The flesh, said Balthasar Hubmaier, was destroyed in the fall and must perish; the soul was damaged and is restored by grace; the spirit remained upright as the image of God in humanity. The second Adam restored what had been destroyed by the first Adam, and more. Since Christ, humankind has had the capacity to be sensitive to good and evil in a way not possible before the fall. Therefore it is better to be in the church of Christ than to have been in paradise.

Original sin, they believed, is not part of the essence of human nature. The fall did not destroy the nature of humankind, though it corrupted it, and this is restored by the finished work of Christ. They distinguished between the consequence of the fall and personal guilt. All suffer death as the judgment of God on the disobedience of the human race. Even children die. But they do not die because of their own sinfulness. Children are the natural children of God; they have not fallen into disgrace because their will has not rebelled against their Creator. God does not create little children only to prepare them for hell. They are born free from *active* sin and guilt by virtue of the atonement. The evil inclination is there, but is not counted against them for Christ's sake until it is expressed in deliberate wrong choices in the mature person.

People can choose between good and evil, but their choices are prone to evil until they have been restored through Christ. This freedom is not simply antinomianism or individualism, but freedom under the guidance of the Holy Spirit. The person in

Christ lives by the love which the Spirit pours into his or her life, making the person eager to do the will of God. The call to holiness is both a command and a promise; the disciple hears the call of God and obeys, but such a person prays for and receives enabling grace to do it. Historically sin is a condition of humankind, but existentially it is an act of will, a rebellion against God deliberately carried out.

The nature of grace

For most Anabaptists, but particularly for Pilgram Marpeck and Balthasar Hubmaier, grace is understood on two levels—the natural knowledge or conscience, by which people know right from wrong and regeneration. In no case is it sacramentally substantive, a "thing," but God coming to people in Spirit and in power. It is never separated from the coming of Christ as Savior and Lord. The possibility of holiness is, consequently, not based simply on following the example of Jesus, but on the work of Christ who sets people free to respond to him.

Regeneration is an inclusive term describing repentance, conversion, and the continuing process whereby the grace of God works an actual transformation in the very nature of the believer. Forensic grace, the declaration of divine justification of the sinner without the sinner's response in declared obedience, declared Hubmaier, makes carnal Christians instead of cross-bearing Christians. Humankind is not simply pronounced righteous, but grows in righteousness under the tutelage of the Holy Spirit.

The beginning of regeneration or salvation is not a confession of sinfulness, Menno said against Luther, but repentance. And he added, "But if you wish to be saved, by all means and first of all, your earthly, carnal, ungodly life must be reformed. For it is naught but true repentance that Scriptures teach.... If you do not repent there is nothing in heaven or on earth that can help you.... We must be born from above, must be changed and renewed in our hearts.... Wherever true repentance and the new creature are not.... there man must be eternally lost."[11]

Conversion means to turn around and start on a new way. It is repentance, the beginning, not the end of faith. Dirk Philips wrote, "No one can be born again or spiritually quickened, and no one can believe the Gospel except he first sincerely repent, as the Lord Jesus Christ himself testifies (Matt. 3:2), for he taught the people repentance first of all and then faith, and so he also commanded his apostles to do."[12]

Repentance is not joyful trust, as Luther described it, but fear and remorse, which alone are the beginning of the Christian life. Fear, said Menno, "is the power which expels, buries, slays, crushes, and destroys the sins of believers, and is the first part of true repentance."[13] This fear is produced by the law. To preach faith first, without repentance, or to preach the gospel without law, is a false faith, attractive only for those who walk "on the broad way."

Preaching the law is a necessary first step to conversion. Pilgram Marpeck wrote, "Without the knowledge of sin which is brought by the law, the sinner is not driven to Christ, the true physician, who alone can heal him with his grace."[14] Hans Denck wrote, "No one can satisfy the demands of the law who does not know and love Christ in truth."[15]

Because of this emphasis on the preparatory role of the law the Reformers often accused the Anabaptists of work-righteousness. But they replied that feeding the hungry and clothing the naked was not work-righteousness. Menno wrote, "How miserably the priests have had us poor people by the nose. . . . God be praised, we caught on that all of our works avail nothing, but that the blood and death of Christ alone must cancel and pay for our sins. They strike up a psalm . . . while beer and wine verily run from their drunken mouths and noses. . . . If someone steps up in true and sincere love to admonish or reprove them for this, and point them to Christ Jesus rightly . . . and to show that it is not right for a Christian so to boast and drink, revile and curse; then he must hear from that hour that he is one who believes in salvation by good works, is a heaven stormer, a sectarian agitator, a rabble rouser, a make-believe Christian . . . or an Anabaptist!"[16]

This enabling grace works a change in people whereby the lost image of God is restored. A divine power enters their hearts and lives, making it possible for them to live as they could not live before. The believer becomes a partaker of the divine nature itself, as Dirk Philips wrote, "Now although men become participant in the divine nature, . . . they yet do not become in being and person what God and Christ alone are. On no! The *creature* will never become the *Creator*, and the flesh will never become eternal spirit. . . . But the believers become gods and children of the Most High through the new birth, the impartation and fellowship of the divine nature . . . they . . . will be taken up into glory even as God is in glory. But men are and remain there as creatures, and God alone [is] creator and ruler."[17]

Menno used the analogy of the vine and the branches. Through the new birth the believer is joined to Christ, "so like unto Him, so really implanted into Him, so converted into His heavenly nature. . . . For how can the twig of the vine bear fruit different from that of the vine from which it springs?"[18] He said elsewhere, "For all who are in Christ are new creatures, flesh of His flesh, bone of His bone, and members of His body."[19]

Thus in their understanding of both sin and grace the Anabaptists affirmed the possibility of holiness, the call to holiness, and the command to holiness. Sin was no longer a disease for which there was no cure, since Christ, the Spirit, would always bring fruit in the lives of the faithful. Yet few Anabaptists moved on to teach sinlessness. They were too conscious of the ethical expectations of a righteous and holy God. Sinlessness belonged to God alone.

Jesus as Lord of history

A church-world dualism is basic to Anabaptist thought, brought about internally by the vision of building a church "without spot or wrinkle," and externally by the pressures of persecution. After its initial thrust, Anabaptism soon withdrew geographically, whenever possible, and theologically into quietism. With this came a quick loss of missionary zeal, except among the Hutterites, where it continued to the early seventeenth century.

Because of these developments the Hutterite movement has most frequently been interpreted as rejecting all responsibility, or even concern, for the social and political affairs of their environment. Their citizenship, they were said to believe, was in heaven, and the church, the new community of grace, was a colony of heaven on earth. At the heart of this stance was nonresistance, it is believed. Coercion is necessary in sinful society, but outside of the perfection of Christ, so the withdrawn church becomes the new frame of reference for the life of the believer. Sometimes believers must be hostile to the world because they see it as a personification of the devil. Sometimes they are simply indifferent to it, but never is the world affirmed as *here*, as a part of the believer's real work; it is always *over there*, separate from the things that really count in a believer's life.

This picture may well be a distortion of the evidence from the sources, at least of the first generation. The Anabaptists did not hold changing society as their primary goal, except for the radicals of Münster. They had no programmatic vision for a new social order into which they wished to lead Europe. They were conscious of the evil in people and society and had no utopian vision. But they did not write off humankind because of it. They did propose the church of true believers as a bold new social option, but they also admonished rulers to live by their own professed standards of law and justice.

Two texts which were used to justify their total concern for humankind are, "The Spirit of the Lord is upon me, because he has anointed me to preach good news to the poor. He has sent me to proclaim release to the captives and recovering of sight to the blind, to set at liberty those who are oppressed, to proclaim the acceptable year of the Lord" (Lk. 4:18-19); "Go therefore and make disciples of all nations, baptizing them in the name of the Father and of the Son and of the Holy Spirit, teaching them to observe all that I have commanded you; and lo, I am with you always, to the close of the age" (Mt. 28:19-20).

Their message and action contained an eschatological

passion which interpreted the present in the light of that which was about to come. Yet the kingdom had already come in Christ and his body, the church, which was to be Exhibit A of the new age. For this conviction Luther charged them with wanting to make a heaven on earth; if this were heaven, he said, we would all be angels; if hell, devils; but it is earth and we are both sinner and saint at the same time. They rejected Luther's belief that the Sermon on the Mount was meant for another age because they believed that this new age was here.

Suffering

One of the signs of the new age was the suffering to which the believers were called. In his *Foundation Book* of 1539 Menno wrote: "Therefore comfort not one another with senseless comfort and uncertain hope, as some do who think that the Word will yet be taught and observed without the cross. I have in mind those who know the Word of the Lord, but do not live according to it. Oh no! it is the Word of the cross and will in my opinion remain that unto the end.... Therefore, tear from your hearts the harmful thought that you may hope for another time, lest you be deceived by your vain hopes. I have known some who waited for a time of freedom, but did not live to see it. Had the apostles and fathers waited for it, the Gospel of the kingdom would to this day have been silent, and the Word of the Lord unpreached."[20]

Dirk Philips wrote much about "the last and perilous times," of which false teachers are a sign, as are suffering and the cross. Suffering was the mark of the faithful church; wherever believers were willing to endure hardship for the sake of the kingdom, there Christ was Lord and the kingdom was at hand.

Powerlessness

Another sign of the new age was the willingness of the believers to be powerless. History was in the hands of God. God ruled the nations with justice. All evil would ultimately receive its judgment. Since the Anabaptists really believed this, they did not need to coerce people to make history come out right. They were content to leave that concern in the hand of God.

Conrad Grebel said, "True Christian believers are sheep among wolves, sheep for the slaughter; they must be baptized in anguish and affliction, tribulation, persecution.... Neither do they use worldly sword or war, since all killing has ceased with them—unless, indeed, we would still be of the old law."[21]

Menno Simons added, "All who are moved by the Spirit of Christ know of no sword but the Word of the Lord..., Our weapons are not weapons with which cities and countries may be destroyed.... Iron and metal spears and swords we leave to those who, alas, regard human blood and swine's blood about alike."[22]

Nonresistance did not mean "please leave me alone," but a turning of the other cheek, vigorous confrontation of enemies, trying to win even the executioner on the way to the stake. It was what George Fox later called the *Lambs War*. They refused to take the cross at the short end and make a dagger out of it because love, not violence, was the new key to life.

Economic sharing

Another sign of the new age was the rejection of property as an end in itself. While Hutterian communalism was the most visible evidence of this, it is found in the writings of most of the leaders. They lived lightly. Jesus, the Lord of history, had promised to care for them (Mt. 6:33). In 1538 George Schnabel of Hesse wrote: "Economic practices in the congregation of believers are thus, that everyone who has food and clothing to spare shares it with his poor brother."[23] Another said that when we pray "Our Father" we say thereby that what we have is not mine but *ours* under God.[24] Another wrote, "The true Christian should not possess so much on the whole earth as a place on which to set his foot."[25] This did not mean Christians could not own property, but that they held it in trust from God for the use of all in need.

Balthasar Hubmaier wrote, "Concerning community of goods, I have always said that everyone should be concerned about the needs of others, so that the hungry might be fed, the thirsty given to drink, and the naked clothed. For we are not lords of our possessions, but stewards and distributors. There is certainly no one who says that another's goods may be seized and made common; rather, he would gladly give the coat in addition to the shirt."[26]

Mission vision   *apoc, context?*

Another sign of Anabaptists' belief in Jesus as Lord of history was their missionary concern. The time was short; to them had been given a sacred trust. The new age was at hand in its fullness to make all things new. Hans Hut, one of the greatest witnesses, said, "The last and most dangerous time of this world has now come upon us."[27] Jacob Hutter wrote, "One child of God wakes another and thus many are brought to God."[28] Hans Schmidt wrote from his prison cell, "God has revealed His counsel to the Church. The primary and greatest task is to bring this counsel to the unknowing nations . . . to proclaim repentance to the sinner . . . so that at the last there may be no excuse."[29]

Menno wrote, "My heart trembles in me; all my joints shake and quake when I consider that the whole world, lords, princes, learned and unlearned people . . . are so estranged from Christ Jesus and from evangelical truth and from eternal life."[30]

He said elsewhere, "Therefore, we preach, as much as possible, both by day and by night, in houses and in fields, in forests and wastes, hither and yon, at home or abroad, in prisons and in dungeons, in water and in fire, on the scaffold and on the wheel. . . . For we feel His living fruit and moving power in our hearts. . . . We could wish that we might save all mankind from the jaws of hell, free them from the chains of their sins, and by the gracious help of God add them to Christ by the Gospel of His peace."[31]

Believers were the building stones of the new age, the vindication of the cross of Christ, the climax of the plan of God since time began. And so the Anabaptists said, in effect: "All time is in the hand of God, our past, our future, and the present moment. His kingdom is coming and is here. Join it while there is time. Repent and be baptized into the true church of believers." Suffering (the cross), powerlessness in the midst of a violent society, the free sharing of possessions, and a passion for the lost were not their works, but the fruit of the Spirit who was making all things new.

The New Testament church restored

At the heart of this newness was the church of believers. The Anabaptists of the sixteenth century wanted to restore the life, faith, and even practice of the early church. For Menno Simons this meant six things:[32]

(a) An unadulterated, pure doctrine. Deuteronomy 4:6; 5:12; Isaiah 8:5; Matthew 28:20; Mark 16:15; John 8:52; Galatians 1.

(b) A Scriptural use of sacramental signs. Matthew 28:19; Mark 16; Romans 6:4; Colossians 2:12; 1 Corinthians 12:13; Mark 14:22; Luke 22:19; 1 Corinthians 11:22,23.

(c) Obedience to the Word. Matthew 7; Luke 11:28; John 7:18; 15:10; James 1:22.

(d) Unfeigned, brotherly love. John 13:34; Romans 13:8; 1 Corinthians 13:1; 1 John 3:8; 4:7,8.

(e) A bold confession of God and Christ. Matthew 10:32; Mark 8:29; Romans 10:9; 1 Timothy 6:13.

(f) Oppression and tribulation for the sake of the Lord's Word. Matthew 5:10; 10:39; 16:24; 24:9; Luke 6:28; John 15:20; 2 Timothy 2:9; 3:12; 1 Peter 1:6; 3:14; 4:13; 5:10; 1 John 3:13.

This desire for *restitution* instead of *reformation* was based on their despair over the possibility of effectively reforming the church as they saw it all around them, but even more on their understanding of the Bible as authoritative for faith and life. The church in the Bible was not some embryonic beginning which was meant to develop institutionally and doctrinally through the centuries to come; it was the norm for all ages, the one certain reliable point of reference. To depart from it was to depart from the intention of Christ, the head of the church, his body.

Baptism

The way to be a believers' church, the Anabaptists were certain, was to admit only true believers into it's membership. They needed to be persons who had counted the cost and were able to make a commitment of will with mature judgment and responsibility. That alone would be sufficient to rule out children, not to speak of biblical teaching about children. First comes hearing, said Hubmaier, then believing, and then baptism. The 1527 Schleitheim Confession said, "Baptism shall be given to all those who have learned repentance and amendment of life, and who believe truly that their sins are taken away by Christ, and to all those who walk in the resurrection of Jesus Christ."[33]

No child could "walk in the resurrection." Jesus himself had been thirty at baptism and set an example for his disciples. Only those who had been born again could enter the kingdom. "One seals an envelope only when one knows the content," said Leonard Schiemer. Menno wrote, "It is clear that the regenerate do not willfully live in sin, but through faith and true repentance were buried by baptism into the death of Christ, and arose with Him to a new life."[34] Baptism gives a new identity to the believer, with all other identities second. It was a sign of hope, of victory over evil, an eschatological sign that the new believer would be a participant in the Lord's victory on the last day.

Admonition

But baptism was more; it was also a sign, an affirmation by the congregation of believers that they recognized the gift of the Spirit in a member, and it assured that person that he or she was within the covenanted people of God. Because Satan does his best to bring believers to fall, those being baptized asked, as part of the ceremony of baptism, for the help and admonition of the others, that they would warn them when they saw them err and submit to their discipline to bring them back to the kingdom if they sinned. The rule of Christ was clearly spelled out in Matthew 18:15-18. So Conrad Grebel had written to Thomas Müntzer in 1524: "Go forward with the Word and establish a Christian church with the help of Christ and his rule, as we find it instituted in Matt. 18:15-18 and applied in the Epistles."[35]

Discernment

All of life was really a baptism for the Anabaptists, and discipline was required for the narrow way. The true church was a community of disciples. True, Jesus had walked the way for them, but truth was not a formula; it was a person to be followed, a way to tread in *participation* with, rather than *imitation* of Christ. Menno Simons said, "For this is the greatest delight and joy of believers: that they in their weakness may walk and live according to the will and Word of the Lord."[36]

The will of God could be known by testing the witness of the Spirit with the brotherhood. The Spirit was able to speak more clearly through the interacting process of a group than it could to one alone, or at least the witness of the Spirit could be more accurately understood together. Franklin H. Littell quotes Hans Umlauft on this as follows: "How can there be a Christian community where no Christian order and command is [maintained], with separation, the ban, discipline, brotherly love and other [practice]; further that one after the other may speak openly, give of his gifts and insights freely before the people at the appointed time, 1 Corinthians 14:30-31?"[37]

Menno Simons wrote in his *Meditation on the Twenty-fifth Psalm:* "Then if I err in some things, which by the grace of God I hope is not the case, I pray everyone for the Lord's sake, lest I be put to shame, that if anyone has stronger and more convincing truths he through brotherly exhortation and instruction might assist me. I desire with my heart to accept it if he is right. Deal with me according to the intention of the Spirit and Word of Christ."[38]

This was more than democracy; it was disciplined listening to each other, courageous but loving admonition as members of one body. The will of God could be known sufficiently to live obediently.

Summary

We have discussed the Anabaptist understanding of the good news under three headings: first, the possiblity of holiness, with reference to the nature of sin and grace; second, Jesus as Lord of history, with reference to suffering, powerlessness, rejection of property as an end in itself, and missionary concern; and third, the New Testament church restored, with reference to baptism, admonition, and discernment. Within Anabaptism the first concern gathered up private and public morality, giving a clear witness where it was sorely needed; the second concern centered in the Christian hope and its implications for daily living in this world; the third spoke to the resources God gave in the congregation of believers. Where Christ was obeyed, there the kingdom had come.

That witness was given 450 years ago. It represented, those Anabaptists believed, a witness first proclaimed nearly 2,000 years ago by Christ himself. By the power of the Spirit the apostles became their contemporaries; there was no time lag, no need for apostolic succession to preserve orthodoxy and purity. They lived in the presence of the living Christ.

The moral needs of individuals and society are not too different today from those of the sixteenth century; the need for holiness cries out on every hand. In a time of increasing violence and the potential for total destruction of the human race, the time is *now* to affirm to all who will hear that Jesus is the Lord of history. We all, the church, the nations, are in his hand. And in a time when people are seeking for those who care, for those who can help them make sense out of the experiences of life, the congregation of faithful believers is needed more than ever before. May we be found faithful as we follow where the Spirit leads us.

3

Reformation and Missions: A Literature Survey

John H. Yoder

When Pietism and a series of related "awakenings" had brought about a widespread allegiance on the part of European and North American Protestants to the world missionary enterprise of the church, a new challenge was put to Protestant self-understanding. Protestantism had been looking to the sixteenth century as the age of its origin.

Even those denominations with no sixteenth-century fathers to look back to—Methodists, Congregationalists, Baptists— claimed a share in the heritage of Luther and Calvin. But how could the longtime loyalty to the Reformers be linked with the newfound vision for missions? Why did missions need to be found anew? Why had the Reformers not sent out missionaries? They lived after Columbus and Vasco da Gama, simultaneous with the work of great Catholic missionary orders; why did Protestantism have to await Pietism to bring about actual overseas sending?

John H. Yoder, Elkhart, Indiana, is professor of Theology at University of Notre Dame. Among his writings are Karl Barth and the Problem of War *(Abingdon, 1970),* The Original Revolution *(Herald Press, 1971), and* The Politics of Jesus *(Eerdmans, 1972). This chapter is reprinted by permission of the editor of* Occasional Bulletin of Missionary Research.

Protestant interpretations

The first answer to emerge, the simple one, was that the Reformers did not get around to it. The sixteenth-century Reformation had a sixteenth-century agenda. In any case, the great Protestant fathers need to be saved from later generations' tendencies to hagiolatry; they did enough other great things that we can afford to admit their limits. In this spirit, beginning with Gustav Warneck, the first great historian-interpreter of the modern missionary movement, a charitable yet critical explanation could develop.

Warneck[1] was careful to recognize the Reformers'[2] indirect contribution to missionary renewal in clarifying the substance of the gospel message, in fostering what he called "a mighty testifying Spirit," and in disavowing the crusading attitude toward "the Turk." Nevertheless, the absence of overt missionary thought and of actual sending still stands, and must be explained. Warneck noted numerous reasons:

> 1. The Reformers were preoccupied with the internal reform of the church, in the restoration of proper doctrine and practice.
> 2. The Reformers were almost crushed by external conflict with the Catholic princes; militarily and politically they were on the defensive and had no resources left for outreach.

In addition, the Reformers held that:

> 3. The pope and the Turk being apocalyptic figures, the two forms of antichrist, the shadow of their rebellion was cast over the peoples they dominated, which were all the near neighbors of the Protestant countries. One does not expect the conversion of antichrist.
> 4. The last day was at hand.
> 5. The Great Commission had been given to the apostles and they had discharged it; the church was already everywhere.
> 6. Reformation, when seen as the conversion of the baptized unbelievers within Christendom to the correct evangelical faith, was already the essence of mission.
> 7. The best known colonial-missionary work was a popish, monkish, and Spanish monopoly, disqualified by its association with such sponsors.
> 8. The Germans had no direct contact with heathen peoples; they had no non-Christian neighbors.

Warneck noted that the first two handicaps have obtained in other ages as well without interrupting missionary movement. Nor would considerations 4 or 6 have had an anti-missionary effect if it were not for number 5, which thus becomes relatively the most important. He might have added that points 3 and 8 are partly contradictory.

Warneck's greatest successor, Kenneth Scott Latourette, has taken over Warneck's explanations and added a few more:[3]

> 9. Social power was in the hands of princes who did not care for missions as much as Catholic princes did.
> 10. Protestant nations' budding colonial interests were in the hands of trading companies who considered missionary concerns a waste of resources or even a threat to their income.
> 11. The Protestants had no monks, since, for theological reasons, they had downgraded the idea of a special religious vocation.

If we look back at the entire list, it is somehow not enough. With the exception of point 11, each of these arguments could have applied as well to the Catholics. Catholicism too was undergoing reform, purifying doctrines and clarifying structures; but the renewers and reformers (Erasmus, Ignatius, Trent) made Catholicism more missionary. It is true, as Latourette wrote, that Italy and Spain were not fighting Protestant princes in their homeland; but neither was Scandinavia fighting Catholics. The exceptions balance out. Why were Catholic kings and traders in favor of missions, and their Protestant counterparts not,[4] when according to the standard Reformation concept of vocation the opposite should have been the case? Even the absence of the religious is a strange excuse, for was not the heart of the Protestant message and of its critique of monasticism the distribution of priesthood, vocation, and mission throughout the whole people of God?

The Warneck analysis has called forth touchily apologetic reactions from those who prefer not to relativize the Reformers. One way people have defended the Reformers has been to accept Warneck's vision of the missionary imperative, but to argue that the fathers did better than Warneck knew.[5] In the vast bulk of Luther's writings, for instance, statements can be found which speak of "winning the heathen" to faith in Christ, which seem to call for a sending of some kind. Such statements are largely, but not wholly, subject to the limitation that (see point 6 above) both heathen and sending can be understood as internal to Christendom.

Specifically, Luther saw the possibility that Christian prisoners of war in Turkish hands might convert their captors. Two generations later this grew into the vision that evangelical Slavs in southeastern Europe might win their Turkish rulers, so that the promotion of Protestantism among the Balkan Orthodox can be interpreted as mission to Islam.

If we strip the definition of mission to its root, understanding it as someone being *sent* from somewhere, from one's geographical or cultural home, with a mandate to testify in some other home, and if we strip the literature in favor of the Reformers' missionary vision of its touchy tone, two cases remain. (Warneck knew about both.) Once in 1559 and again in the next century, the Protestant sovereigns of Sweden resumed a ministry to the Lapps, begun before the Reformation, which seems not to have included learning the local language.[6] The other case is the participation of a handful of French Calvinists and Genevans in an attempt to colonize Brazil under the aegis of an adventurer who soon returned to Catholicism, banished some of the Protestants, and killed the rest. Instead of going to the Indians, those who were banished returned to Europe.

Careful reading of the polemic against Warneck seems thus to conclude in his favor.[7] The more *statements* one finds in Luther's writings which would *imply* missionary concern,[8] the clearer is the absence of deeds. When a generation later the Wittenberg theology faculty was actually asked about the matter, and explicitly rejected the idea of sending, no remembered body of Luther tradition existed to stop them. These apologies do, however, add a few further significant elements to the explanation.

12. "The obverse of Luther's faith is the obedience, which leaves it to God to provide the 'open door' for the course of the Word."[9] Obedience does not mean doing something as God's instrument, but keeping hands off so that the work can be all his.

13. All people, including Christians, are basically heathen. "The position of man before God is always and everywhere that of the 'pagan,' even in Christendom; salvation comes for all only through the justification of the godless...."[10] This makes a doctrinal statement of what before was a pastoral one (point 6 above).

14. The Christian church is in the whole world.

This last affirmation states as simple fact what before (point 5) had been the trust that the apostles had done their duty. Werner Elert[11] further explained the absence of formal sending by reference to what he called "the religio-geographical knowledge of the age." He cited a "World Mission Survey" of Philip Nikolai (1597) who compiled extensive data on episcopal sees around the known world, supporting "the firm belief that no land and no nation was without Christians." To call such Christians to Reformation (cf. the Balkan example above) is thus the best way to evangelize the heathen in those same lands.

Another line of response to Warneck turns the tables of the argument. Rather than accepting the positive evaluation of missions which the centuries since Pietism had given us and arguing that the Reformers came closer to it than Warneck saw, Walter Holsten has argued that instead the missionary movement must be judged by the Reformation: "First modern missions must be exposed to the judgment and the claims of the Reformation."[12] The Reformation as the most normative statement of the gospel since the New Testament, and Luther as the most adequate definer of the Reformation, must "challenge and show new ways"[13] to modern missions.

The institutional missionary enterprise stands guilty, Holsten contended, of the theological error of modernity, i.e., of a concern with human deeds and human piety which was already a threat within the Reformation, except in Luther himself. The enterprise thereby falls under the verdict of similarity to Catholicism, the ascetic thrust of which it shares. Even the word *mission* is suspect, as it came from the Jesuits. "Modern missions" concentrate, wrote Holsten, on institutionalizations *(Veranstaltungen)* rather than on propagation *(Ausbreitung)*, on spreading the Christian religion instead of "the gathering of the elect from all peoples and their religions." With regard to each of these dualities Holsten has left us ignorant of how either element can be achieved without the other. In short, the author's preoccupation was to affirm the priority of a correct Lutheran concept of the church as bearer of the "external word of God" and of religious institutions as works of human piety.[14]

After clarifying how the question must be put, Holsten documented numerous statements in Luther about Christians' obligation to communicate their faith to non-Christians they encounter. This might occur if Christians were taken prisoner or their territories occupied by "the Turk." Toward this end, Christians whose territory is likely to be taken should study their catechism, especially the second article.

Holsten's descriptive analysis of Reformation texts then moves on to the other—in his mind less correct—Reformers: Bucer, Zwingli, and Bibliander. Having a less critical view of human wisdom, these earliest Reformed reformers thought both more often and more highly of non-Christian people. Bucer assigned missionary duties to the Christian government, though he made no formal proposals to the governments under which he served. The conversion of Jews had a special place in his eschatology, and he sincerely thought that the legal measures discriminating against Jews in Protestant Europe would help to convert them.

Zwingli and his successor, the Hebraist, Arabist, and comparative religionist Bibliander, developed on the other hand a Renaissance-humanist vision of the essence of all religions, and held that especially the noblest figures of Greco-Roman antiquity had true insights and access to the divine. Election, being a sovereign divine act, cannot be denied to people outside the visible church. A meaningful missionary duty remains: to learn to show Muslims through linguistic and comparative cultural studies how the truths they already hold (i.e., their agreement with Christians) call for the complement of the remaining truths they have not yet heard. This should be especially possible through the Christian prisoners in Turkish lands, whom European traders could visit. Bibliander once tried to persuade the authorities of Augsburg to send him to Egypt for such contacts. Holsten believed the examples of Bucer and Bibliander supported his thesis that formal missionary sending—even as a concept—arose only when reformation was diluted with humanism.

In summary, what has been said here about the official Reformation, as interpreted by its friends,[15] strikes the observer from another continent and another tradition as much by the commonality of its context as by the difference of conclusion. Warneck's pietism is just as genuinely Lutheran as is the neo-Reformation theology of Elert or Holsten. All three presuppose much that other Protestant churches and missiologies would exclude: pedobaptism, state church, identification of the missionary enterprise with specific overseas sending agencies distinct from the church.

Believers' church perspectives

This observation leads one to suspect that a more adequate analysis of why the Reformers were not more missionary might better come from a more distant or more independent cultural perspective. A logical alternative would be the other major Protestant structural option, besides establishment and pietism, namely the believers' church.[16] From this perspective a new set of answers to Warneck's question arises.

15. Subservience to the state and subsequent provincialism.

By entrusting to local government the implementation of reforms in the visible church, the official Reformation[17] committed itself unintentionally to a provincial definition of the church's mission. Their *thought* about church and state was drawn from pre-Reformation models, and therefore dealt ideally with the state *as such* or the universal state of Christendom. But neither the metaphysical definition of the state as such, nor the historical Holy Roman emperor, was accessible to them when it came to applying that theory. When they appealed instead to the *local* state, this introduced an element of provincialism of which they were not at the time self-critically conscious.

Medieval Catholicism had already subjected the church to the state in many ways, but at least the vestiges of universality remained—in the papacy's claims and in the universality of the episcopate. Such vestiges of the church's otherness from the state, and therefore of her universality as transcending a given people, were sacrificed by the Reformers' appeal to the princes.

Much more is involved here than a simple geographic narrowness. There followed as well a concept of the *Volk*, incorporated in its politico-religious authorities, as the subject of religious decision and therefore as the object of missionary proclamation. A nation was Protestant or Catholic, according to the decision of its prince. Thus for Nikolai, the naming of a few Spanish bishops on the coast of South America assured the presence of the church on that continent; the *Land* or *Volk* as a unit was represented in its head. A theory of the *Völker* as objects of mission concern was long to remain important in Lutheran missiology.

16. The disappearance of personal decision.

The counterpart of national unity is the individual's inability to decide for him- or herself whether to be a Christian. Pedobaptism was only the outer, formal sign of the assumed ethnic unity of the visible people of God. The individual was still free to decide whether *truly* to believe—and Luther, like his father Augustine, was no optimist about the relative number of true believers—but authentic personal experience and commitment were not to be a precondition for being a member of the visible Christian community, for baptism or communion. Properly, for the sake of its authenticity, true inner decision must be left hidden, a secret between each person and God. Not until the coming of Pietism was there a call for conscious decision and open expression of it, and then (significantly) in structures which were not called church.

Medieval Christianity of course had long since merged church and society in pedobaptism; yet the repeated criticism by the monastic reforms and the invitation to monastic vocations had kept alive—albeit in unevangelical form—concepts of responsible adult decision and of such adult decisions involving a distinctive life loyalty. With the Reformation's rejection of monasticism the last vestiges of the responsible otherness of Christian commitment were gone. The Christian call at home had no visible social meaning—only the appeal to the already baptized to appropriate inwardly the faith that their fathers had confessed for them in their baptism. No wonder there was no self-evident need or opening to call men and women of other peoples to a faith contrary to that of their birth.

If these factors do help explain the lack of missionary understanding in the official Reformation, then we should expect to find a kind of missionary vision in that branch of the Reformation which challenged those two formal axioms. For there was another side to the Reformation in the sixteenth century, though neither Warneck nor Elert, nor even Latourette[18] nor Gensichen[19] or Neill noted it. The anti-establishment, anti-pedobaptist wing of the Reformation did, as a matter of fact, develop in Luther's lifetime both the theory and the practice of evangelistic sending, proclamation, and church planting,

   —despite the need for internal organization,
   —despite political pressures from outside,
   —despite their seeing the pope and Turk in an apocalyptic
      light,
   —despite their expectation of an early end of the world,
   —despite their ignorance of geography.

Following briefer analyses by Wilhelm Wiswedel[20] and Franklin H. Littell,[21] Wolfgang Schäufele published in 1966 his lengthy Heidelberg dissertation on Anabaptism as a missionary movement.[22] Beginning with the phenomenon of the rapid rise and spread of Anabaptism despite the hostility of both churches and states, both Catholic and Protestant, Schäufele sought explanations in both theory and practice, with special attention to South German sources.

The missionary *consciousness* is analyzed with reference to a vision of history, of the nature and commission of the church, of the place of the Great Commission and of baptism, the eschatological component of evangelism. The analysis of missionary *activity* gives attention to the personality type of the Anabaptist apostle, to the shift from the restless itinerancy of the 1520s to the planned expeditions of the 1540s, to financing, communication tactics, the formulation of the message, baptism and church-planting, lay participation....

The capacity for formal organized sending based in stable home congregations was rare for the Anabaptists, existing only in the Moravian communes; but the same missionary vision, rooted in the same ecclesiology, prevailed where freedoms were fewer and banishment was often one of the modes of sending. The earliest Zürich Anabaptists, when they escaped from prison in March 1526, discussed whether they should go "to the red Indians across the sea."[23] The Moravian missionaries, in addition to roaming the German-speaking territories, went beyond them into Lorraine, Scandinavia, Poland, Italy, and Hungary.

From the official viewpoint, of course, this missioneering was not that at all, but sedition, for the lands the Anabaptists traversed were Christian, with Christian princes and Christian pedobaptism. Since the homeland was already Christianized, sending could apply only beyond its bounds. The Warneck debate within official Protestantism is then only about where those boundaries are and whether any untouched territory remained beyond them.

The Anabaptist originality on the other hand was their rejection ✓ of the Augustinian visible/invisible division which could say at the same time that the bulk of Europe's populace were baptized Christians and that they were not true believers. Consequently, Anabaptists rejected as well the sacramental and institutional practices (pedobaptism and establishment) which maintained the self-evidence of that ecclesiology.[24] The Anabaptists claimed they were rereading the New Testament as their norm, taking as exemplary its description of a missionary, minority, nonestablished church. It could also be said that they were anticipating the age of disestablishment when even the church of Wittenberg or of Lambeth would need to stand without the birthright of the sovereign's support or the birthrights of the sacral village.

4

The Anabaptist Approach to Mission

Hans Kasdorf

The Swedish historian Gunnar Westin points out that beginning with the apostolic era God's *ekklesia* consisted of free independent minority fellowships within Jewish and pagan societies. This *ekklesia* was free from governmental control, separated from the world, voluntary in terms of membership, bound together by a sense of fellowship among its members, submissive to the authority of Scripture in matters of theology and ethics, and strong in missionary outreach.[1] These were precisely the characteristics that captured the attention of the Anabaptists during the Protestant Reformation, as both European and Anglo-American scholars have pointed out.[2]

Their primary objective was not to reform the Constantinian-Theodosian structures of the territorial church, but to restore the primitive-apostolic model of the believers' church with its implicit theology of discipleship under Christ's lordship and explicit evangelistic witness in the power of the Holy Spirit. This led them to unqestioned obedience to the risen Christ's mandate to "make disciples of all peoples" (Mt. 28:19). "No words of the Master," contends Franklin H. Littell, "were given more serious attention

Hans Kasdorf, Fresno, California, is Associate Professor of World Mission at Mennonite Brethren Biblical Seminary. He spent five years of missionary service in Brazil and taught college level languages for fourteen years. He has written Christian Conversion in Context (*Herald Press, 1980*) *and numerous articles.*

by the Anabaptist followers than His final command."[3]

So central was the Great Commission to the total life of the Anabaptists that it became a key factor to enhance their understanding of history and the world, the church and the kingdom, discipleship and witness.

The missionary mandate and radical obedience were considered to be inseparable ingredients for a life of discipleship under Christ's lordship. This found its clearest expression in Anabaptists' engagement in world mission which in turn reflected an advanced concept of a mission strategy.

Mission strategy may be defined as the way and manner in which the church carries out the Lord's command to make disciples. Every strategy must be in harmony with biblical teaching, relevant to the time in which it is used, and effective when applied to mission situations. This implies adequate goals, appropriate time and place, well-defined methods, the right kind of people, and, above all, the dynamic and power of the Holy Spirit, without whom no person can be a witness in this world, as the Lausanne Covenant points out.[4] The Anabaptists firmly believed in this kind of mission strategy. Although these terms were not used, the principles they expressed undergirded the entire Anabaptist mission program. Thus the application of contemporary mission concepts will enhance our understanding of—and appreciation for—the dynamic mission movement of sixteenth-century Anabaptism.

Setting definable goals

The Anabaptists firmly believed that it was significant to observe carefully the order laid down by the Lord in the Great Commission for the sole purpose of making disciples of all peoples: (1) *going* into all the world; (2) followed by *preaching* the gospel to every creature; (3) upon preaching, a sense of *anticipation* that humankind will respond by believing in the gospel; (4) then *baptizing* those who respond by faith, having the promise of being saved; and (5) subsequently *incorporating* the saved into the fellowship of believers, the true Christian church.[5]

The Anabaptists dealt in depth with the concept of making disciples. No other Christian movement between the apostolic era and the modern mission period has articulated and demonstrated more clearly the meaning of discipling than have the Anabaptists. While mainline Reformers rediscoverd the great Pauline term *Glaube* (faith), the Radical Reformers rediscovered the evangelists' word *Nachfolge* (discipleship). People cannot, they maintained, call Jesus Lord unless they are his disciples indeed, prepared to follow him in every way. This was the message they preached, the code they lived by, and the faith they died for. This was a unique message, one of reconciliation and forgiveness. But it was a costly message, one people heard mainly from the Anabaptists. Harold S. Bender (1897-1962) has described the Anabaptist concept of discipleship in these words:

> It was a concept which meant the transformation of the entire way of life of the individual believer and of society so that it should be fashioned after the teachings and example of Christ. The Anabaptist could not understand a Christianity which made regeneration, holiness, and love primarily a matter of intellect, of doctrinal belief, or of subjective "experience," rather than one of the transformation of life. Repentance must be "evidenced" by newness of behavior. "In evidence" is the keynote which rings through the testimonies and challenges of the early Swiss Brethren when they are called to give an account of themselves. The whole life was to be brought literally under the lordship of Christ in a covenant of discipleship, a covenant which the Anabaptist writers delighted to emphasize. The focus of the Christian life was to be not so much the inward experience of the grace of God, as it was for Luther, but the outward application of that grace to all human conduct and the consequent Christianization of all human relationships. The true test of the Christian, they held, is discipleship.[6]

The missionary objectives emerge from the Christian's life which is, as the Anabaptists understood it, that of being a disciple. This, in turn, means multiplication of that life by making more disciples who not only enjoy the privileges, but also participate in the responsibilities and share in the cost which such life entails.

Selecting responsive population groups

Some evidence suggests that the Anabaptists operated on what

some missiologists today call the homogeneous unit principle.[7]
That means that the missionaries sought to witness to people with
whom they had things in common. They concentrated their efforts on peoples who were of similar social and economic status as
the missioners themselves. Thus the lay missionary was sent to
rural areas, winning whole family units to Christ; the artisan evangelists were sent to people of their profession, leading them to
profess Jesus as Savior and Lord; the educated were sent to the
cities where they were bound to meet the sophisticated and secular elite, introducing them to Christ.

Time and place were equally significant in finding people
who readily responded to the claims of Christ. This became
particularly crucial in view of existing ecclesiastical and civil laws.
To preach the gospel outside the framework of either the Roman
Catholic or Protestant Church and by people not authorized by
ecclesiastical and state officials was punishable by one or more of
the following measures: confiscation of property, expulsion from
the land, imprisonment, or death. But multitudes of people were
not reached through the institutional channels, and the
Anabaptists felt responsible to witness to them, even if that meant
suffering the consequences. This meant that prudence had to be
exercised in selecting time and place for evangelistic gatherings.
That is precisely what they did, as a German historian has con-
vincingly pointed out:

> Usually they had their gatherings in a forest. In the Forest of
> Strassburg, for example, they had as many as 300 people in one
> single meeting. They also met regularly in the Ringlinger Forest at
> Bretten, in the Schillingswald between Olbronn and Knittlingen,
> and in the Forest of Prussia near Aachen. These meetings were
> held between 10:00 p.m. and 2:00 a.m. In the section of the forest
> called *Bregehren* at Walkerbach in Wuerttemberg one can still
> find a pulpit-like rock known as *Gaisstein* where they conducted
> their worship and gospel services with the aid of two lanterns to
> dispel the darkness. In addition, they met in isolated mills, such as
> the one at Kleinleutersdorf in Orlammunde, or at the sawmill in
> Zorge on the Harz and in similar places. Peter Valk preached in a
> sheep barn at Saal in Thuringia. Enders Feckelein preached to a
> number of people sitting there with open Bibles around two tables
> in a blacksmith shop. Sometimes they gathered for meetings at

places that would allow them to escape quickly from the hands of persecutors in the event they were found out. In Tirol, for example, they met on remote farms, in sand pits, and in the shelters of huge rocks. But not all places were hideouts. There were at least two castles where the Anabaptist missionaries evangelized. One was the Schloss Munichau at Kitzbuhl and the other the Schloss Neuhof at Brunneck in Tirol. The records also show that these meetings generally drew large crowds.[8]

Applying relevant methods

We will consider the Anabaptists' missionary methods in terms of an earlier spontaneous expansion and a later strategized expansion. The first period covers about three-and-a-half years. It began on January 21, 1525, when the unavoidable breach between Zwingli and his most faithful disciples occurred over the issue of the mass and ended with the famous Missionary Conference of Augsburg (also known as the Martyrs' Synod), held from August 20-24, 1527. From this time on every mission endeavor of the Anabaptists became increasingly marked by a deliberate mission strategy that aimed at evangelizing all of Europe and the whole world.

Spontaneous methods before August 1527

Historical records point to at least four specific methods the Anabaptists used to make known their faith.

Preaching pilgrims. During the early period the Anabaptist faith spread much like that of the apostolic church. "Anabaptist leaders at first wandered as pilgrims, seeking relief from persecution, and shepherding from time to time the little groups of the faithful. As persecution grew more savage, hundreds of families took to the road, moving slowly eastward toward the Moravian settlements. A whole people thus became pilgrims, exiles for Christ."[9]

Wherever they went these persecuted, wandering Anabaptists preached the gospel of the kingdom, calling men and women to repentance, forgiveness, and reconciliation. They may well have learned this method from Zwingli, whom they respected as a dynamic preacher.

House meetings. The Anabaptists' objective was to reach whole households with the gospel. Fritz Blanke records a number of house meetings held during the week of January 22-29, 1525. At times these were the spontaneous result of a casual visit; at other times they were planned by believers. Sometimes these meetings resulted in the conversion and baptism of all adult members who then celebrated the Lord's supper together. These meetings frequently manifested the typical characteristics of a spiritual awakening. Fritz Blanke comments:

> When we seek a caption for the inner processes of these eight days, the concept "revival movement" presents itself. We thereby understand the sudden occurrence of a religious awakening, in which not just a few individuals but a considerable number are gripped by a personal Christian disposition to repentance and break through to the joy of salvation.
>
> This happened in Zollikon. We can still clearly see the process of repentance in sequence from the protocol of the hearings (Nos. 29, 31, 32). . . . Here we meet the reformational understanding of sin, and that not just as abstract theory but as personal experience.
>
> The impact of this experience is underscored by the strong emotions accompanying it. These farmers, who otherwise certainly were accustomed to hide their feelings broke out in wailing and weeping.[10]

Professor Blanke concludes that the "soul struggles" of countless ordinary nameless Christians of this period were crowned by forgiveness and sealed by baptism, the visible sign that God has pardoned the sinner.[11]

Bible reading and lay evangelism. Since the leaders of the awakening were quickly arrested and banned, the responsibility of spiritual care and continued evangelism was transferred to local farmers and artisans. Those who could read began to read the Word of God to nonliterates as they met in homes and barns and village churches. When people confessed Christ, lay brothers performed the rite of baptism. Hans Bichter, for example, baptized thirty believers within a week, and Jörg Schad baptized forty in a single day—in the village of Zollikon.[12] A significant benefit these new Christians shared with other reformers was Luther's New Testament which had gone through at least twelve editions between 1522 and 1525.

Persecution. Persecution was severe, and only two or three of the sixty leaders who met in Augsburg for the missionary conference in August 1527 lived to see the fifth year of the Anabaptist movement.[13] Some of the early Swiss leaders did not even live to see the 1527 conference. As one pages through the *Ausbund*,[14] the first Anabaptist hymnary published in 1564, one reads time and again a biographical note about the author, including such execution data as burned 1525, beheaded 1528, drowned 1526, hanged 1537. Many of these songs not only told the story of the martyrs and their deaths; they also were a powerful evangelistic message to the executioners and those who witnessed the executions. The appeal was to repent and be converted and reconciled to God.

A few excerpts translated from song Number 12, written in 1550, serve as an example. Followed by a fairly long narrative conversation between the official accusers and the Christian accused, the latter vindicates his case by saying, "We speak of these things only from the Word of God." Then he adds in rather unsophisticated but in no uncertain terms this appeal:

> We do not want you to forego
> The truth which we ourselves do know;
> That by erroneous teachings
> And even by decrees,
> By falsehood and deceptions
> You have been totally deceived;
> For thirteen hundred years
> You have these lies believed.

> I plead, please let me say to you
> That wolves are anxious to pursue:
> They come clad in clothes of sheep—
> With subtle stealth and guile
> Deceive the poor in spirit.
> To count the cost they do refuse,
> They see not their reward;
> In death their life may lose.

Oh hear the call from God, our Lord,
The apostles' teaching of His Word
With compassionate voices
Wooing to Him to come.
So knock and call now on Him,
He will open wide the door,
Will break your prison walls.
Oh praise Him evermore! (My translation)

Donald F. Durnbaugh states that "in the duchy of Württemberg in the sixteenth century, all of the Anabaptist men were expelled or executed," and "only women with small children were
allowed to remain at home." That is not to say, however, that the
authorities considered the women less dangerous than the men in
spreading the "illicit faith." In fact, the government chained the
women in their homes "to keep them from going to their relatives
and neighbours to witness to their faith," as was their custom.[15]

Despite such stringent measures, the martyrs and evangelists
seldom recanted. Their testimony made a lasting impression on
many executioners and spectators, so that not a few came to accept the same faith they had tried to resist and obliterate. Yet by
1527 all Anabaptist founding fathers in Switzerland had either
been executed or banished and all followers so successfully exterminated that the movement became more dynamic in other
European countries than in Zürich and Zollikon. As the movement spread through the pilgrim witnesses, the biblical message
was so winsome, so overpowering, and so appealing to the masses
that, as one recent German historian has put it, "often a few hours
at a new place were sufficient to found a new congregation."[16]

Strategic methods after August 1527
This section highlights several missionary methods between
1527 and 1565, covering the time from the first missionary conference in Augsburg to the so-called golden age of the Anabaptist
movement in Moravia. I will not discuss this golden age which
was intitated after 1565 under the dynamic leadership of Peter
Walpot. Walpot headed "the greatest missionary organization of

the epoch maintaining an extensive correspondence and guiding a large and effective corps of lay missionaries."[17]

Evangelizing Wandermissionare. This method of preaching by the wandering missioners continued past the second half of the sixteenth century. Like the famous Irish *peregrini* almost a thousand years before them, these Anabaptist preachers wandered from place to place and proclaimed the gospel. But unlike the *peregrini,* these Anabaptist missionaries baptized new converts, established Christians in their faith, and gathered them into local congregations. One such preacher was the ex-priest Georg Blaurock (1492-1529). He was no doubt the greatest evangelist of the time, traveling far and wide throughout Europe. During the four years from his conversion under Zwingli in 1525 until his death at the stake in 1529, he baptized at least a thousand (some say 4,000) new converts and planted many new churches.[18]

Systematic sending of missionaries. The Anabaptist churches discerned and systematically sent out many apostles. The designation *apostles* was deliberately chosen for those who were sent out in apostolic teams. Generally, such teams consisted of three people who were commissioned to specific places for the sole purpose of evangelism and church planting. Hans Hut (d. 1527), one of the chairmen of the 1527 missionary conference in Augsburg, had already been instrumental in sending apostles to many parts of Europe. But by then the Augsburg church was behind the program in evangelism, and the Anabaptist apostolate took on new shape and form.

Due to intensified persecution, these apostles were convinced that time was running out for their missionary efforts. The sending church of Augsburg shared this conviction of the missionaries and urgently called for commitment to evangelism. Within two weeks (from the termination of the conference on August 24, 1527, to the issuance of a new mandate by the Augsburg authorities against the Anabaptists on September 6) the Augsburg church recruited and sent out more than two dozen missionaries to strategic centers in Germany and Austria. But what had happended to the dynamic mission centers in Switzer-

land a few years earlier now became the fate of the sending
church in Augsburg: It was choked by fierce persecution. Three
years after the conference only two or three of the sixty leaders in
attendance had escaped the hangman's scaffold. That is why history has ironically recorded the first Protestant missionary conference of August 1527 as the Martyrs' Synod.

Dynamic lay witness. Early Anabaptism operated on the
principle of the priesthood of all believers. Lay people were missionaries. Schäufele has likened this method to that of the primitive church where the bearers of the gospel message were pre-
dominantly the common folk, not the ordained leaders. The sociologist Max Weber (1864-1920) is reported to have said that
Luther's principle of the priesthood of all believers was actualized
"in Anabaptism with its revivalistic character, on the basis of its
sect sociology."[19] Durnbaugh observes that the Reformation
churches have scarcely anything like it to set over against the
Anabaptist phenomenon. This applies to both the ministry of mission to the world and the ministry of care in the church.[20]

With lay evangelism, one authority notes, the Anabaptists
made use of three specific channels to point people to Christ. One
of them was the web of family relationships. Schäufele comments:
"Family relationships played an important role in the expansion
of the Anabaptist revival in the years 1527 and 1528 in
Augsburg."[21] Thus an old Anabaptist calendar of the time reports
on the lay ministry of a certain Endris Fachlein near Stuttgart who
is said to have won almost his entire relationship to the Anabaptist
faith. The historical record offers interesting illustrations as to how
one family member won another to Christ and how the faith con-
tagiously moved on to cousins, uncles, and aunts.[22]

Another channel for lay witness among the Anabaptists was
to neighbors and other acquaintances. Bible study groups met in
homes and invited unbelievers from the neighborhood with the
objective of winning them to the Lord. Social events such as wed-
dings and similar community affairs, as strange as it may sound to
us, provided excellent opportunities to make new acquaintances
and to invite people to a Bible Reading.

"There is indeed impressive evidence," says one historian, "that most members felt the call to convince and convert others, relatives, neighbors, strangers. The rapid spread of the movement is otherwise inexplicable. The well-known Martyrs' Synod of 1527 staked out separate areas of mission responsibility in a 'grand map of evangelical enterprise.' "[23]

Occupational contacts provided another channel for lay missionary outreach. The Anabaptist employer sought to win employees to a life of discipleship under Christ. When Katherin Lorenzen, who later became the wife of Jacob Hutter, had to testify in court about her faith, she said that her employer, a Christian baker, as well as other believing employees had witnessed to her and persuaded her to join the Anabaptist sect. Records also show that laborers and artisans took their evangelistic tasks seriously in everyday contacts with people. Since many of them were banned from their cities and states, they had to search for employment elsewhere, either in the craft of their occupation or with farmers on the land—at least until 1539 when the Decree of Regensburg made it illegal to hire an Anabaptist. Until that date the Anabaptist workers witnessed to their masters and fellow workers.[24] Thus, sent missionaries and laity alike made a deliberate and conscientious effort to form what we might call extension chains for the spreading of the gospel and the planting of believers' congregations.

Sending responsible agents
These people were at the right time in the right place, employing the right methods to achieve the goal of making disciples and multiplying churches. The Anabaptist annals record several characteristics of those who were committed to present the claims of Christ to the lost in the world.

Compelled by the Great Commission
The great Anabaptist missionary Hans Hut often preached to large crowds. Upon baptizing large numbers of those who repented of their sins and confessed Christ as Lord, Hut wou'

challenge each one to obey the Great Commission and tell others
the good news. Those who obeyed always went under the shadow
of the cross, "where the representatives of the state churches
dared not go, and for the Gospel's sake were made pilgrims and
martyrs throughout the known world." When asked what compelled them to go, they answered without hesitation: the Great
Commission.[25]

Convicted by a deep sense of calling

The Anabaptists called it *Berufungsbewusstsein.* Nothing is
more apparent in the Anabaptist missionaries than their deep
sense of calling to the task. This call, as they understood it, always
had two dimensions: One is internal, the other external. They
explained this experience as a direct call from God inwardly
perceived and a call from the church outwardly confirmed.[26]

In the first place, the Anabaptists placed great emphasis on a
specific spiritual gift for the missionary task. "It is God who sends
us, but the Holy Spirit who gives to us the apostolic gift for the
preaching of the Gospel of Christ." Again they said, "The Spirit of
God tells our spirit that we are called and must go and preach . . .
for it is for that purpose that He has given us to possess the gift of
the Holy Spirit."[27]

Second, the call contained an external dimension. Schäufele
states that in addition to the inward charismatic call, the
Anabaptists followed Luther's principle of the authority of the
local congregation to discern the inner call and then to commission people to the ministry to which they felt called.[28] In the early
Anabaptist document known as *The Schleitheim Confession*
(February 24, 1527), we find the instruction that the local church
has the responsibility to choose the right person for the right task,
whom the Lord has thus appointed. Once the persons had been
discerned, the congregation publically confirmed their calling and
sent them on their way as missionaries.

Commissioned by a supporting church

The Graner Codes, found in the so-called Brunner Archives,

describe in some detail an Anabaptist commissioning service.[29] First, the candidates reported to the congregation how God had called them into mission work and to preach the gospel in other lands. This was followed by a session of admonition and encouragement. The missionaries asked the congregation to remain faithful in their local tasks, visiting the sick and imprisoned, and providing for the poor and unemployed. In conclusion the missionaries asked that they themselves be remembered with prayers and material provisions. In response the people of the congregation pledged their support, wished them well, and prayed for God's mercies upon their ministry. Thus the commissioning service was actually a kind of covenant between the commissioning body and the commissioned team.

Since singing played a significant role from the inception of the Anabaptist movement, and since hymns were often written for specific occasions, I have selected and translated several verses from a twenty-five stanza song used for an early commissioning service.[30]

As God his Son was sending
Into this world of sin,
His Son is now commanding
That we this world should win.
He sends us and commissions
To preach the gospel clear,
To call upon all nations
To listen and to hear.

To Thee, O God, we're praying,
We're bent to do thy will;
Thy Word we are obeying
Thy glory we fulfill.
All peoples we are telling
To mend their sinful way,
That they might cease rebelling,
Lest judgment be their pay.

And if thou, Lord, desire
And should it be thy will
That we taste sword and fire
By those who thus would kill
Then comfort, pray, our loved ones
And tell them, we've endured
And we shall see them yonder—
Eternally secured.

Thy Word, O Lord, does teach us,
And we do understand;
Thy promises are with us
Until the very end.
Thou hast prepared a haven—
Praised be thy holy name.
We laud thee, God of heaven,
Through Christ, our Lord. Amen!

The entire congregation observed the commissioning ceremony. In most cases the missionaries were married men, leaving families behind; occasionally wives went with their husbands. In the event that the missionaries would be executed by "sword and fire," as expressed in the song, the church was committed to take care of the widow and the orphaned children.[31]

All this speaks of a profound *Sendungsbewusstsein* or sense of sentness. According to the late professor J. A. Toews, Sebastian Franck (1499-1543) was both friend and critic of the early Anabaptists. He was so impressed by their consciousness of mission that he described this aspect of their life as follows: "They wish to imitate apostolic life . . . move about from one place to another preaching and claiming a great calling and mission." Some of them were so sure of their calling, wrote Franck, that they felt "themselves responsible for the whole world."[32]

Committed to a high view of discipleship

The missionaries sent out from the main centers in South Germany, Switzerland, and Moravia were all of noble character. Since they were committed to the concept of the believers' church as a visible structure within society, they insisted that their converts live exemplary lives. "No one can truly know Christ," they said, "unless he follow Him in life."[33] This was precisely one point of tension between the Church of the Restitution and the *corpus christianum* of the Reformation. The emphasis in the latter was on faith, but the Anabaptists stressed faith plus *holy* living. That is why all missionaries had to undergo rigorous tests as to ethical character before they were sent out by the church.

The Moravia churches (after 1565) had a special mission committee, a kind of sodality, whose members were well informed about both the missionary's character and the needs and opportunities for mission work. The task of this committee was to screen each of the candidates on the basis of call, gifts, and moral and spiritual qualifications. Their concept of discipleship under the lordship of Christ covered all these areas.

Called to carry out the apostolic task

We find a close correlation between the call of the missionary to the apostolic task and the responsibility felt by the sending church to help individuals carry out the task. Whenever possible, the area of service was clearly defined by the church, taking into account such important matters as education, trade, social status, culture, and language of the candidates.[34]

As already noted, the missionaries were sent in apostolic teams to carry out their task. Since persecution was almost inevitable, the missionaries were usually sent in teams of three: First was the *Diener des Wortes*, or minister of the Word. That person was the preacher and the teacher. Second came the *Diener der Notdurft*, the servant to the needs of others, a type of deacon. Finally was the *gewöhnliche Bruder*, or common lay brother. These as well as their families were supported by the sending church. Professionals (such as architects or engineers) sometimes worked as tentmaking missionaries, supporting themselves.[35] In the event that one of the team members was apprehended, the church was immediately notified so that reinforcement could be sent and those in prison visited and their needs supplied. The task of the common lay person was usually to serve as liaison between the church and the missionaries.

Measuring the resulting harvest

As we look at the missionary effort of the Anabaptist movement we are naturally interested in measurable results, in terms of both quantity and quality.

Quantitative results

Unfortunately, sixteenth-century church records are unavailable or incomplete. Then, too, many records are inconsistent. Furthermore, no statistics are available concerning some of the best-known leaders of the Anabaptist movement. Yet from the fragmentary records that have been preserved we can measure, at least in part, Anabaptists' fruitful mission work.[36] (See chart on page 66)

Most of these missionaries died a martyr's death, and their short time of service was interrupted by days, weeks, and even months of persecution and imprisonment. Nevertheless, congregations of believers sprang up almost overnight in many parts of Europe, especially after the 1527 mission conference. By 1528 Austria was dotted with Anabaptist churches. From 1532 to 1539 the Tirol area was literally permeated with missionaries and young congregations, the number which grew daily.[37]

The famous social philosopher-theologian Ernst Troeltsch (1865-1923) has written extensively on the impact of the Anabaptists, whom he calls "an early premature triumph of the sectarian principles of the Free Church." Troeltsch underscores their drive for missionary expansion in these words: "The whole of Central Europe was soon covered with a network of Anabaptist communities, loosely connected with each other, who all practiced a strictly Scriptural form of worship. The chief centers were Augsburg, Moravia, and Strassburg, and later on, in Friesland and the Netherlands."[38]

The historians Wiswedel, Littell, and Schäufele record similar achievements of the Anabaptist mission movement. Like Troeltsch, these scholars point out the growth of the church in Europe and add that scores of missionaries were sent from these centers in all directions. By the middle of the sixteenth century

Name of Missionary	Known Number of Converts Baptized	Time of Baptism	Estimated Total	Time of Service
Jakob Gross	35	1 day		1525
Jörg Schad	40	March 12		1525
Wilhelm Roubli	60	1 day		1525
Balthasar Hubmaier	360	Easter	6,000	1525-28
Conrad Grebel	"a whole procession of men and women"			1525-26
Johannes Brötli	"nearly a whole village"			1525
Hans Bichter	30	March 8-15		1529
Martin Zehentmaier	40			1527
Leonard Dorfbrunner	100 (about)	few mts.	3,000	1525-29
George Blaurock	1,000		4,000	1525-29
Hans Hut	100 (about)	2 weeks	12,000	1527-29
Georg Nespitzer	22	2 years	4,000	1527-29
Leonard Schiemer	200 (over)	6 mts.		1527
Michael Kürschner	100 (about)	11 mts.		1528-29
Jacob Hutter	19	August '35		1533-35
Leenaert Bouwens	10,378	31 yrs.		1551-82
Hans Mändl	400 (about)		4,000	1561

Anabaptist missionaries were preaching in every state of Germany, Austria, Switzerland, Holland, France, Poland, Galicia, Hungary, and Italy. Several even went as far as Denmark and Sweden in the north and Greece and Constantinople in the south. The record of a conversation among early Swiss Anabaptists states that on one occasion they talked about going "to the red Indians across the sea."[39]

Qualitative results

The cost of obedience to the Great Commission, however, was high. Over 2,000 Anabaptist martyrs are known by name. One authority estimates that 4,000 to 5,000 "men, women, and children fell prey to water, fire and sword."[40] To this Roland Bainton adds:

> Those who thus held themselves as sheep for the slaughter were dreaded and exterminated as if they had been wolves. They challenged the whole way of life of the community. Had they become too numerous, Protestants would have been unable to take up arms against Catholics and the Germans could not have resisted the Turks. And the Anabaptists did become numerous. They despaired of society at large, but they did not despair of winning converts to their way. Every member of the group was regarded as a missionary. Men and women left their homes to go on evangelistic tours. The established churches, whether Catholic or Protestant, were aghast at these ministers of both sexes insinuating themselves into town and farm. In some of the communities of Switzerland and the Rhine valley Anabaptists began to outnumber Catholics and Protestants alike."[41]

Concluding lessons

Every biblical mission strategy calls for total obedience on the part of a missionary people in every generation. As the Anabaptist of the sixteenth century, so the members of the believers' church in the twentieth century must view with equal significance the ethical teaching of the Sermon on the Mount and the *magna charta* of the Great Commission. The one is a call to discipleship, the other a command to make disciples. Both are given by the same Lord. Both are rooted in his abiding Word. Both must find expression by *telling, being,* and *doing* in the lives of Christ's disciples, the people of the way (cf. Acts 9:20). Unless we learn from history, history's record has been written in vain. From the annals of our Anabaptist forebears come several lessons.

Radical obedience

The Anabaptists' uncompromising obedience to the Great Commission is best understood in the light of their concept of discipleship on one hand and their view of Christ's lordship on the other. Robert Friedmann (1891-1970) has pointed out that the Anabaptists lived by an implicit, relational—rather than by an explicit, creedal—theology. Such a theology of *being* and *doing* finds its clearest expression in discipleship and obedience, yet not without a verbal witness.

Obedience, however, does not emanate from a servile or legalistic attitude, but from an attitude of freedom of the will which is in harmony with the Lord's will. "If God gives commands in His Scriptures, they are meant to be obeyed and not only to be looked at as something unattainable and paradoxical."[42]

The test of discipleship stands or falls with the ancient question, "What think ye of Christ?" (Mt. 16:13-16). Hans Denck (1500-1527), one of the early Anabaptist missionaries, maintained correctly that to know Christ means to follow him; to follow him means to know him.

Harold Bender (1897-1962) attempted to answer the question of who Christ really is in Anabaptist thought:[43] Christ is more than a prophet or moral teacher of an ethical code—though he taught ethics; he is more than the second person of the Trinity included in a liturgy of praise and worship—though he is worthy of our highest adoration; he is more than an exclusive Savior who gives the gift of forgiveness and the blessings that go with it— though he is the only Savior reconciling people to God. Christ is the prophet and teacher to be listened to, the Son of God to be worshiped, the Savior who saves from sin. He is all that and more: Jesus Christ is *the Lord* who makes the believer his disciple who follows and obeys him. Radical obedience is the key.

Priority of mission

As the believers' church is Christocentric, so its mission is ecclesiocentric. The Lord said on one occasion, "As the Father has sent me, even so I send you" (Jn. 20:21). As Christ maintained a consciousness of being sent by the Father, so the members of the believers' church in the New Testament tradition maintain their deep awareness of *sentness* for *witness*. Their sense of priority of mission found expression not only in a conviction of *being sent* by the Lord, but also in a recognition of responsibility *to send* missionaries into all the world across social, cultural, linguistic, economic, religious, and geographical frontiers. Mission always implies the crossing of frontiers from faith to unfaith.

Legitimacy of the apostolate

The Anabaptists retained the New Testament concept of apostle and applied it to their own missionaries. In fact, they considered the apostolic band of a Paul and Barnabas to be a legitimate model for the proclamation of the gospel as a means to extend and expand their newfound faith and life in Jesus Christ, their Redemptor and Master.

Living witnesses

The Anabaptists looked to the mission of the apostolic era as the golden age of evangelism. All believers have the power of the Holy Spirit in their lives and are, therefore, living witnesses to give expression in relationships with others of the divine life within. As believers witness by *telling, being,* and *doing*—and even by dying for their faith—unbelievers become believers. Whether people come to Christ through spontaneous expansion or through strategically planned evangelization, those who believe, the Anabaptist maintained, must be baptized and gathered into local congregations. New converts were taught all the things which the Lord commanded pertaining to both discipleship and lordship (Mt. 28:20). They were being equipped to worship, honor, love, serve, and *obey* the Lord between his ascension and coming again.

5

The Missionary Vision and Activity of the Anabaptist Laity

Wolfgang Schäufele

The missionary activity of the ordinary members of the Anabaptist brotherhood was an important factor in the spread of the movement. It is true that the chief carriers of the activity were the missioners and the elders (*Vorsteher*), who traveled from place to place filled with a strong sense of mission, and with flaming zeal proclaimed the gospel, everywhere founding new congregations and winning new adherents to the movement. The astonishingly rapid spread of the Anabaptist "awakening" or "revival"[1] in the years following 1525 is primarily to be attributed to their work.

In spite of this, Anabaptism would not have been able to spread so rapidly and to take such firm roots if the missionary activity of the leaders had not been vigorously supported by the missionary activity of the ordinary members. These lay members did not simply turn over to the ordained missioners and elders the task of spreading the faith, but they themselves as individual members spread the message in the framework of their own contacts with their environment. The new converts frequently

Wolfgang Schäufele is a teacher in the Gymnasium in Karlsruhe, Germany. His essay is based on his doctoral dissertation at Heidelberg University, 1962. Reprinted from Mennonite Quarterly Review, XXXVI:2, April 1962, 99-115.

reported the Anabaptist doctrine to their families and to the circles of their neighbors and occupational comrades. Most of the members of the brotherhood in one way or another contributed to the spread of the message.

This "apostolate of the laity" was, of course, conceivable only in a movement in which the members had committed themselves to follow Christ at a responsible age through repentance, faith, and baptism.[2] "*Fiunt, non nascuntur Christiani*" (they became—were not born—Christians), the familiar phrase from Tertullian, characterizes strikingly the clarity of decision, without which a true Christian life according to the Anabaptist concept was impossible. The emergence of a brotherhood of earnest and committed Christians in which more vigorous religious energies could develop more naturally than in the later state churches is due not only to the requirement of a conscious commitment to be Christian, but also to the Anabaptist doctrine of sanctification, the practice of the ban, and the pressure of persecution.

In the Anabaptist brotherhood, as is well known, there was no distinction between an academically educated ministerial class on the one hand and the laity on the other. Each member was potentially a preacher and a missionary, and each single member had equal opportunities for advancement according to his own competence, just as was the case in primitive Christianity. Luther's "priesthood of all believers" became a practical reality in Anabaptism with its revivalistic character, on the basis of its sect sociology (Max Weber). For this reason the concepts "laity," "lay" mission, and "lay" missionary are really not applicable to the Anabaptists. When they are used in the present essay, in accord with traditional usage, they are meant only in the sense of referring to the ordinary member of the church who was not a bearer of office such as missioner or *Vorsteher*.

The sources
The abundant Anabaptist sources contain much material bearing directly on the question of the lay mission, material which affords highly interesting insights into the life and thought of the

Anabaptists who came largely from the lower class of people, and also gives important help in understanding the detailed operations of Anabaptist expansion, whose ultimate ramifications thus become tangible. In this connection, it should be noted that most of our knowledge of the Anabaptist lay mission comes exclusively from the court records and trial examinations. While it is true that one would expect persons on trial to report their own actions in the best possible light in order to avoid serious consequences, nevertheless the court records give the impression that the complete integrity of these simple Christians, who were fully convinced of their faith, very seldom permitted diplomatic statements of self-protection, so that the documents reflect honestly and dependably the spiritual attitude and acts of the persons involved.

The lay missionary commission

We find in the sources indications that not only the Anabaptist leaders, but also ordinary members were obligated to contribute to the spread of the message. An illustration is Augustin Würzlburger, who later became a missioner; he testified that at his baptism, which occurred several months before his ordination as a missioner, he was charged with the obligation "henceforth to sin no more" and to bring as many as possible to the "right way."[3] Another rebaptized person, of the Markgrafschaft Ansbach-Bayreuth, reports in a trial record that "he had been commanded to speak the gospel to others."[4] The members were commonly challenged by their spiritual leaders "to confess the Lord"[5] and "to be stewards"[6] of the truth that had been committed to them. In many cases such an appeal was not necessary, since the religious dynamic dominating the Anabaptist revival movement, which pressed for expression, automatically led the individual believers to lay missionary activity.

To be sure, the actual Great Commission of Matthew 28:19-20 and Mark 16:15-16 could be carried out in totality only by Anabaptist office-bearers since baptizing was a part of the Commission, and since—apart from the very beginning of the movement—no ordinary member was authorized to baptize.[7] The lay missionary activity of the ordinary members of the brotherhood therefore was limited essentially to the oral proclamation of the Anabaptist message of repentance and salvation which they themselves had accepted, and to which they conformed their own lives. Repeatedly imprisoned Anabaptists state in the trials that they had baptized no one, but had admonished their fellowmen to repentance. This was stated, for instance, by Peter Elster of Plauen, a tailor's apprentice who was baptized in Linz about 1529, when he said that he was neither called nor sent to preach or to baptize, but he condemned vices when he saw them.[8] Bernhard Zurgkendorffer, of Göggingen near Augsburg, reported in a trial that he had baptized no one himself but that he had admonished all who came to him in his house "to repent" and "to depart from blasphemy, drunkenness, and similar things."[9]

Many lay members manifested a notable zeal in their lay missionary activity. A peasant named Hans von Rüblingen, who had been arrested in Passau in 1535 along with other fellow believers on the way to his earlier home in Hohenlohe following the expulsion of Anabaptists from Moravia, replied to the question of the judge whether they had sought to win followers to their Anabaptist movement: He and his comrades had compelled no one to join the movement, "but wherever they traveled or lived they spoke the word of the Lord."[10] A citizen of Heilbronn said in a period of testimony before the court in 1539 that he had earlier fled from the Anabaptists as from the devil, for "they would gladly have persuaded all of us."[11] Only seldom does one find evidence in the sources that an Anabaptist had deliberately concealed his faith.[12]

The extraordinary missionary-expansionist energies which were to be found among the common members are proven by the Passau court records in which the members of the Anabaptist congregation at that place confessed that they were merely waiting for the arrival of a *Vorsteher*, whom they would then receive and lodge, in order to help their suppressed movement to a fresh breakthrough in the city. These people as ordinary members felt themselves responsible for the spread of their teaching in their city independently of the leadership of the *Vorsteher*, and actually undertook measures to accomplish their purpose.[13] It should also be noted that in Anabaptism it was a common occurrence that ordinary members read the Scriptures publicly and no doubt expounded them at meetings held in homes when no *Vorsteher* was present.[14]

Channels of lay missionary activity

The regulation found in the Schleitheim Confession of 1527 concerning "separation" from certain aspects of the ungodly world[15] brought only minor restrictions upon the possibilities for lay missionary activity by the Anabaptists in the German-speaking world. In spite of the prohibition of such things as attendance at the state-church services and taverns and accepting of bondsman obligations and similar duties, many and various connections with the "heathen" environment still remained. Hans Feygenbutz, an active member of the Esslingen Anabaptist congregation, stated in his trial examination that he had "always maintained friendly relations with everyone and never had separation from anyone and does not now."[16] Such an openness to relations with the non-Anabaptist population was, of course, the indispensable condition for passing on to others the message of salvation, of which one was himself completely convinced.[17]

The following social groups were natural channels through which the Anabaptist revival was extended by the activity of the lay missionaries: nearer and more remote family connections; neighbors and other acquaintances; occupational connections.

The nearer and more remote relatives

Family relationships played an important role in the expansion of Anabaptism.[18] This is particularly obvious in the expansion of the Anabaptist revival in the years 1527 and 1528 in Augsburg. Simbrecht Widemann, a shoemaker, stated in his trial examination that his brothers-in-law and relatives came to him in his home. In addition to the common meals which they had together they discussed questions of faith and read from the Bible.[19] According to the statements of Simprecht Mair, a peddler of Augsburg, his entire clan was involved "in the matter."[20] About the same time Anabaptists in the canton of Zürich were seeking to win their relatives for the Anabaptist teaching. Those who were approached for this purpose were obviously unhappy about the attempt.[21] The Württemberg Anabaptist Calendar of 1570 contains a charge against an Anabaptist by the name of Endris Fäcklin, of Schmiden near Stuttgart, who was active in spreading Anabaptism and had won almost his entire relationship to the Anabaptist faith.[22]

The following family relationships can be noted as a channel of effective work in the lay missionary activities: (a) the husband persuades his wife to join Anabaptism. For instance, Herman Anwald, Eitelhans Langenmantel's servant, who had been baptized, urged his wife to be baptized likewise, whereupon she decided to take this step.[23] (b) The wife wins[24] her husband for the brotherhood. (c) Anabaptist parents[25] influence their children to become Anabaptists. Furthermore illustrations are the brother,[26] the brother-in-law,[27] the male cousin,[28] and the female cousin,[29] in which cases the remaining family members of these relatives were also reached.

A vivid picture of lay missionary activity through the channel of the relatives is found in the Anabaptist records of Regensburg.[30] About Shrove Tuesday in Lent of 1528, Augustin Würzlburger (by occupation a teacher), before his ordination as a missioner, visited his brother Hans, a butcher in Landshut. A second visit took place in early April. Augustin, who was sitting at the table, read to his brother several chapters from the New Testament which he had brought with him, attacked infant baptism and the typical church faith, and summoned those present to the obedience of faith toward God's Word. Specifically he summoned his brother to accept baptism, "to die to the world and to serve God." The outcome of this attempt was, however, rather discouraging. Neither the brother nor the other family members responded to his suggestion. The brother simply explained evasively that he wanted to consider the matter.

Nevertheless Würzlburger's endeavors were not completely in vain. At the first house meeting in the butcher's residence a cousin named Hans Sedlmair had taken part, whose son was working as an employee for the butcher in Landshut. Sedlmair invited the Anabaptist propagandist to come to his home village in Lower Bavaria. Here Würzlburger found open ears for his teaching. At his first meeting, which was during Lent, he criticized both the church practice of fasting and infant baptism, in connection with which he used Mark 16:16 as a support for his teaching that one must be baptized after coming to believe in Christ. With the promise that he would come soon again the Anabaptist teacher left. On his next visit—he had meanwhile been appointed as missioner by the Augsburg Anabaptist congregation—he baptized his cousin, the cousin's wife, two sons, and a daughter, besides another man.

Neighbors and other acquaintances

Neighbors, friends, fellow residents, and fellow citizens of villages and towns furnished good objects for lay missionary activity in the same way as relatives did. For instance, Jacob Breitiner, an Anabaptist in Zollikon, Switzerland, who had rooms to rent, acquainted the teacher Peter Forster, who was renting a room in his house, with the new brotherhood.[31] Neighbors, who had most likely been invited, took part in the Anabaptist meetings held in Martin Pschysser's home in Esslingen.[32] Michel, a shoe-maker of Getzenberg (Pustertal), took his friend Niclas Praun and the friend's wife, Appolonia, to an Anabaptist meeting which Jacob Hutter held in the forest of Taufers in August 1535. Both were deeply impressed and were at once baptized.[33] Adam Bauder of Urbach, Württemberg, reported in his trial examination that he had decided to accept baptism at the instigation of an Anabaptist neighbor in the village.[34]

Philipp Jakob, of Creglingen (Oberamt Mergentheim), in his trial examination in 1530 described the circumstances which had led to his joining the movement. He said that he had taken part in a wedding in another place, but when he was about to join the dance the "son of Mulhansen," obviously an acquaintance, invited him to his father's home. There he found three Anabaptists reading the New Testament who involved him in a discussion on matters of faith. To their question whether he, Philipp, would not also want to learn the "right truth," he answered affirmatively. After two further meetings, which soon took place in his own home, he was baptized.[35]

The circle of occupational contacts

Occupational contacts also furnished a variety of opportunities for lay missionaries. The Anabaptist employer sought to persuade his employees to join the movement. This was the case, for instance, with Katherin Lorenzen, later the wife of Jacob Hutter. While she was working for Paul Gall, a baker in Trens (Pustertal), about 1532, she was "persuaded and led to join the Anabaptist sect" by her employer as well as by the baker's assistant, Paul Rumer, and other members of the movement, as she stated in her trial examination in 1535.[36]

Far more frequent, however, were the cases where the Anabaptist employees sought to influence and win their employers and fellows to the Anabaptist faith. An interesting case is that of Valtein Luckner, a master shoemaker of Taufers in the Tyrol. Luckner possessed a New Testament, which he often read. His journeyman, Matheis, who was an Anabaptist, made use of Luckner's Bible reading as a contact point for a lay missionary attack. He asked the master whether he practiced what he read, and added that one must believe in God. When Luckner answered that he believed, Matheis ventured a decisive attack: "There is more to that."

Later in his trial examination Luckner summarized the statements of his employee: "One must live according to the will of God and be baptized according to faith. Infant baptism is from the pope, but the present baptism was established by God, and he, Valtein, had to be baptized in order to be obedient to God." As happened so often, the Anabaptist message given in the shoemaker's words was combined with criticism of the ruling church.

Luckner was persuaded and asked where he could find a
Vorsteher who would baptize him. Matheis gave him further
instruction in the faith and told him about the Anabaptist center
at Augsburg. "Thereafter he, Valtein, had no rest but thought
more and more about the matter," said Luckner in his examination. In April 1530 he was baptized by Jacob Hutter.[37]

    Not only were employers objects of lay missionary activity
but also fellow workmen. Julius Lober, of Zürich, later a
Vorsteher, was introduced to Anabaptism by a comrade in the
Strasbourg tailor shop in which he was working, "who pointed out
the Scripture to him." This talk by his fellow workman became for
Lober the impulse for his own reading of the Bible, which ultimately brought him to acceptance of baptism.[38]

    The reason why laborers and craftsmen played such an im-
portant role in the spreading of Anabaptism was that Anabaptists
who were expelled from their homes frequently accepted employment in another place in a similar occupation either in a craft or
with farmers. The fear of the authorities regarding the spread of
Anabaptist ideas by this route is evidenced by a series of decrees,
especially by imperial cities, in which the citizenry was forbidden
to employ Anabaptists as servants (men and women). A decree of
the Regensburg Council of 1539 obliged the master craftsmen to
thoroughly examine the journeymen whom they were then
employing as well as prospective employees, to determine
whether they had Anabaptist tendencies. Should this be the case
they were forbidden to employ such persons.[39]

    But it was not only the journeymen who were regularly em-
ployed by the masters who carried on a successful lay missionary
activity, but also the independent persons who normally traveled
about in their trades, such as tailors. One Jacob Moer (or Taisler)
of Leutershausen near Ansbach was won to Anabaptism about
1530 by an Anabaptist tailor whom he had commissioned to make
a coat for him. "Now he had requested to have the coat tailored
handsomely and in a proud style," he reported in his trial examination, "whereupon the tailor then had said, 'what are you saying
about pride? God will punish pride.' Such and other good words

had moved him thereto."[40] An interesting case is that of a well-driller employed by an inhabitant of the Reichstal Harmersbach in Baden. The man, who was a convinced Anabaptist, "seduced" the two stepsons of his client so that they avoided any further attendance at the church service and participation in the sacrament and refused to take the oath of allegiance to the authorities.[41]

The role of women in the Anabaptist expansion

The participation of women in the spread of the Anabaptist faith is of special interest. It is true that women members were forbidden to preach and to baptize, and that they were not permitted to take part in the election of the *Vorsteher*.[42] On the other hand, the sources give valuable information about the religious activity of Anabaptist women who, being certain of their faith on the ground of a personal decision and acceptance of baptism, not only defended their faith tenaciously over against their husbands, but courageously confessed their faith and spread it in the circles of their relatives and neighbors.[43] The woman in Anabaptism emerges as a fully emancipated person in religious matters and as the independent bearer of Christian convictions.[44] A farmer's wife, Elizabeth Sedelmair of Egenhofen in Bavaria, who had been staying in Augsburg since Shrove Tuesday of 1528—the height of the Anabaptist revival—not only visited many Anabaptist families in the city, but sought to persuade non-Anabaptists to accept the faith. She went with her distaff (her handwork) to Anna Butz and her tenant Madlena Seitz and persuaded both to be baptized. Thereafter she brought the *Vorsteher* Claus Schleiffer of Vienna into the house, who baptized both women and Anna's son Hans.[45]

The audacity with which many Anabaptist women engaged in their lay missionary activity is demonstrated by a further example from Augsburg. On Easter Day of 1528 an Augsburg resident named Dorothea Tuchscherer was on the way to the Sunday service in the Holy Cross Church. On the way the Anabaptist maid of the shoemaker Widemann met her. After an introductory question as to where she was going, the servant girl persuaded the woman on the spot to give up going to the church and instead to take part in an Anabaptist meeting which was to be held on the same morning in the home of the sculptor Adolf Ducher.[46]

Even toward the end of the century and later, the Württemberg government considered the propaganda activity of Anabaptist women, who spread their faith through word of mouth or through booklets,[47] so dangerous that married women who could not be expelled on account of their little children were chained at home, so that they should not lead other people astray. This, of course, did not eliminate the possibility that visitors who came into the house might be infected. Often the woman who had been chained worked herself loose or was freed by her husband from her unhappy state.[48]

The manner of life of the Anabaptists:
An aid to evangelism

The successes which the ordinary members of the Anabaptist congregations, as well as the *Vorsteher* and missioners, continued to achieve in the spread of their faith were aided by the Anabaptist manner of life, and can scarcely be comprehended except against this background. Countless testimonies by contemporaries, especially by theologians, confirm that the Anabaptists on the whole led a blameless and exemplary life.[49] Amid the general corruption of morals of the sixteenth century a group of convinced Christians were living out the ethical principles of the gospel in daily life.[50] There is no doubt that the exemplary behavior of many Anabaptists gave a strong emphasis to their word-of-mouth appeals, and preached more loudly than the exegetically and theologically correct sermons of many a pastor who could not point to any "saints" in his church. In 1582 in Lörrach, Baden, a citizen who was close to being an Anabaptist declared to the local pastor at his court examination that he believed that there was no group of people who lived a better life than the Anabaptists. They were pious, God-fearing, prayed diligently, did not curse, and harmed no one. "He would wish that he could be a true Anabaptist like some he had learned to know, such as his late brother-in-law."[51]

On the other hand, it is important to remember that the missionary activity of the ordinary members of the church, as well as those of the *Vorsteher* and the missioners, was carried on under continuous persecutions, especially in the early days of the movement and in the Catholic territories. The ordinary members of the movement were threatened daily with imprisonment, torture, and death, unless the pressure of the persecution and the fear of what might come resulted in a recantation, which actually occurred frequently. Such recantations were seldom given apart from persecution. Under these circumstance open confession and active work in spreading a faith which was forbidden by the authorities required courage.

The special case of Moravia

The previous examples which I have reported concern Anabaptists in the empire, who up to the time of their arrest usually remained in constant contact with the non-Anabaptist environment through a variety of family or occupational connections. In Moravia conditions were quite different. The refugees who from 1526 on gathered from the territories of the empire into the relatively peaceful and protected Anabaptist paradise in the East—this was especially true of the Hutterite brotherhood, which in the course of time absorbed the smaller competing Anabaptist congregations—lived in a brotherhood which was relatively isolated from its surroundings. Those who joined the refugees in Moravia were separated from their unbelieving relatives, neighbors, and fellow citizens, whereas the Anabaptists who stayed behind in the empire had to continue to live together with such people.

The economic system of the Hutterite brotherhood—a strictly organized and to a large extent self-sufficient production group—developed a situation in which most of the members had hardly any contacts with the surrounding world. Furthermore, most of them lived in a Slavic language area[52] and therefore had to depend upon translators in their contacts with the native population.[53] The Hutterite Bruderhofs for the most part were located in Czech areas. Unintentionally, therefore, the emigration to Moravia led to a loss of most of the social contacts with the surrounding world. This was the price paid for greater personal security.

It dare not be overlooked, to be sure, that many of the Hutterian Brethren worked among "the heathen"[54] scattered over the whole of Moravia, especially as millers, dairymen, waiters, physicians, and barber-surgeons in the service of the nobility.[55] The Hutterite carpenters and masons were highly regarded among the nobility and citizens in Moravia, Austria, Hungary, and Bohemia because of the mills and breweries which they built for the native population at low rates.[56] Although because of religious reasons they fundamentally refused any business dealings with the Roman clergy, including the acceptance of commissions for craft work, and even the greeting, they normally maintained good relations with the "other unknowing heathen," either through a greeting or through friendly words.[57] In times of dearth or famine, the Hutterites aided the native population with material relief.[58]

But on the whole, the numerous lay missionary contact possibilities which were to be found everywhere in the empire in great variety were reduced to a meager amount for the Anabaptists in Moravia. Real contact with those of other faiths was possible only for the representatives of the Bruderhofs who were responsible for the purchase of material and the sale of the wares which had been produced, or for those members who worked outside in their trades. But even the testimony of these persons was very likely in many cases handicapped by the language difficulties, so that all that remained was the influence of the manner of life and of their cheap and good labor. As a consequence practically no missionary breakthroughs were achieved among the Slavic population; only a very few of such persons joined the brotherhood.[59]

This situation was given a theoretical justification in the theology of the Hutterian Brethren. The brotherhood, as the "bride of the Lord," who sanctifies herself in the desert and waits for her coming Lord, had to maintain its isolation from the world and its defilements in radical "separation."[60] From this eschatological point of view the attitude of the Swiss Brethren in the empire, who were involved in many ways with the unbelievers and therefore failed in the matter of separation, was expressly criticized.[61] The establishment of communal living, which contributed so much to an isolated way of life, was likewise grounded on religious principles.

In spite of this particular specialized development in the sociological and theological area, the Hutterite community maintained the original expansionist impulse of the Anabaptist movement in undiminished strength.[62] The brotherhood systematically sent out missionaries into the empire, into whose hands the evangelistic activity ultimately was exclusively placed, whereas the ordinary members occupied themselves in a diligent and rationalized production system and thus furnished an economically secure basis for the sending out of missionaries and for their evangelistic activities.

But even the lay missionary impulse was not fully extinguished. A few channels of personal influence upon their fellowmen still remained for the use of the lay members, which were gladly used. The ordinary members took frequent advantage of the possibility of sending along with the missionaries who went into far countries letters of invitation and appeal to their relatives in the empire. In these letters they challenged such persons to a change of mind for the purpose of joining the Anabaptist movement and emigrating to Moravia.[63] Many of these letters manifest a moving missionary zeal. One Jonas Maler, for instance, an old man, wrote in 1592 from Maskowitz in Moravia to his brothers in Esslingen as follows: "We would like very much to have you also emigrate to us to this pious people and thus better your life and also be concerned regarding that which is necessary and good for your salvation so that you may be able to stand before the Lord on that day." At this point, said Maler, it was not necessary to write very much since he had already done this earlier. If the recipients of the letter would want further information the bearers of the letter would be at their disposal.[64]

In another letter a mother explained to her son who had

remained behind in Württemberg while she emigrated with two other children to Moravia, concerning the errors of the Lutherans: "You should know that your Christianity of which you pride yourselves, as well as you yourselves, are far from the way of truth, from the commandments of God, from the pure teaching of Christ, and from the right faith, and that all your Christian ways and customs are perverted." The teachings of the church as well as the moral degradation of the members of the church are scourged in harsh language.

To this unsparing criticism the mother adds the following plea to her son: "You should convert yourself out of such corruption and great error of the world, forsake it and separate yourself from it and change your life. For God desires to have a separated people. And Christ says: Who is not born again cannot see the kingdom of God, that is, who does not manifest a different life of another sort and another way and another spirit and meaning, he cannot inherit the kingdom of God."

Consequently, the mother continues: "Therefore, my beloved son, think over my writing, beg God for mercy and understanding day and night, let nothing hold you back, convert yourself to God and join his people. For we have no doubt that this is the people of God, the right way, the narrow gate, the true faith, through which one becomes pious and saved in Christ Jesus our Lord and Savior. Will you not do this, you and your wife and my two daughters . . . this is our sincere appeal."[65] The recipients of the letter of course furnished the missionaries who brought the letters a contact point for missionary activity.[66]

Another possibility of direct solicitation for the Anabaptist faith and for the emigration to Moravia became possible for the ordinary members when they made their none too frequent visits to the empire on various errands.[67] On such occasions it was possible without difficulty to point the relatives and friends to Moravia and the church of God there, and to the necessity of a personal convincement of faith.[68] In this connection it should be remembered that the persecution which broke over the Anabaptists in Moravia in the year 1535 resulted in the return of many

Anabaptists to the empire. Thereby a veritable lay missionary wave poured over the land since the returning emigrants gave abundant witness to their faith on the way back and in their homelands.[69]

Summary and perspective

As a consequence of the general priesthood of believers which was realized in Anabaptism, and as a result also of the religious intensity which ruled in this great revival movement, the ordinary members participated actively in the spread of the Anabaptist faith. Ordinary lay people, craftsmen, peasants, servants, solicited their fellowmen to attend the meetings, to change their life, to accept baptism. The gospel was carried in aggressive and emphatic offer into everyday life. The "sacred area inside the church buildings" disappeared as the only place where salvation is mediated. The offer of the Anabaptist message of repentance became possible everywhere, in the workshop, in the house, in the field, on a journey.

The very fact of membership in a bitterly persecuted sect which was forbidden by law was an inescapable, unavoidable testimony of great power. How much more impressive were the exemplary manner of life of many Anabaptists, the convincing certainty of faith, the bearing of persecution, and the brave attitude with which repeatedly even the simple members of the brotherhood went into death.

The spread of the Anabaptist faith by lay missionaries is to be noted not only in the beginning years of the movement but also in later decades, and not only in the empire but also in Moravia.[70] Women as well as men participated on the basis of their own independent religious convictions. Family members, relatives, neighbors were won for the Anabaptist revival movement through personal conversations and invitations to the meetings. In their occupational relationships employers acquainted their journeymen and maids with the Anabaptist faith. More frequent is the reverse channel, since many Anabaptists who were driven out of their homes or who fled to other places found a new place of employment and were able to spread their faith further in a new occupational circle. Members of the Moravian Anabaptist brotherhood, whose social contacts with those of other faiths were reduced to a minimum because of the manner of settlement in a Slavic-language area, endeavored to make good the loss of their opportunities for personal mission activity by solicitation letters to their relatives in the empire as well as occasional visits thither.

However, alongside the activities of the ordained Anabaptist leaders, the lay missionary activity, in spite of its real importance, constituted only a complementary and more restricted and even hidden factor in the expansion of the movement; it was not so evident outwardly. In addition it should be remembered that particularly active lay members, who seemed to the brotherhood qualified for greater assignments because of their activity, were normally very likely soon chosen as *Vorsteher* or missioners. Consequently at a certain point the activity of the lay missionaries almost automatically resulted in ordination to a fully commissioned missionary status, of course based upon an election by the congregation.

In spite of this an astonishing thing about Anabaptism is not so much the activity of the ordained leaders, who usually were chosen out of the laity (the Lutheran Reformation also at the beginning used many lay people in the spiritual ministry, both craftsmen and educated persons),[71] as the missionary commitment of the ordinary members. The Reformation churches have scarcely anything like it to set over against the Anabaptist phenomenon. How full of spiritual energy and vision the Anabaptist congregations must have been, if so many of their ordinary members were active as missionaries. This is one of the foremost reasons that the healthy center of early Anabaptism is today rightly seen by church historiography as a genuine revival movement. It is deeply to be regretted that as a result of the bitter persecution "a great wealth of living piety, much genuine enthusiasm ... was forcibly suppressed and defamed as *Schwärmerei* and *Rotterei*" (fanatics and schismatics).[72]

With its lay missionary spirit Anabaptism circles back over

the centuries of the medieval period in which the laity was normally a lower-class, spiritually unimportant church mass in contrast to the mighty clergy (exceptions were the Albigenses and Waldenses) to early Christianity, whose expansion in the first centuries was almost exclusively the result of the activity of lay people.

> The bearers of the expansion of Christianity in the first five centuries were largely, and soon after the end of the first century exclusively, nonprofessional missionaries. . . . The members of the house churches worked from person to person. Alongside the relatively few professional apostles, prophets, and teachers were the slaves, the merchants, the deportees, the soldiers, the travelers, and especially the women who were the most successful missionaries. . . . More important than the sermons to the heathen were the conversations which came to pass through natural contacts and whose effect was strengthened by the life of many simple Christians.[73]

Historically, there was on the one hand the Anabaptist movement with its practical realization of the priesthood of believers and its lay activity, and which thus was very near to primitive Christianity. (Other parallels could of course be cited.) On the other hand, Anabaptism led to similar phenomena in Pietism, in the revival movements of the nineteenth century, and in the modern *Gemeinschaft* movement in Germany. With Zinzendorf the lay element already had a great role to play. The pietistically spirited organizations for Bible publication, tract and missionary societies, the YMCA, and the Christian Student World Federation were founded by laity. In the "left wing" of the Reformation, which was suppressed in Germany, but then was able ultimately to build its own churches in Holland, England, and the United States, a powerful lay impulse lives on. Mennonites and Baptists long considered themselves as lay movements in contrast to the state churches of the old world.[74]

6

The Missionary Zeal of the Early Anabaptists

H. W. Meihuizen

When Wolfgang Schäufele finished his Heidelberg dissertation in 1962, he was aware, as reflected in the subtitle,[1] that he had confined his research into the missionary passion and work of the Anabaptists to the sources available to him out of the Swiss-South German and Austrian regions. Only on a rare occasion did he base his conclusions on documents from the Northwest stream. It appears to me that in this year [1980] when we want to call attention to the fact that 450 years ago the first congregations in the Netherlands came into being as a result of the missionary witness of the earliest co-workers of Melchior Hofmann and shortly thereafter of Hofmann himself, we will profit from an examination of the testimonies out of the Lower Rhine and East Friesland-Westphalia areas. We will discover similarities in content and formulation between the two areas. But we will also notice differences in

Hendrik W. Meihuizen, (1906-1984) was a Dutch minister and lecturer. He served Mennonite congregations at Wieringen, Veendam, and the Hague and taught at the Mennonite Seminary in Amsterdam (1965-76). Publications include Galenus Abrahamsz *(1954),* Menno Simons *(1961),* Dat Fundament des christelyken leers of Menne Simons of 1539/40 *(1967), reprinted with an introduction and explanatory footnotes,* Van Mantz tot Menno *(1975). This chapter, translated by Roelf Kuitse and J. C. Wenger, is from* Doopsgezind Jaarboekje 1980.

nuance which, if considered, can illuminate the value of our tradition more clearly.

The publication of Schäufele's dissertation in 1966 caused surprise among those who knew little about Anabaptism. They did not know that the movement had spread "with tumultuous alacrity."[2] Apparently within two years after the first baptisms on confession of faith on January 21, 1525, congregations had been established in places as far away as Vienna. At least three more years after that the Melchiorites appeared in Amsterdam. Yet we may with reason be surprised at the speed with which the principles reached the Netherlands and the remarkable missionary passion with which these propagandists worked in this region. Before 1530 there were no Anabaptist congregations north of Worms. Although Hans Denck had taken refuge there in June 1527, he worked quietly at a translation of the prophets of the Old Testament and did not engage in efforts to establish congregations. Melchior, by whose work baptism upon confession of faith would be introduced into the Netherlands, was still in Strasbourg in April 1530, but by the next fall he baptized 300 people in Emden. Two of the elders whom he appointed there preceded him—almost immediately after their ordination—to the Low Countries. The first one, Sicke Freerks, died as the first martyr already on March 20, 1531, in Leeuwarden. The second one, Jan Volckertszoon Trypmaker, to whom Melchior entrusted leadership of the congregation at Emden before he returned to Strasbourg, arrived at Amsterdam in November 1531. His work resulted in his imprisonment and death at The Hague on December 6. Not much more than a year after his appearance, Anabaptism had already gained a firm footing in the Netherlands.

One may ask: Where did this missionary urgency spring from in the East as well as in the Netherlands? Why was this recruiting effort of these "Christian knights"—a term from Erasmus adopted by the Anabaptists—so successful? Indeed, the number in the Northwest actually exceeded those in the Southeast. If Balthasar Hubmaier prided himself on having baptized 300 people on one day in Waldhut, then Melchior Hof-

mann did the same thing in Emden five years later. Hans Hut
may have brought into the congregation at Waldeck a hundred
people during a fairly long period of time, and during his three
years of ministry he may have won a thousand converts. Leenaert
Bouwens must have been the most prolific. He baptized 10,378
believers in the area between Emden and Kortrijk in the years
between 1551 and 1582. No doubt for both branches of the
Anabaptist movement missionary passion sprang from the conviction that the end of the world was near.

The Roman Catholic Church all through the Middle Ages
emphasized dread of the last judgment. The rediscovery of the Bible, and in particular of the New Testament—especially the
Revelation of John—inevitably led to an emphasis on the "signs
of the times" as pointing to the approaching judgment.
Anabaptist missionaries had arrived in the eschatological "nick of
time." The day of the Lord would come "as a thief in the night"
(Rev. 3:3 and 16:15 and elsewhere in the New Testament). That is
why Hans Hut said in his important book about the mystery of
baptism that now "the last and most dangerous period for the
world" had come because "all that from the beginning by the
prophets, patriarchs and apostles was predicted, now was
realized"[3]; and Menno Simons opened his *Foundation*, after citing several Bible verses, with these words: "Because we observe
and out of experience perceive that the prophecies of the prophets
and apostles about the horrible and frightful oppression, distress
and want, the persecution, perils, fear and false doctrine of the last
day appear to be so oppressively and terribly true, that we ask our
readers now at last to take notice of our arguments."[4]

Consequently a second question arises: How was it possible
that the principles of the movement could be so strikingly similar
even though the two regions were separated by great distances?
There is so much similarity of thought and formulation between
Hans Hut's book just mentioned and certain passages out of
Menno's tracts that one would be inclined to suggest that the
Dutch elder must have known of the writings of his South
German colleague, even though it is difficult to trace the channels

by which it would have been brought to the Northwest. Of course, it is possible that the propagandists knew whole passages by memory. People at that time often had sharp memories! We know about this oral tradition through the oldest account of this early period of our history by one who had experienced it personally, Obbe Philips, who reported that everything he said in his confession he heard from Melchior's followers who "daily traveled to and from him in Strasbourg." The same report[5] also mentions that those at Leeuwarden regularly received Melchior's writings.

Melchior was a prolific writer indeed. Besides two publications on the last days and what God would do at that time, he published an essay in 1530 about God's commandment which he had instituted and confirmed by his Son concerning baptism, the Ordinance of God.[6] The German original has been lost, but it is not impossible that Melchior himself brought the manuscript to the Netherlands where he had it translated and printed. It is not difficult to show parallels with it in Menno's work. Melchior said, "The sixth trumpet has been blown; now is the hour before the false teachers, apostles and prophets with their wrong doctrine will seduce the third part of the people."[7] Menno used that same image from Revelation: "He who has created heaven and earth by his word, has blown his trumpet and beaten his drum; he has proclaimed his punishment, anger and eternal death through his prophets, Son and apostles."

Elsewhere Menno spoke clearly, as did most early Anabaptists, about the severity of God's judgment. Sometimes the suggestion was expressed that fear of the divine sentence, without the possibility of appeal, was the primary incentive for conversion. This may have been true for many but not for all. Conversion often was a response to the experience of God's grace. "For it is impossible," Menno said, "that I would not and should not love him from the depths of my soul and through that love would not willingly serve, honor and follow him all the days of my life."[8] Even if it is true that all converts in fact do reckon that their sins will be charged against them, yet they do not stay with the law but entrust themselves to the gospel. They love the Lord because he has loved them first, and they return that love on the basis of what God did in the life of the individual. They like to say with 1 Peter 2:9 that he has called them out of darkness into his wonderful light—in what one in general calls conversion or what the converts experience as rebirth. Most Anabaptists spoke about this as the renewal of life. This means that they had learned to see how superficial and inadequate their former way of life had been, that they in fact had not reckoned at all with God and thus, in essence, they had been turned away from him as sinners. Only after a person started to focus on the only correct attitude toward God and neighbor could one begin to respond to the intention of the gospel that had indeed been hidden during many centuries but was now again brought to light.

That is why the rediscovery of the gospel had its reverse side, too, as we see in Melchior's interpretation of Revelation 9:15: The proclamation of the end times would be accompanied by such powerful temptations that even the elect would almost be led astray and apostasize again. Thus Melchior[9] and Menno speak: "God sets one family against the other and one friend against another. He makes some wander in far away countries for the sake of his holy word, he makes others suffer want, burning, drowning and being killed by the sword. He gives signs: earthquakes, wars, pestilence and many kinds of diseases."[10]

All this is more or less summarized in the prologue to *Offer des Heeren:* "The most merciful God and Father has in his inscrutable grace and goodness in this last, most dangerous time allowed that his blessed, only and eternal Son, Jesus Christ who has been unknown for so many hundreds of years, now before the eyes of the conscience of a few people took shape and caused those who were dead in all kinds of sin and ungodliness to arise and claim eternal life. He has saved the poor, bewildered, starved sheep out of the hands of the perfidious shepherds and out of the jaws of the ferocious wolves and led them out of the dry unfertile pastures of human teaching and laws to the green, fat grasslands of the mountains of Israel, guarded by their only and eternal shepherd Jesus Christ."[11] These words and images could have been taken straight out of the books of Melchior and Menno; as a matter of fact such good biblical sounds are heard wherever Anabaptists have written.

Many times in those days when a crisis arose the Anabaptists appealed to Matthew 9:38: "Pray the Lord of the harvest that he might send laborers." Michael Sattler wrote in 1527 to his congregation at Horb, which within a short time was shepherdless by virtue of his martyr's death: "Pray, that reapers will be pressed to the harvest work, because the time for threshing has come."[12] When Menno called to mind his appointment as elder, he remembered well that the six, seven, or eight who with him possessed the same spirit and conviction had asked him to take pity on "the great misery and distress of poor oppressed souls; the hunger was great and faithful stewards were few."[13] But Menno remained well aware of the fact that he had at his disposal a "little talent" and thus with reason asked God "to give him a manly heart." Yet he was strongly convinced that he taught nothing more than what "Christ Jesus, the heaven-sent teacher, the mouth and the word of the most high God" himself had taught.[14]

That is expressed with somewhat more modesty than what Jacob Hutter, the influential leader from Tyrol, after whom also a whole group is named, exhibited in his farewell letter: "God has entrusted his godly, eternal word to me, has placed it in my heart and in my mouth and granted to me the heavenly blessing of his godliness and his Holy Spirit." Thus God had appointed him as "guardian, shepherd and steward of his holy people, of his elect holy Christian congregation, which is the betrothed and bride, the lovely and beloved spouse of our dear Lord Jesus Christ."[15] Another equally assured Tyroler expressed himself when facing his interrogators at the time of his imprisonment in Aken: He had not put himself in office, but "God and his Spirit in the congregation had done it, because as God had sent his beloved Son into the world and the Son his apostles, thus he was still sending his servants through his Spirit."[16]

Of course, all Anabaptist missionaries believed they were called by God, and it was not a matter of self-exaltation. When

Melchior was about to begin his long imprisonment, he said that he at his coming liberation "with outstretched finger shall indicate him who had sent him." But already then doubt was beginning to grow concerning whether one can be really sure of the Spirit's call. Obbe voiced this doubt most bitterly when he wrote that he at his commission as elder indeed had heard the words being said and felt the hands laid upon him, but he had not experienced anything of the Holy Spirit.[17] Menno, whom he later ordained as an elder in the ministry, subsequently stated that only "the one urged by the Spirit could be called by a Christian, orthodox and irreproachable congregation."[18] In his rather much-revised *Foundation*, Menno remarked about this: "The commissioning and calling of the Christian preachers happens in two ways—many occur without human mediation, being called by God alone, but many others are called through the faithful."[19] In the course of time the call received from the congregation was considered to be the guarantee of divine approval on one's holding office.

What did the office in fact entail? Hans Schmidt of Rommelshausen, elder in Württemberg, explained at his trial: "This is the greatest and most important work: to visit the ignorant nations, to proclaim to them God's will, to be a light to the world, to lengthen the cords of the tabernacle (Is. 54:2) and announce forgiveness to sinners in order that the number of the saints might be completed."[20] Melchior emphasized the calling together of the converts: "Now, in these last days, the apostolic messengers of the Lord Jesus Christ will gather the elect, calling by means of the gospel the bride of Christ to the spiritual desert (Rev. 12:6, 14) and through baptism be united with the Lord."[21] Menno spoke more directly: "I and my dear brothers in the faith are laboring with no other intention than that we may bring the poor, blind and bewildered congregation by the Lord's grace, Spirit, and word back again to the true shepherd, the authentic sheepfold, on the right road to true faith, to the correct sacraments, a sincere obedience to God and to an irreproachable life."[22]

Something can be said yet about method and tactics of the early propagandists. In the Southeast region some began with the clergy believing that if they were won for the faith they would win their parishes. It is possible that the so-called "Wassenberger preachers" in the Northwest were converted by representatives of Jan Matthijs. We can hardly close our eyes also to the fact that Menno had been a priest and Dirk Philips a monk. But for the most part it must have happened as in Leeuwarden where Obbe tells us that "fourteen or fifteen people, both men and women had come together to hear the summons to peace and suffering; they should not be anxious about or afraid of the great tyranny, because no Christian blood would be spilled any more and God would before long destroy all those who shed blood and were god-less. Thereafter they were all baptized that same day."[23]

Baptism, then, was more or less as a matter of course con-nected with the resolute intention to henceforth walk in "newness of life" (Rom. 6:4). Melchior impressed on his adherents that "the command and order of the law of the Lord for his apostolic messengers was that through the true sign of the covenant, the cleansing by water in baptism, they would entrust and unite themselves with the Lord Jesus Christ."[24] Baptism for him, ac-cording to these words, is apparently the sign that signifies, and, if one wants, symbolizes the covenant with God. Going into the water made visible the covenant and pointed to baptism as administered in the time of the apostles. Baptism thus was the es-chatological sign, the "sign on the doorpost" of the day of the Lord, the very insignia of God.

That elder whose influence has too often been underesti-mated, even more often denied, but who for a period of time was Menno's equal, David Joris, in one of his many songs thought of baptism as the insignia of the true people of God: "The Lord has lifted up his hand; let the trumpet blow and the sign of Israel be written on his servants."[25] Menno used the same text from Ezekiel 9:4 in his first booklet on spiritual resurrection: "Those who with Christ have risen out of their sins, have the mark Tau, with which the servants of God have been marked on their foreheads."[26]

But more important than all of this is the answer to the ques-tion of what in fact gave such convincing power to the missionary labors of those early Anabaptists that they could enlist so many into their ranks. It seems to me that no clearer disclosure can be found than in the words of Jörg Haug von Juchsen, farmer-preacher in Thüringen. Even though he likely had not yet come around to identifying himself with the movement through the new and only true baptism, the Moravian brothers included his writing on the beginning of a true Christian life in their collection of Christian literature as being from an unquestionably congenial spirit. He wrote in that booklet—which seems almost modern and which in 1527 was published together with an essay by Hans Denck—this passage: "Only the person who is converted is able to give insight to others concerning how one fares when he comes to faith and knowledge of God, the suffering he has had to go through and how bitterly difficult it has been in his own heart before truth has triumphed over unbelief. Because he has sailed through the sea of antagonisms, he knows the way and the dangers one has to pass through. Therefore, out of experience he can show others how the beginning leads to the end."[27]

This originates in the school in which Hans Hut had learned the principles of the Christian faith, the school of mysticism, also familiar to Thomas Müntzer. He was considered by the original group, the one in Zürich in which the first baptism upon confession of faith had been administered, among the "purest preachers of the gospel." They emphatically declared that Thomas's writings had greatly strengthened them in their convictions that only through suffering could believers come to submission, that they should have felt God's "plowshares" in the field of their hearts[28] before they would be prepared for true surrender to God and true knowledge of the bitter Christ. Hans Denck said that that was reserved only for the one who wished to follow him [Jesus Christ] in life,[29] or as Hans Hut, completely in the spirit of Müntzer, remarked: "Nobody can obtain the truth unless he pursues the footsteps of Christ and his elect in the hard apprenticeship of tribulation."[30] That was the condition for accepting the missionary task and the secret of the results of that passion for mission to which our congregations owe their existence.

7

Sixteenth-Century Hutterian Mission

Leonard Gross

In view of the many creative movements that regularly surface throughout church history, it was to be expected that an intense reaction to magisterial Protestantism arose among those who understood Christianity as a gathered church, free from magisterial control. But also in Roman Catholic lands, individuals and groups continued to react against a church in need of reformation "at its head and among its members." These reactions to both Protestantism and Catholicism resulted in the wide-flung and tenacious Anabaptist movement, one manifestation of which was the birth of the Hutterian Brotherhood.[1]

The community of peace as the Anabaptist response to "world"

One distinction between the Protestant and Anabaptist political outlooks is basic for the movement depicted in this essay: Luther—and the other Reformers as well—chose to retain the

---

Leonard Gross, Goshen, Indiana, is executive secretary of the Historical Committee of the Mennonite Church and director of its archives and historical research program (1970-   ). He had a Mennonite Central Committee youth-work assignment in North Germany (1955-57), taught at Bethany Christian High School in Goshen (1959-64) and at Western Michigan University, Kalamazoo, and was a research associate to Robert Friedmann (1968-70). He is editor of Mennonite Historical Bulletin *and has written* The Golden Years of the Hutterites *(Herald Press, 1980) and other articles on Anabaptists and Mennonites.*

concept of *corpus christianum*, where society was by and large
equated with the established church, making society and church
in effect coterminous. Hence the idea of *world* in the New Testament sense of the term was neutralized and was therefore a self-
contradiction. On the other hand, the idea of the narrow gate (Mt.
7:13-14), a way of life set apart from society at large, was central
to Anabaptist thought. Such a path led to a voluntary community
of committed Christians bound together by God's Spirit, who
lived in peace and love and shared one another's burdens. The
concept of mission was integral to such a gathered church. The
Anabaptists believed themselves to be on this narrow path,
whereas society was on the broad path leading to destruction.
They equated society with the unregenerate world, within which
lived seekers after God's truth, souls who desired the strength of
God's kingdom of peace. Anabaptist mission was set up to locate
these seekers.[2]

The Protestant churches worked on the basis of an ultimate
responsibility for all of society within a given territory; mission
was defined in terms of political boundaries. The Anabaptists on
the other hand held to an ultimate responsibility for the kingdom
of God, which they understood to be separate from the world. Although they also felt a responsibility for all people in the world,
and often gave their own lives to fulfill this responsibility through
mission, they considered the pattern and political organization of
general society—including its established church—to be one with
the kingdoms of this world. In fact the all-pervasive decadence
and the constant warfare within the kingdoms of this world, the
Anabaptists felt, militated against the fulfillment of the peace
which Jesus established upon earth.

But in God's kingdom peace was commanded and could
reign. Hate and war were contradictory to the very concept of the
kingdom of God, where Christian love as a way of life was made
possible through the reigning of God's Spirit. The church consequently could not fully participate in the life of the kingdom of
this world and its ruler (Jn. 16:11).

Such a lofty ideal remained central for the Anabaptists, as

God's will for his people. Yet solid evidence from Anabaptist as well as non-Anabaptist sources indicates that a high degree of peace and unity had indeed been established within Anabaptist circles. The Great Chronicle of the sixteenth-century Hutterian Brotherhood affords us the following insights:

> Many were convinced, and praised them as a devout people, and that it must have been established by God. It would otherwise have been impossible for so many to live together in such unity, whereas among others, where only two, three, or four live together, they are daily in each other's hair and dissatisfied until they finally leave one another.[3]

Such peace and unity characterized the Hutterites in Moravia during much of the sixteenth century.

Mission, the natural concomitant of community

The firm emphasis upon establishing a kingdom of peace did not deter the Anabaptists from continuing to carry out the Great Commission. The gathered church became the base from which the call to discipleship and community was to go out through mission. After 1527, Anabaptist mission continued to contain a consciously apocalyptic note; but counter to the earlier, revolutionary nature of many other dissidents who wanted to overthrow the existing regime, the Anabaptists held to the New Testament as programmatic, including a nonviolent approach to effecting Christ's kingdom. They were accused—in a sense, correctly—of wanting to tear down the old church establishment, but the alternative they were suggesting they believed to have been successfully established early within Christian history. It was by no means either a Renaissance utopia, or an illusory dream, or simply a precipitate explosion, the void of which God himself was to miraculously fill. The earliest documents fully substantiate that there was nothing vague in Hutterian doctrine about the kingdom of God. Granted, the Hutterites were dissenters who practiced civil disobedience at times, accepting suffering and persecution as part of the way of Christ. They affirmed only a conditional obedience to the magistracy, but an unconditional obedience to God.[4]

Integral to obedience, to be sure, was the Hutterian concern for the world. Mission was the natural Hutterian response throughout the sixteenth century, extending into the far reaches of many European lands and beyond.

Hutterian mission during the golden era
of Hutterian history, 1560 to 1590

The nature of Hutterian mission

The Hutterian concept of the brotherhood-church as found during the Hutterian Golden Era (1560 to 1590) would be inconceivable without a highly developed mission program. Mission, the concomitant of brotherhood, was a necessary corollary of the command to love God. For a cultural enclave such as the Hutterites, it was one method of showing love to the peoples of an unregenerate world. For the Hutterites, the Great Commission was just as valid during the sixteenth century as it had been for the Christian church during the early, formative decades of the Christian era.

Looking back to the Golden Years, the author of the Great Chronicle takes note of the mission activity and its justification in Peter Walpot's time:

> Christian mission was established, of which the Lord commands and says: "As my Father has sent me, so send I you." And also: "I have chosen and placed you that you go out and bear fruit." Therefore, servants of the gospel and their helpers were sent out annually into the lands where there was reason [to hope for success]. They visited individuals who desired to change in their way of living, who sought and inquired after truth. They led these out of their land by day and night according to their desire, not considering constable and hangman nor that many sacrificed their heads, bodies, and lives for this reason. Thus they gathered the people of the Lord in a manner befitting good shepherds.[5]

During these Golden Years the missioners spread out into most of Europe. For example the Great Chronicle records for 1570 the journeys of Jörg Rader to Tirol, Hans Langenbach to the Rhine, Claus Braidl to Württemberg, and Peter Hörich to Silesia.

Hutterite missioners not only trekked through all parts of the German lands, but also to Switzerland, the Low Countries, Italy, Poland, Bohemia, Slovakia, and even as far as Denmark. Although the Hutterites tried to keep careful record of their mission program, government sources yield evidence of a far greater outreach than the voluminous Hutterian codices would indicate.[6]

These missioners, if apprehended, received a variety of punishments. Some were simply threatened and admonished. One missioner heard that he might be sent to the galleys. A short entry for the year 1567 in the Great Chronicle is by no means atypical: When Burckhart Bämerle, an aged minister, was imprisoned along with his companion, Bärthl Ringel, no ordinary hundredweights were hung on him, but rather the whole earth; for a ring was fastened to the earth, Bämerle's feet were tied to the ring, and the unfortunate prisoner was pulled up "so that the sun could have shone through him." The prisoner remained steadfast, was later released, but died the same year at Tracht, Moravia.[7]

The Hutterites' great antagonist, the Catholic missioner Christian Erhard, described the "damage" brought about by the Hutterites and their missioners, who, he reported,

> sneak about in the country and secretly commit serious crimes. Just look at the huge heap of wasps in Moravia; that is where they annually seduce the people. . . . And these Hutterites are the very same Anabaptists who are hanged and drowned in Tirol, the region of Salzburg, Bavaria, Switzerland, etc., and are scorched and burned according to their deserved reward. Other Anabaptists are not able to seduce the people so secretly, quietly, and treacherously.[8]

Erhard's vituperation not only shows his disapproval of the toleration accorded the Hutterites in Moravia, which is what he intended, but also demonstrates the effectiveness of Hutterian mission.

The method of Hutterian mission

Hutterian mission strategy took many forms. Personal encounter was the usual method used, but group evangelism also oc-

curred, usually held in secret in the open, in barns, and in homes.[9]
Missioners were sent out into the world around Easter, and again
in the autumn. They met with seekers wherever and whenever
possible, sometimes in cellar recesses, sometimes in forests, and at
times, at night.[10] An insight into a missioner's arduous travels is
provided by the experience of Valentin Hörl. With several other
brethren he was sent out in 1571 to determine how many souls
were left in Tirol who were seeking God's righteousness, and who
were desirous of reforming their way of living. Hörl's three
comrades had already toured the upper Inn and the Etz valleys,
and Hörl had made inquiries at various localities, including the
Adige. The group was planning to meet at a certain place, but
something went amiss. Hörl then searched for his comrades in the
Puster Valley, and found them on the road just above Schöneck.
Because they were finding no one who desired to give him- or
herself over to divine obedience they went to Stertzing, and from
there directly to Moravia, so as not to misappropriate their
funds.[11]

Mission was also carried on through written communication.
The mission activity of Hans Schlegel and Simon Kress in the
early summer of 1574 in the area of Maulbronn, Württemberg, is
an example of both personal and epistolary mission. Kress told
Schlegel of his visit to a man whom we know only as Caspar, who
had shown genuine interest in Hutterian Christianity. But instead
of visiting Caspar, Schlegel merely wrote a letter to him. The
probable reason was that circumstances necessitated Schlegel's
"hurrying to another place," in all likelihood because the authorities had caught wind of his work. At least Schlegel was able
to lend Caspar a printed copy of the Brotherhood *Rechenschaft*,
which he was to return in two or three weeks. The letter expressed
Schlegel's hope that the work would bring Caspar blessing and
eternal peace. Schlegel apologized for not coming in person, testifying that he was indeed responsible to contact any person showing interest in true righteousness and that he wanted to witness to
the truth to the degree that God's grace resided within him.
Realizing that Caspar might find the *Rechenschaft* difficult to

comprehend at places, he asked Caspar not "to desire to understand it with flesh and blood, for flesh and blood cannot reveal
[truth] since flesh and blood must lose its own will at this point
and die to itself if man is to obey and be made a living person in
Christ."[12]

Schlegel further suggested that this is why Christ com-
mended for his followers the narrow way, where few were able to
enter, since "the entrance and way to heaven is called the gate of
death. Christ himself is this path and entrance, a way full of deri-
sion, pain, and suffering."[13] It was behind this gate that Christ
stood "with his poverty, with his bloody garment and crown of
thorns, and with the cup of the bitter cross and suffering." Christ
presented this way of life to those who desired divine inheritance.
Yet many attempted some sort of compromise to this narrow way,
"bending Scripture back and forth so that one might find a wide
road that is not so hard, and desiring to break open another gate
into heaven." Such persons however were only thieves and rob-
bers. Schlegel suggested therefore that if Caspar desired to seek
the kingdom of heaven he should seek it correctly.[14]

The Hutterites carried this same missionary message to their
relatives living in the "world." In April 1574 Margarete Endris, at
Wastitz, sent such a letter to her non-Hutterite son Elias, in Hor-
ren, Württemberg. Two other children of Margarete, Gretl and
Jörgle, had already joined the Hutterites in Moravia. Elias had
just written that his two sisters were planning to make the
journey. Margarete responded that this would bring her real joy if
they came with good intentions and desired to live according to
God's will.[15]

But Elias also had wondered on what grounds his Hutterite
mother opposed his Protestant faith. Margarete replied that he
was deviating from God's truth and the teachings of Christ by
turning baptism into child's play, and by transforming the Lord's
supper into idolatry and financial gain, communing and sharing
with participants who might still be living in sin, contrary to biblical teachings. Furthermore, she continued, a Christian was a
godly person, and this was not the case with Elias, who was

instead traveling down the broad way of the devil, thereby demonstrating the works of the flesh. God did not want such "Christians," who only confessed a "holy Christian church" with words but in reality were part of an unholy congregation which disgraced his name. Indeed, her son's congregation did not even demonstrate mutual aid![16]

Margarete expressed the hope that her son would leave the world and change his manner of life, accept the new birth, and separate himself from the world. She pleaded with him not to hesitate:

> Become converted to God and come to his people. For we have no doubt that this is the people of God, the correct way, the narrow gate, the true faith through which one becomes godly and is redeemed in Christ Jesus our Lord and Savior. May you desire to submit to this, you and your wife, and my two daughters if they are still out there. This is our heart-felt request.... From me, Margarete, your loyal mother.[17]

The content of the mission message

Hutterite missioners proclaimed a uniform doctrine wherever they were active, based on the Brotherhood *Rechenschaft*, printed in the 1540s and again in 1565. However, a growing tradition built upon the written reports of cross-examination also contributed to the growing refinement of the mission message. One solid tract entitled "Noble Lessons and Instruction on How to Turn Unbelievers from Their Error" was composed specifically for missioners, probably by Leonhard Dax during the 1560s.[18] The document begins with an analysis of humanity's lost state and God's proffered redemption. Adam is to blame for the lost state of humankind; but through Christ, salvation has again been realized for the true disciples who remain in his teachings. The redeemed Christian community, composed of these very disciples, remains in conflict with the world. The conflict is partly the consequence of mission, for the world does not desire to acknowledge God or his messengers, but rather persecutes them. Although the world claims to be Christian, it demonstrates by its actions, such as persecuting innocent missioners, that it is not Christian; and God, at the appropriate moment, will cast down his vengeance upon such ungodly people.

The document continues with a discussion about the world and its magistracy, which exists without God; unfortunately, there is a close relationship between it and the established church, whereas actually the true nature of Christianity and its way of peace lies hidden from the world. Furthermore, the false prophets of the established church, with their claim of Christian truth, cause the magistrates to believe their words, and in this manner lead them to transcend their rightful bounds.

A general appeal is then made for people to turn away from the ways of the world and enter the Christian way of life. For, as the argument continues, the world has created havoc out of biblical precepts, such as the Lord's supper. Indeed, anyone who eats with an unrepentant sinner shows himself not to be of God's holy community, the church. Partaking in the Lord's supper, correctly understood, means acknowledging complete agreement and fellowship with one another. Baptism too is of the greatest import to the devil, for if infant baptism were rescinded, then much of his power would be broken, since he "knows that when a person allows himself to be baptized in the Christian manner, he then completely renounces service to the devil." [19] As for marriage, the priests—who do not even enter into it—lead wanton lives, which to them is better than to break the man-made rules of celibacy.

In short, the Hutterites believed that the world simply did not allow Scripture to bring people to repentance and the forgiveness of sins. The result was evident: God's punishment continued to prevail in the world. But at the opposite pole of this retribution lay God's redemption. Christians were to see to it that the world and its evil—namely, the false prophets, persecution, and martyrdom—did not overcome them. For God granted salvation to his true children, who remained steadfast until the end.

The tract closes with a final appeal to those living in the world. The nature of Christian mission is defined by contrasting the nature of the Christian way of life to that of the world. The mood of the appeal is captured in the following paraphrase: The

world wants to claim for itself what the Lord has promised only
for the godly, to whom he has shown his grace. The world wants
to cover everything over with the mercy of God, and avoids
perceiving to whom he wants to be merciful—namely, not with
the ungodly. But sin earns only death, not the grace of God. One
is to follow Christ, who said: "Where I am, there shall my servants
be." One who lives the life of Christ's goodness will receive
eternal life; one who lives a life of evil will receive damnation. But
this does not imply salvation through good works, for salvation
rests only within the atoning power of Jesus Christ. Yet good
works are surely to be there, for Christ is the example. Christians
are to do as Christ did and keep his word by loving one another,
which is the sign of discipleship. For the Christian has died, and
his or her life is hidden with Christ in God, with victory lying at
the end; although for the ungodly, raging hell will be the
reward.[20]

In this tract one may note the Hutterian view of salvation,
where a distinction is made between the discipleship-mandate of
Christ that entails bearing fruit, and a works-religion which the
author believes he experienced as a former Catholic priest. The
Hutterian call to mission was an appeal to divine mercy, founded
solely upon Christ's redeeming act. But by accepting this mercy,
the Christian could not help but demonstrate the Christian
experience of a transformed life pattern.

The missioners' farewell service

At the time of departure of one or more missioners, the community held a special farewell service. A poem, still extant, was
sung for the occasion, entitled "A New Song, Written in 1568, on
the Theme of 'When the Brethren Depart for Other Lands.'"
The impressive ceremony developed as a sort of prayerful litany in
which the missioners, in dialogue with the gathered community,
solemnized under God the commission placed upon them.[21] The
following résumé offers an insight into what must have been a
most meaningful experience to both church and missioners, the
latter perhaps never to return.

First of all, attention was called to the original mandate for mission: God has granted his salvation through the coming of Christ to all who accept his counsel and follow his teachings. Hence, as the Father sent Christ, so Christ also sent his disciples to proclaim the gospel. God continues to send his disciples so that people may turn from their evil ways. The message these disciples are to proclaim is that everyone without exception must someday appear before God and account for all deeds and for every idle word.

Then followed a petition to God for perseverance in proclamation, and for divine guidance in scriptural interpretation, that God's covenant be preserved, that the missioners refrain from idle talk in their striving to seek God's honor and glory, and that the people far and wide might hear the message of the need to repent by separating themselves from the sins of the world in order to enter into salvation.

Next a reminder was given about the stark reality of divine punishment: Whenever God had desired to punish people, he first warned and taught them. If they did not repent, he brought on punishment. But God is still sending out his Word, proclaiming to the people how they should change in their ways, separate from the worldly Babel and all its impurity, submit to God, and become part of his community. Since the last hour is near, the godly are to be prepared. They are to gather Christ's chosen ones according to his command.

Attention then turned to the missioners themselves: They, God's chosen emissaries, will have to bear the pangs of misery within the world, confident of gathering the fruit resulting from the proclaimed seed.

At that point the missioners responded to the gathered community, acknowledging their call and requesting the continuing prayers of the church, so that God would comfort the missioners with the presence of his Spirit and protect them from suffering.

Another Hutterian document found in a seventeenth-century codex sheds light upon the farewell services of missioners and the nature of later Hutterian mission.[22] A missioner goes to the front of the assembled congregation and announces that he and others have been chosen through the counsel of the Lord to go out into foreign lands to gather a church. The missioners acknowledge the immensity of the task and the limitations of human resources; yet God has demanded obedience in service to the church. Indeed, since God has previously been able to use simple folk for his work, the missioners hope that God may grant them renewed opportunities.

The farewell service brought various points to the attention of the community. If mission was to be successful and bring people to Moravia, the Hutterites would constantly have to keep in mind that they were to be living examples of a unity wherein life and doctrine merged. The newcomers were to be accepted with joy. Patience was to be the rule in case the incoming people did not immediately comprehend their new vocations. There were not to be hard words such as "Oh, you coarse Swiss; you cavilling Rhinelander; you bad Hessian!"[23] Rather humility was called for toward everyone. For each person should consider how he or she had been accepted into the community with love and friendliness, and that the stranger was unaccustomed to everything: the language, the work, even the food and drink.

The missioners then admonished the youth to follow the instruction of the adults, to learn from them, and even to accept punishment and counsel with gratitude. They were to commend themselves to the elders as they would to parents, not begrudging them their food and drink, but trusting them and accepting their advice. The missioners admonished the adults to care for the sick, the elderly, the widows, and orphans.

At this point the missioners asked for the prayers of the church, and for pardon if they had caused any hurt. They thanked the community for the love shown them from the time of their youth. Then in closing they announced that the missioners would soon depart.

After this a member from the congregation arose and praised the missioners, referring to them as sheep among raving wolves, as people facing possible death, as mirrors to the world. They acknowledged the possible harsh treatment of prison towers and chains. Then there was prayer for successful mission.

Finally, following apostolic custom, the congregation accompanied the missioners to the town gates. There, after the missioners were blessed, the parting became stark reality, leading to certain hardship, probable persecution, and possible death.

If the missioners returned, they were received "as if he were the Lord himself." The successes of the mission were lauded, and the reports of imprisoned missioners eagerly awaited. Prison epistles were handed over to the addressees, greetings delivered, and reports made, some of which found their way into the Great Chronicle.[24]

The results of Hutterian mission

The majority of those thousands of recruits finding their way to Hutterian communities adopted the new way of life. The Hutterian way was a way to eternal salvation, but also a way out of material poverty for many.[25] Many types of immigrants converted to Hutterianism. During the late sixteenth century, some complaints surfaced about the lack of drive among some converts; they were nevertheless accepted in the expectation that both spiritual growth and physical dexterity would gradually become manifest. The continuing strength of the brotherhood suggests that the Hutterian hopes were realized.[26]

The Brotherhood's capability of receiving total strangers into its close communal system is also substantiated by no less a figure than the bold Catholic, Christoph Andreas Fischer. Fischer's compliment, obviously intended as an attack, witnesses to the continuing success of the mission program into the seventeenth century:

> Just as doves fly out and continually bring strange doves back with them, the Anabaptists also send out their false apostles annually to seduce the people, both women and men and bring them into their dove-cotes—as I have been told that in 1604 they enticed more than two hundred persons out of the empire, leading them into their dove-cotes. And just as newly captured doves are pampered with wheat, honey, and other things during the first days,

until they become accustomed [to their new environment], the
Anabaptists also give their new accomplices rich foods and roasts,
and very sweet hypocritical words. But afterwards comes the time
to "go and work, and be satisfied with cabbage and beets."[27]

It was incomprehensible to populace and magistrate alike
that well-to-do farmers would voluntarily forsake productive
farms by night for no apparent reason but to join with the distant
Hutterites. A passion for private riches and prestige was
transformed into a desire for total surrender to God and a life of
complete sharing within a brotherhood. On the other hand, economic reasons led some poverty-stricken families also to make
their way to Moravia, the "promised land" of the Hutterites.[28]

Although most of the converts became a part of the expanding Hutterian movement, adapting themselves willingly, a few
disenchanted souls returned to the land of their birth. In the
winter of 1577, for instance, a handful of young men went to
Moravia to look around, returned to their homeland disillusioned,
and told the magistrates that they had no desire to return to
Moravia. Others, however, returned once again to the Hutterite
fold, sometimes bringing with them their families or other acquaintances.[29]

Hutterian mission fields

Five distinct Hutterian mission fields developed in the course of
the sixteenth century, which together suggest the breadth and
depth of Hutterian mission. Three of these fields were defined by
the religion of the land, Catholicism, Lutheranism, and Calvinism—although it was not with convinced individuals of these
faiths that Hutterite missioners met, but with seekers open to the
Hutterian way of life, who lived in these territorial-church areas.
In addition, the Hutterites entered into serious dialogue with the
Swiss Brethren (and also with the Polish Brethren) about the
possibility of effecting closer ties. Aspects of the first three of these
encounters are lifted out, not primarily to highlight confessional
differences, but simply to define further the Hutterian theology of
missions.

Hans Arbeiter and the Jesuits

Hans Arbeiter, while on a Hutterian mission in 1568, was captured at Hainbach, in the Roman Catholic bishopric of Speyer. During his imprisonment at the Kierweiler Castle, Arbeiter was questioned at various points and later released. He wrote a detailed resumé of his imprisonment and cross-examinations; at several points he was asked about the Hutterian rationale of mission.

The following account lifts out one aspect only of Arbeiter's position on mission which focuses upon his awareness of being a member of a free church, separated completely from the magisterial organization which governs society in general.

The main point of contention between Arbeiter and the magistracy in fact centered in Arbeiter's very presence in foreign territory, which in itself challenged the claim of the established church to be the true church of Christ. For here was one who proclaimed implicitly, and at times explicitly, that the established church had no right even to call itself a church. Since there was close interaction between the church and the magistracy, the magistracy also felt threatened by the potential revolutionary force such dissent might, and at times did, provoke.

Arbeiter admitted from the outset of his imprisonment that he had been called to the office of teacher and apostle by his brotherhood in Moravia for the purpose of pointing others to the way of redemption. As a missioner his mandate was to confront the people of the world with their sins, their abominations, and their vile living—and this with the Word of God. He proclaimed that the individuals leading such a life could in no way be saved unless they repented and took the cross of Christ upon themselves (Heb. 13:13).

Arbeiter also asserted that no earthly magistrate had the right to forbid God's missioners from setting foot on their land, for the earth was the Lord's (Ps. 24:1), and the Lord had called the church to mission. Therefore God was to be obeyed and people disobeyed where such prohibition was demanded by rulers and their mandates.[30]

Paul Glock and the Lutherans

Another aspect of mission surfaces in the prison experience of
Paul Glock, which extended continuously from 1558 to 1576 in
the castle-fortress of Wittlingen, in Württemberg. Glock also was
finally released, after recounting many a prison episode to his
brethren back home in Moravia through prison epistles, most of
which are still extant. For Glock, mission could be understood
only from the perspective of the brotherhood-church.

Glock's definition of the church is unequivocal: "There have
always been two peoples, the godly and the ungodly." Denying
the Lutheran idea of the invisible church, Glock believed that the
godly formed a visible church, composed of identifiable disciples
and founded on Christian love. Since Glock knew of only one such
brotherhood, which was in Moravia, it was there that God's
people, in disciplined obedience and mutuality, could grow in
faith and love by following the example of Christ. The tending of
this flock of Christ required constant vigilance to preserve unity in
the Spirit.

Entrance into the church was through baptism, and baptism
was for believers. Glock believed it quite simple to show this view
of baptism as the biblical position: Faith stems only from hearing
the Word being taught (Rom. 10:10, 17). Salvation is based on a
person's confessing that Jesus is Lord (Rom. 10:9). Therefore,
since baptism (entering into the body of Christ) is integral to salvation, and since faith follows teaching, an individual's baptism
does not precede either having been taught or the personal
confessing of faith; baptism instead follows from this. Furthermore, baptism, as a covenant of a good conscience with God (1
Pet. 3:21), demands that the convert understand what he or she is
entering.

Mission consequently meant searching out those who desired
to live among God's gathered people in his kingdom, bringing
them to Moravia, and sharing with them the good news that
God's kingdom indeed existed. But Hutterian mission included a
more subtle witness as well. God's people, as the body of Christ,
emanated something of Christ's Spirit simply by living in

brotherhood; all members also reflected this same Spirit wherever their paths led. Part of this witness lay in the concept of truthfulness and genuineness, as when Glock refused to break his promise not to escape, although he was advised to do so by the Hutterian leaders. Even in prison it was natural for Glock to share the good news of the kingdom of God.[31]

Leonhard Dax and the Calvinists

In the cross-examination of the Hutterite missioner Leonhard Dax in 1567 and 1568 at the Alzey prison in the Palatinate, the two sides of the issue of mission clash in a way which underscores the radical difference between the Calvinist view of the church and its mission, and that of the Anabaptists.

The thought of the Calvinist superintendent who interrogated Leonhard Dax, as condensed from Dax's reconstruction of the prison debate, takes on the following argument: Since the church in the Palatinate is correctly established upon Calvinistic dogma and the truth is proclaimed throughout the whole territory, there is no need for Anabaptism (Hutterianism) to make its appearance in the land. The Anabaptist missioners are consequently attempting to lead astray any and all people who yield to the witness of Anabaptism, people who are already of the right persuasion. And given the peculiar Anabaptist doctrines such as baptism, (Hutterian) community of goods, and the view on the nature of church and the magistracy, the whole Anabaptist idea of mission is based upon human—not divine—action. Furthermore, since the Hutterites confess, with the Calvinists, the foundation of Jesus Christ and his justification, there really is no reason why the Hutterites should form a separate church body. They should actually join the Calvinist church.

The thought of Dax, highly condensed, takes on the following argument: Hutterian mission justifiably extends into the Palatinate, because the church there is by no means correctly established, and the proclamation of God's truth must go forth. Even though the Hutterian creed and view of justification by faith seem on the surface to be similar to that of Calvinism, the Hut-

terites in fact stand a world apart from the Calvinists on many important issues that determine the authenticity of the church. The
differences are serious enough to merit a separation of God's
people not only from the world, as the term is usually defined, but
also from other so-called churches, which are churches in name
only. Such mission results in a gathering together of the faithful
into a godly community where a communal sharing takes place on
all levels among believers who have freely committed themselves
through baptism to be God's people, the church. But separation
from the world also entails political consequences in light of the
fact that God's kingdom, not being of the world, is established
upon voluntarism and love, not upon the sword. The church consequently relates to the magistracy on a conditional basis only.
Furthermore, separation at times may also have a bearing upon
unequally yoked marriage partners, for even marriage is conditional to a higher obedience to God, which conceivably could (although in general practice does not) lead to separation of husband
and wife.[32]

Mission as protest to the corporate world
       The radical dualism of the Hutterites which defined their
mission to seekers also determined their witness to the secular authorities. In the late 1570s, after half a century of suffering and
persecution, one anonymous Hutterite writer composed a bitter
rebuttal to those individuals and rulers who were intent on
destroying the brotherhood. The book-length document is titled:
"Charges and Allegations of the Blind, Perverse World and All
Ungodly People, Who Constantly Agitate Against the Devout
Witnesses of God and his Truth, and Blaspheme Against the
Truth in Them, Thereby Bringing upon Themselves Eternal
Perdition. (Revelation 15)."[33]
       The work is a Hutterian answer to the world's hostility, in the
form of an incisive apologia, coupled with a prophetic message of
judgment. After the refutation of thirty accusations by the world,
the author concentrated on one basic demand the world placed
upon the Hutterian brotherhood: to recant.

Writers, in using Scripture, open their eyes to those parts of the Bible which speak to their situation and times. The author of "Charges and Allegations" took a careful look at the Old Testament passages portraying God's wrath poured out upon the wicked world and concluded that once again a righteous God would ultimately punish those who committed obvious sins during the decadence of the sixteenth century.

There is another important reason for prophetic dissent at this time. The Hutterites were a Christian version of the Old Testament "people of God," separate from other peoples and separate from the world. Their firm conviction was that the prophetic remnant of Isaiah, culminating in the new covenant remnant of God, was again realized in Zürich Anabaptism of 1525 and was brought to its original purity within Hutterian Anabaptism in Moravia. Within this promised land the elect and separate people of God again underwent persecution as Scripture promised, because they adopted a biblical, theocratic organization, founded upon Christian discipleship within a disciplined brotherhood. As a German-speaking minority in a Slavic culture, the Hutterites could identify more readily with the Old Testament people of God than could other churches or brotherhoods whose members were not cultural foreigners to their society. The Hutterites had also been able to develop a program of mission where seekers were invited to share in a unique kingdom-of-God experience. Although the Hutterites were still sparing no effort in carrying the mandate of mission throughout Europe, now, at a point in history where their mission was at low ebb, they found biblical precedent for the reverse side of the mission message: "We have given you a chance, you have not responded. God's judgment will fall upon you: Woe, woe, thrice woe!"

The defiant mood of "Charges and Allegations" is evident from the outset. The power which the beast of evil is able to unleash against the godly (Rev. 12), the Hutterites believed, was now being unleashed in an attempt to wreak havoc among the people of God. Consequently the godly, who at times are to keep quiet, are also at times commanded to speak out; Christians must be bold to answer where truth is blasphemed and scorned. The author intends to carry through with this commission, maintaining a spirit of friendliness, although also promising to mix in a goodly dosage of salt, as Paul himself suggested (Col. 4:6).[34]

The first part of the writing, composed of thirty "dialogues" between the people of God and the world, holds forth a positive redemptive note, although the author makes clear that true Christianity is not a surrender to the world either through compromise or through living in an individual ivory tower of quietistic pietism. Instead, the sharp Hutterian prophetic utterances found in "Charges and Allegations" even breathe an air of superiority, suggesting that the people of God indeed have the upper hand in their relationship to the world, and that life in the present world is after all an important part of God's kingdom which needs defending.

Part Two of the document begins with an extended, pointed polemic against the world which, as interpreted by the Hutterites, says to God's people:

> [*The World:*] Desist from your error and your sectarianism.... If you were devout you would have remained in your own land.... You want to fathom the Godhead much too far and be far too holy. It is not so serious; one can still find redemption.... After all, we also believe in God; you could well come to the church too and take the sacrament, and eat it with any interpretation you wish; keep your own faith in your hearts. Don't be so obstinate, but do as other people who also call themselves brethren ... who still follow us; they are not as headstrong and stubborn as you. They pay war taxes and hangmen's fees. They live separately in their own little homes, and not all in a heap like you.... Soon it will produce a king and fight against us as they did in Münster.... You are called Hutterites. You think your faith is the only right one. Yet it is a new faith; ours is centuries old.... You call us all ungodly and sinners and claim to be better than we. Are we to tolerate that? You must rather all be burned! You are seducing the people. It is we who will teach you to believe![35]

In reply the Hutterites asserted that words cannot express what the devil does among his children of the world, trying with lies and fabrications to break the people of God away from divine truth; the whole world is full of lies and guile, as is shown throughout Scripture.[36]

Then follows a detailed analysis of the contemporary situation, the pressures placed upon the brotherhood by the world: In the face of the ever-present danger that the Hutterian community might be torn apart by outside forces the Hutterites resolve never to abandon Christian community, where there is one heart and soul among all the faithful people of God. They reject the demand of the world to halt their program of mission, for to keep silent about Christian faith would amount to pure hypocrisy, and would be denying the Lord God. "Oh you crafty and poisonous and treacherous snakes," the Hutterites cry, "disappear from us with your deceit! For you shall not succeed—so help us God—in deceiving us."[37]

We note, by way of interpretation, that by the 1570s the Hutterites had experienced the consolidation of Protestant forces and the countering strategy of the Catholics, eventuating in open and bitter conflict between these two Christian churches. Hence, the ever graver political situation in itself was one of the strong signs of the times. The Hutterites with their sense of history and awareness that sin is finally found out not only for individuals, but for churches and nations as well—were able to utter a prophetic message suitable to the times. They perhaps were anticipating the outbreak of the Thirty Years' War fought among Christians, which would leave Germany a shambles, most of the population to perish from warring and pestilence. The *corpus christianum*, the Hutterites believed, had forsaken its New Testament mandate to be the reconciling body of Christ. It had betrayed its Master, whom it was to follow in love and peace and unity.

Hutterite missioners had traversed much of Europe with the message of reconciliation and peace; most people and their lands remained unrepentant—indeed, they had constantly harassed, persecuted, and martyred the faithful Hutterite missioners. If the world only knew that the time was so near, and that it was only God's Word that kept the devout who trusted in God. This is the message which surfaces at the end of "Charges and Allegations," where the Hutterite author makes a final pronouncement of woe upon those who made up the world, those sinners and ungodly people who do not grant a listening ear to God's voice. God would punish them, avenging the blood of his missioner-witnesses:

> Oh you wicked and dissolute world! God will someday teach the mockers to confess that he is Lord, and he will talk with them in his wrath and will frighten them with his terror.... These people believe this life to be an amusing game, and that the human's walk and living is to be compared to a fair or circus, where one pursues gain and benefit ... profiting from all sorts of evil (Wisdom of Solomon 15a).[38]

For the Hutterites, the fulfillment of life lay in another sphere, in the reality of God's Word, which preserves his people. The quotation from the Wisdom of Solomon, which the Hutterite author presents near the end of his "Charges and Allegations," serves well as a final pledge of Hutterian allegiance; it also forms an appropriate conclusion to this chapter:

> For the creation, serving thee who hast made it, exerts itself to punish the unrighteous, and in kindness relaxes on behalf of those who trust in thee. Therefore at that time also, changed into all forms, it served thy all-nourishing bounty, according to the desire of those who had need, so that thy sons, whom thou didst love, O Lord, might learn that it is not the production of crops that feeds man, but that thy word preserves those who trust in thee (Wisdom of Solomon 16:24-26, RSV).[39]

8

From Anabaptist Missionary Congregation to Mennonite Seclusion

N. van der Zijpp

Missionary zeal in the beginning

The early Anabaptists were biblical Christians. One even called them radical Scripture readers. Indeed, they read their Bibles faithfully and wanted to be obedient to what the Scriptures directed them to do. This also meant that they knew they were called to preach the gospel when building up their congregations according to the example of the early Christian church.

The oldest Anabaptist congregation was a missionary congregation. In Professor F. Blanke's enjoyable book, *Brothers in Christ*, we can read how strong this was in the very first Anabaptist congregation of Zollikon, near Zürich, in January 1525. The leaders, Grebel, Manz, and especially Blaurock, knew they

Nanne van der Zijpp (1900-1965) was a Dutch Mennonite minister and professor. He taught Mennonite History at Amsterdam Mennonite Seminary and was a professor at Amsterdam University. He wrote Geschiedenis der Doopsgezinden in Nederland *(Arnhem, 1952). This chapter is a translation of* "Van doperse zendingsgemeente tot doopsgezinde beslotenheid," Stemmen, *Jaargang 7:4 (1958). It was translated by Rita Romeijn-Hogeweg and Els du Rieu, with assistance from Nelson P. Springer and Roelf S. Kuitse. It is reprinted with permission from* Doopsgezinde Zendingsraad.

were sent as new apostles. They read the Scriptures in the houses of the farmers of Zollikon; they exhorted, baptized, and celebrated the Lord's supper. During an evening discussion at the home of Ruedi Thomann on January 25, 1525, some people who were impressed by Blaurock's preaching became converted and were baptized. The young farmer Marx Boszhart could not come to a decision yet. During the following night he reflected again upon all Blaurock had said: "He did not know any other way out than to ask God to give the correct insight. Toward morning the understanding he had prayed for broke through with convincing power." Marx Boszhart arose early in the morning, awakened Blaurock, and asked him for baptism upon his faith. Shortly after that, Boszhart left as a missionary to bring the light to others in the Zürich Highland just as he himself had received the light from Blaurock.

And after Felix Manz was drowned as a heretic and George Blaurock was burned, others were ready to take over their task, "to go therefore and teach all nations, making them disciples of Jesus" (Mt. 28:19). Thus, the oldest Anabaptist congregation was a missionary congregation. Due to its missionary awareness, the movement expanded from Zürich to other Swiss cities and villages, to Bavaria and Baden in Germany, to Tyrol and Moravia in Austria. And the South German and Tyrolean *Täufer* in their turn became missionaries who carried forward the gospel: no temptation of rest or earthly well-being, no threat of torture or death could keep them from being preachers of the good news.

Earliest Dutch Anabaptism was no different. Again and again we hear from imprisoned Anabaptists how they knew they were called by God to preach the gospel. Many of them were constantly on the way spreading the gospel, wherever the opportunity presented itself, until the Inquisition laid its heavy hands on them and after a short trial condemned them to a martyr's death. And even then they were not silent. The two friends, Hans van Overdamme and Hans Keescoper, were executed together in Gent in 1550: "and Hans Keescoper had agreed with Hans van Overdam, that on the scaffold he would take off his stockings and in the meantime Hans van Overdam should speak to the people, which was also done. When the executioner would assist him, Hansken desired to do it alone, so that Hans van Overdam might speak the longer to the people. When this had happened, each was placed at a stake and they sacrificed their bodies to God," as reported in *Het Offer des Heeren.*

Thus it is told of many people: The love of Christ constrained them (2 Cor. 5:14), just as it had constrained Paul and the other apostles in the early years of Christianity. All the time new messengers arose. It looked as if the persecutions made their numbers increase:

> But know (that), where they kill one
> One hundred will rise again!

as goes an old Dutch martyr song. It is well-known how the Dutch "elders" like Obbe Philips, Menno Simons, Dirk Philips, and Leenaert Bouwens put their lives into the service of preaching the gospel, and neither difficulties, nor hardships, nor even perpetual risk of life could keep them from being missionaries for Jesus Christ.

During the years 1551-82 Leenaert Bouwens baptized almost 11,000 people in more than 300 places on his numerous mission journeys, which led him from deep into Holstein to Northern France. Menno evangelized not only in the Netherlands, but also in the vicinity of Cologne, in East Friesland, in Mecklenburg; he even visited Poland. The same applied to Dirk Philips. But not only—and that is very important—were the leaders missionaries, the whole congregation was a missionary congregation: in the Netherlands, in Germany, in Switzerland, in Austria, in every country where one could find Anabaptists, no matter under which names.

Declining missionary zeal

The situation we find in the nineteenth century is entirely different. Then we find no longer in the Netherlands, nor in Switzerland, Germany, France, or Russia a Mennonite missionary congregation, but we find secluded Mennonite congregations—congregations in which the missionary zeal is dead, in which the members do not have an apostolic-missionary élan to share their spiritual gifts with those who are outside the church. The congregation has neither eye nor interest for foreign or home missions. Preaching of the gospel to nations which do not know Christ (missions to the heathen) as well as conscious and intentional evangelization among their fellow countryfolk—and is it really possible fundamentally to separate these two, foreign and home missions?—is strange to them. The congregation has become what I call a closed congregation. The goal of the congregation is, as described in the constitution of one of our Dutch congregations, the reinforcement of the religious feelings and images of its members.

Anyone whose attention is attracted to the great change that occurred between the sixteenth and nineteenth century in our Mennonite brotherhood wonders involuntarily what caused this change and how it could move from an Anabaptist missionary congregation to Mennonite seclusion. Undoubtedly one can point out clearly perceptible circumstances for that, and we will mention a number of them.

As for the Netherlands, in the Northern Netherlands the persecuted Mennonites soon gained some freedom after the outbreak of the Eighty Years' War (between Spain and the Netherlands, 1568-1648). The last martyr in the Northern Netherlands, Reytse Aysesz, died in 1574. (In the Southern Netherlands the persecutions lasted longer. Anneke Utenhove as last Anabaptist martyr was buried alive in Brussels in 1597; at that time in the whole of Belgium none of the formerly numerous Anabaptist congregations was left and hardly a dozen dispersed Mennonites remained.) In that period in the Netherlands the power of Rome and the Inquisition foundered in the heat of the battle against Spain. Although particularly Friesland and Holland contained a rather large number of Mennonites about 1570—at first they even outnumbered the Calvinist Protestants—yet it was Calvinism that took control.

The Calvinists took a different position than Rome toward the Mennonites. Though far from regarding them as equal partners or as "true Christians," the Calvinists did not execute the Mennonites as heretics, although among the Calvinist leaders and clergymen a portion pressed for it; but William I, Prince of Orange, could avoid this both for conscientious and practical reasons. The Mennonites were tolerated, and by the Union of Utrecht (1579) it was decided that "every individual will be allowed to have religious liberty," and no one would be "hunted down or persecuted" because of religion. Thus freedom of conscience came. But freedom of conscience did not yet mean freedom of worship. The word *individual* from the above-cited formulation in the Union of Utrecht clearly shows that, although one did not persecute a person any more for being Mennonite, yet one did not want to grant the right to have worship services together with like-minded people, let alone to propagate their principles and opinions. The Calvinist practice, protected by the government until 1795, was in conformity with this.

The so-called Later Union of Utrecht (1583) had already decided that "the Calvinist religion will be maintained and protected throughout the united provinces, excluding the public teaching or exercise of any other religion." The Mennonite congregations—just as the Roman Catholics—came under the control of the government, which, stirred up continually by the Calvinist synods and church boards, guarded against papist and Mennonite audacity. Not always and everywhere did the local magistrate show the forceful intervention which the watchful Calvinists wished for—particularly in Amsterdam Menno's people had much freedom—but the Mennonites came and remained under control, and that not only formally, as history shows clearly. Again and again Mennonite ministers were molested because they acted too boldly or because they attracted members of the Calvinist church to their congregations; Mennonite "preaching-houses" could not be built in places where they had not previously existed; if they were built anyway they were sometimes demolished by order of the government, as happened in Sap-

pemeer and Visvliet; in addition there were a number of embar-
rassing and humiliating regulations for Mennonites regarding
marriage and right of inheritance. And a Mennonite minister of
Barsingerhorn still experienced serious difficulties in 1756 because
he catechized a girl of Reformed origin. This "bloodless persecution" of the Mennonites lasted till late into the eighteenth
century. The Mennonites were only tolerated, *geconniveert* (con-
nived with), as the old term says. They had to keep "silent and
quiet." This restricted their old missionary zeal. They could not
spread their wings anymore.

It was the same elsewhere. In Switzerland severe persecutions, which caused a heavy loss of life until the end of the
seventeenth century, had pushed the Mennonite movement back
to distant mountain valleys, where only small congregations could
hold their own in secret. In Tyrol and Moravia, just as in Belgium,
the Mennonites were exterminated entirely. In the Palatinate and
some other parts of Germany, where many Swiss *Täufer* had
found their refuge since the middle of the seventeenth century,
the Mennonites often had a hard time as well. Here times of
peace alternated with periods of persecution, and continuously
there was threat and oppression. The Archives of Amsterdam still
hold a large number of letters from congregations in the
Palatinate, which picture the distress.

From every new elector the special protection had to be
bought again with extra poll tax. As in the days of Israel in Egypt
the number of Mennonites could not exceed a stated maximum;
in 1744 the number of Mennonite families was fixed at 200, and
when it appeared that there were 244 families, 44 were expelled
from the country, while besides it was provided that henceforth all
young people who contracted a marriage had to leave the
country. Usually the government refused to give consent for mar-
riages, sometimes even permission for burials, so that people were
forced to bury their dead privately on their own land. It goes
without saying that under these circumstances all attempts to win
people of different beliefs over to the congregation were severly
punished. Roman Catholic as well as Lutheran and Calvinist elec-

tors, who followed each other in colorful succession in the Palatinate, maintained these restrictions against the Mennonites, of whom the vast majority emigrated to Pennsylvania after having suffered severely in the course of the eighteenth century.

In Prussia the situation was definitely better. Mennonites from the Netherlands and Flanders had been settling there since 1540. They were even sought by the government and religious liberty was allowed, on condition that they should reclaim the marshland around the river Vistula. This benevolence is the more striking since West Prussia in that time (until 1772) belonged to the kingdom of Poland and the Polish kings were Roman Catholic. These Prussian Mennonites thus enjoyed a certain freedom, but yet that freedom was restricted, and there were a good many difficulties, especially with the Polish nobility and the government officials, who extorted them and curtailed their freedom again and again. Mission work was categorically forbidden to them. No Roman Catholic or Lutheran was allowed to join the congregation. If this happened sometimes anyway, severe punishments were inflicted on them, consisting of economic reprisals like withdrawal of the market privilege and of free transport of agricultural produce, and high fines were levied on them. Letters in the Archives of Amsterdam also give many details about this.

Yet sometimes people found clever ways out. It happened a few times that a Lutheran young man in Danzig or elsewhere wanted to join the Mennonites. That was not possible on the spot. Then such a person went to the Netherlands for a few months, particularly to Amsterdam; here he was baptized and afterwards left with a letter of transfer to a Prussian congregation.

With the first partition of Poland in 1772, West Prussia (at first without the city of Danzig, but that followed soon) passed to Frederick the Great, king of Prussia. This led to new problems. For this king, who is praised in the annals as the champion of unlimited tolerance, restricted both economic rights and religious principles of his new Mennonite subjects. The result was that many Prussian Mennonites moved to the Ukraine shortly before

ie nationalism and military service

and during the first years after 1800, where through Catherine II and Paul I they were not only allowed free settlement, but also guaranteed "everlasting freedom" to live and believe according to their own view. However, there was one strict condition: They had to be silent citizens and could proselytize neither among the members of the Orthodox Church, nor among Lutherans or Roman Catholics, who lived near the Mennonite colonies.

This brief historical review shows us how all over Europe Mennonites were tolerated in the time between the sixteenth century and about 1800 only if they abstained from any kind of mission and propaganda. Almost everything they did was from sheer need. In this way the missionary congregation became a secluded congregation. Only in young America was the situation rather different. Here Mennonites from different states of Western Europe had settled in William Penn's Quaker state, Pennsylvania, since 1683, and were followed by rather large contingents of Mennonite emigrants from Switzerland and Germany since the beginning of the eighteenth century. Perhaps under the influence of and after the example of the Quakers did Mennonites in Pennsylvania, and soon also in Virginia, concern themselves with the Indians and incidentally carried out missionary work among them. I say incidentally, for this missionary work was far from organized and certainly originated more with some individuals than with the congregations. Also we must not misrepresent the extensiveness of this mission work. Moreover, the Indian tribes went deeper inland with the increase of white immigrants, a result of which the possibilities for contact decreased and the missions came gradually to a standstill.

What is more, when the Quakers had to relinquish control of their Pennsylvania into other hands because of the new immigrations, especially of Lutherans from Germany, the policy of the "new men" was one of extermination, at least of repelling the Indians. Especially since by the War of Independence (1775-83), the American colonies broke away from England, through which a great political activity and a new nationalism arose in the former colonies, the Mennonite congregations in America returned to the old isolation and lived as they did in the Bernese Jura, in the Palatinate, and in Alsace, retiring within their small, secluded congregational communities. Not until "the great awakening" in the middle of the nineteenth century did this situation change.

Some reasons for a decline in missionary zeal

The impulse for missionary work of the first generations yielded to the silent seclusion of the congregations in the following centuries. This situation was imposed on us by external circumstances. But then that one cogent question remains: Why did the Mennonites allow this situation to be forced upon them since about 1570? The generation of the martyrs had also been told: Keep silent! Stop your activities! But they had not complied with that demand. On the contrary, they answered in word and deed that one should obey God above people. "Woe is me, if I don't preach the gospel" was burnt in their hearts. When we ask the question of why later generations have allowed themselves to be forced away from the abundance of evangelical freedom into narrow quietness, there is only one answer: it is because they did not have the faith anymore and, therefore, neither the courage nor the strength that inspired and carried the generation of the martyrs. To state this is not only a judgment on the Mennonites of the seventeenth century, but at the same time on ourselves.

However, it would be unfair not to involve some other factors in this judgment. With this I don't want to revoke or even minimize the expressed opinion that the situation changed because of declining religious strength, but to explain the change into secluded community in more detail and not to accept the often misused "to know all is to forgive all"! Such relativity counts for neither the seventeenth century, nor for us!

I will mention seven of the factors that contributed successively to the change in the character of the brotherhood. These apply specifically to the Mennonites in the Netherlands, to whom I restrict myself in the following. Elsewhere there were other motives, which from within or from without contributed to a similar result.

pwhat · hopes

1. With the first Anabaptists the expectation of the coming
end of the world and the coming of God's kingdom plays a great
role. This was not only the case with the so-called "revolutionary
Anabaptists," such as Jan Matthijs of Haarlem and Jan van
Leyden and their followers, but likewise with the "peaceful"
Anabaptist martyrs. Thus we find in Menno Simons' first edition
of the *Foundation* (1539) continually a strong eschatological
tendency. This is also the case in the testimonies of many of our
martyrs; in their letters and songs they exhort to be faithful, saying that the suffering will be only of short duration. Characteristic
is the last stanza of the song that Anneken Jans composed (1539):

> Rise up, rise up Jerusalem, prepare yourself;
> Welcome your children all alike.
> Will you spread your tents now?
> Behold the throne, receive your kingdom,
> Your King is coming to deliver you.
> He brings his reward for your faith;
> He will rejoice in you.
> We shall see his glory,
> Rejoice, O Zion, with the pure Jerusalem.

One beholds already the throne of God! The Lord is coming and
is bringing us the reward of our faith; we will—soon—see his
glory! This eschatological certitude was certainly beneficial to the
missionary élan. But the final kingdom did not come as soon as
one hoped. As with the early Christians, the second generation
had to change over to find a new attitude toward the world in
which they lived; so it also was with the Mennonites in the
sixteenth century through the cessation of the expectation of the
end, because God's kingdom did not come. It will simply be clear,
that this was not beneficial to zeal for preaching the coming
kingdom and to the call for repentance and conversion.

2. A second factor, closely connected with the previous one,
is the following: After the revolutionary Anabaptist kingdom of
Jan van Leyden had perished in Münster (June 1535), although
not nearly all, yet some peaceful Anabaptists came to lean more
strongly on the existing world order. In their understandable need

moderation for sake of safety

to stress for the sake of their own peace and safety that they had not anything to do with Münster, they were sometimes maybe a little too inclined to "render to the emperor even more than what was the emperor's," in other words, to moderate their evangelization.

However, not all submitted so easily to the worldly authorities. The martyr Jacques d'Auchy, who in 1559 was accused by the inquisitor of having broken the "mandate" (ordinance) of King Philip II, admitted this frankly: "It is of little importance whether I broke the ordinance of the king, for by breaking it I fulfilled the ordinance of the king of kings." Besides, he said, the king does not have the right to make such an ordinance, by which he places himself above God in holding lordship over the consciences of his subjects. But Mennonite writers in later years went to a lot of trouble to show that they wanted to submit themselves to the government, in order to escape the suspicion of Münsterism. Here the compromise already sets in to which we have to return in factor 4 below.

3. In connection with the fading of the expectation that God's kingdom would be realized shortly, we see already since 1540 or soon after that the attention of the leaders of the Anabaptist movement shifted from foreign missions and evangelization to organization of the congregation(s). One can follow this process rather closely in the successive books which Menno Simons published. More and more organizational problems and consolidation of the congregation (rights of the local congregation, matters of discipline, ban and avoidance, etc.) drew the attention of the elders. Through this, something that had been the main task of the elders in the early period, namely the mission, easily took second place.

4. As the persecution quieted down and the government showed in places its willingness not only to tolerate the Mennonites, but even to appreciate them, the Mennonites changed tack. While at first they had drawn a dividing line between "the world" and "Christ," now they built bridges. In April 1572 two Dutch Mennonites, Jacob Frederiksz and Dirk Jansz Cortenbosch,

came and saw the Prince of Orange in his castle in Dillenburg and asked him if they could render him a service. The prince requested that they be willing to raise money for the general welfare.

Cortenbosch and—in the absence of Frederiksz—the minister of Monikkendam, Pieter Willems Bogaert, took a collection among the Mennonites in Waterland and two months later they could hand Prince William a sum of money in his army camp in Hellenrade, for which they received a receipt: "We, William, by the grace of God, Prince of Orange, Count of Nassouw etc., hereby acknowledge to have received from the hands of Dierick Jansz. Cortenbosch and Peeter Willemsz. Bogaerts the sum of a thousand sixty Carolus guilders ... and that from several well-known persons who contributed this money for the general welfare, for which we thank them...." (This receipt is in the Amsterdam Archives.)

This incident shows how much the Mennonites had changed: They showed their gratitude because now in comparison with former times, they were allowed to live quietly and safely in the world. That this change brought certain compromises with it, by which the old Anabaptist "not of the world" got into a tight place, speaks for itself. I do not want to make a value judgment on these compromises—we enter into them daily and we can do nothing else. I only observe the change: The martyrs did not enter a compromise with the world.

5. Does there exist something like a certain Mennonite piety that is different from others? Was and is there among us a certain atmosphere, a certain peculiar character, that differs from that of other Christian churches and communities? Is it this characteristic that has shaped and defined the structure of our congregations up to the present? Does one really have to be "born Mennonite" in order to be "real Mennonite"? It is a fact that nowadays a Mennonite congregation—and in the eighteenth and nineteenth centuries this was the case in still stronger measure—differs much from, for example, a Reformed congregation. I do not have in mind here so much the so-called theological factors as the nonthe-

ological, not so much the doctrine as what is linked up with it, and also not the forms of organization, but the behavior and life as religious community.

A Mennonite congregation is usually small; the members know each other. This results in a community with similar people (family connection, friendly relations—sometimes the contrary as well!) and a special atmosphere that is described by outsiders as sectarian, or as conventicle spirit, and is sometimes called musty and narrow-minded, while Mennonites themselves speak rather of being cozy. By this coziness then—the word is most unfortunate—they mean an interrelatedness and familiarity of the members. Now I want by no means to regard this type as superior over other types of churches, and much less speak for a "biological Anabaptism," by which people would be good Mennonites only if they would be Mennonite from generation to generation.

It occurs to me that joining a congregation on one's own initiative and on personal responsibility is totally in conflict with this; but on the other hand we also have to recognize that all human beings have specific psychic religious natures which make them feel at home in one church and not in the other, or at least make them feel less at home. This psychic nature puts a certain stamp upon the entire religious community. Thus, in the course of time, as Mennonites we developed a tendency to become a secluded congregation. From old the tradition has contributed to that. Already in the first years the Anabaptist congregations—as far as one can speak then of congregations—were small nuclei. The persecution forced the brothers and sisters at all times to meet in small numbers. In this way they assembled, for example, in Amsterdam in 1534 in private houses simultaneously in the evening or at night, rarely with more than fifteen or twenty persons.

When later on the safety indeed allowed them to meet in greater numbers and in the daytime, they still clung for a long time to the small house-congregations, and most Mennonite churches (formerly one spoke of preaching-houses or exhortation-houses) still reflect the old inclination: All Mennonite churches that were built before 1796 do not look—and not only because the

government forbade such!—like a church, let alone like a cathe-
dral, but continued to keep the type of the simple preaching-
house, as we can well visualize by a number of older, still-existing
Mennonite churches, especially when we imagine away the pulpit
and the organ, which were added in later times under non-Men-
nonite influence.

The oldest Mennonite congregations were house-congregations; the consolidated tradition turned us against massiveness.
The Reformed church is different. Although also arising in an era
of persecution, the first Calvinists did not meet secretly in small
groups, but went to field conventicles, where often a thousand
people and more were present. In contrast with the Mennonites
they were oriented to massiveness from the beginning.

6. Among us at all times close attention was paid and much
value was attached to personal faith. However much love went
out to the congregation, and that devotion was usually very
strong, in the last resort the personal relation to God mattered.
When the martyr, Peter Witses of Leeuwarden (1553), answered
to the question of the judge whether his fellowmen are of the
same way of thinking, "What do I know of my brothers; I may
speak of the things God gave me, that is what I know," this apparent crusty answer expresses how at that time the faith of the
Mennonites was already a matter of personal responsibility. Nobody can take away this responsibility from another person, nor is
anybody allowed to determine for another person what he or she
must believe. We express this in the words "accountability of the
believer."

However, in the high principle of personal faith lurked a
danger, namely that one came—also out of horror of what one
saw in "the churches" of unchristian rule over each other's
conscience—to an individualistic atomism, in the manner of
"everyone for himself and God for us all"; not only not minding
the faith of the other, but also not caring for the faith of the other.
This attitude—that every person has to shift for him- or herself
and all have to clear themselves with God—by which one gladly
left alone how every person might be saved, created especially

since the eighteenth century a climate in our congregations that was not very conducive to interest in missions. The Word had only to address the household of faith, who then one by one had to decide on their attitude to it. They could not hear of "a Word for the world"; that would be impermissible meddlesomeness.

7. The following is closely connected with the previous observations. It is striking how little eye or ear Protestantism had in the seventeenth, and especially in the eighteenth century, for Christian missions. Hardly anything was understood anymore of the prophetic-apostolic "Behold, I send you!" As a matter of fact since early times Protestantism, curiously enough, paid little attention to the instruction of Jesus to go and preach. A strong missionary zeal is to be found among the earliest Anabaptists. In the second half of the seventeenth century there is a lively missionary consciousness among the Quakers, and since 1738 there is the active missionary work of the Moravian Brethren, especially in Surinam.

The Anglican church had since 1701 its Society for the Propagation of the Gospel in Foreign Parts, but the activity of this society was restricted by order of the king to the British colonies in North America and practice showed that money and manpower were often pressed more into the service of the British colonial expansion than into the service of Christ's kingdom. Then there was the missionary movement of the English Methodists, the followers of John Wesley, the man who knew in his great love for Christ that the world was his parish. But it is striking how little interest in the heathen missions existed both in Calvinism and in Lutheranism. The climate was too cool to give viability to evangelization, says a qualified critic.

Neither Luther nor Calvin actually occupied themselves with the problem. Luther consoled himself with the thought that the most important part of the world had heard the message of Christ already. In 1651 the theological faculty of Wittenberg declared all motives for the benefit of the heathen missions absurd. In this the Calvinists followed in the steps of Calvin, of whom it is said that he did not come to the full recognition of the

missionary task of the church. The fact that some Dutch Calvinists
in the seventeenth century, like Heurnius and Professor Hoorn-
beek, pleaded the importance of missions, though without being
effective, may be seen more as a wish to compete with Roman
Catholic Jesuit missions than as arising from Christian compassion. However that may be, the majority of Calvinists did not
sympathize with it, and the most peculiar theological opinions
were put forward, for example, that God had cursed the children
of Ham and that therefore it would be against his will to bring
them the gospel!

Certainly it was not this motive that turned the Mennonites
against missions in the eighteenth century. Rather the cultural op-
timism played a part there: The world improved gradually; missions were not necessary. Besides the relativization of Christian
value in the eighteenth century, the myth of "happy
heathendom" arose that would have such a long and tough life.
This, added to the typical Mennonite view that one should not
mind the religious life of others, made the interest in foreign missions among us absolutely sterile for a couple of centuries.

But then, did not our brothers in the era of the Enlighten-
ment know about responsibility for the world in which they lived,
in which they had found such a good place for themselves? In
short I can answer: Certainly! But mission work as a Christian task
was restricted to taking the initiative in or contributing to the
many kinds of socially elevating activities like the Society for
Public Welfare and the like. This is no small matter though! Numerous Mennonites have made important contributions and have
devoted their energies then and since that time to this public ele-
vation and other social work. But among us was minimal interest
in missions proper. This did not change when in 1797 the Dutch
Missionary Society was founded in our country based on the
English example. A few Mennonite ministers were board members in it, and some Mennonites especially from Amsterdam
contributed financially to it for years.

When in 1847 their own Mennonite Society for the Propagation of the Gospel in the Dutch Overseas Territories was founded,

this became a matter, some people said mockingly a "hobby," of a small number of friends of missions. Mission work was not in the line of the secluded congregation and went least of all with the climate of the Dutch Mennonite brotherhood in 1850. During the rest of the nineteenth century and in the first decades of the twentieth century only a small number of the Dutch Mennonites paid attention to and took an interest in missions; in the long run the interest and the required money as well came especially from the Russian, German, and Swiss Mennonites, who also provided the greater number of missionaries.

It may be noted in passing that among the American Mennonites great changes occurred in the second half of the nineteenth century. Under revivalistic influences, later on especially from the Baptist side, their congregations grew from secluded communities into lively evangelizing congregations, so that at present there is among nearly all (Mennonite) denominations a great activity and an enormous readiness to make sacrifices for missions, both home and foreign.

Thus secluded Mennonite congregations developed from an Anabaptist missionary community. Even into the mid-nineteenth century a number of small isolated congregations survived (in Switzerland, South Germany, Alsace this situation still existed until recently and in the Netherlands it is still true) which often had little contact among themselves and which were practically exclusively sustained by the increase from their own circle. These family congregations of quiet people hardly made any sign to the outer world; although they certainly preserved and cultivated in their seclusion a wealth of devotion, in some places more rationalistic-moralistic and in other places more pietistic. They have meant much more for the believer's family and have done much more than is often known (I am thinking of the diaconal aid and the care for the aged in our numberless almshouses and also the large-scale assistance of the Committee for Foreign Needs). Yet with all their loyalty in little things they had lost in a great measure the missionary awareness and the urge for propagating the gospel. Even in the task of sustaining their own membership they did not do well. In the eighteenth century in the Netherlands and in the nineteenth century in Switzerland and Germany—with the exception of Prussia—there was a terrible decline of the membership. In many respects the history of the Mennonites is not very stimulating after its heroic period.

9
Ethics and Mission
José Gallardo

Among Christian churches consciousness is growing of the need to look more seriously at the ethical implications of missions. The history of Christian missions and the more recent investigations on the political use of missionaries show how important it is to think about the ethical aspects of the missionary task. I intend to contribute to this urgent need with the following thoughts that express a deep personal concern that grows out of experience in mission projects in Europe and in South America. I believe that both ethics and mission are essential dimensions of the Christian core and should always be related. When we come to the point of asking about the relationship between Christian ethics and mission, something has gone wrong.

A look at the message
One cannot adequately understand missionary methods and message apart from the methods and message lived and taught by Jesus and the New Testament church. Yet as history shows, often Christians have not been careful about the way they have done missions and about the content of the message they have taken

José Gallardo, Quintanadueñas, Spain, is a pastor in a community of rehabilitation, itinerant teacher, and preacher. He served as president of the Belgian Mennonite Council (1973-77) and as pastor in a Spanish Mennonite Church in Brussels. He also taught ethics at Bienenberg Mennonite Bible School in Switzerland. He has written The Way of Biblical Justice *(Herald Press, 1983).*

with them. They overlooked the distinction between culture and gospel, and presented the "good news" of their country's way of life instead of Jesus' way. Further, they have identified so much with political and ideological forces that the difference between following Jesus and being on their country's side was blurred. Most of the time they were seen as ambassadors of their country's culture and ideology and not of Jesus. For this reason, when the country's official representatives have been asked to leave, Jesus' representatives also have had to leave.

This has happened in most Third World countries that have come to national independence after years of colonial rule. Christian missions were seen as another form of colonialism—and in most cases they were. It is true that leftist anticolonial regimes which have taken control of many countries (especially in Africa) have ideological prejudices against religion *as such*, but one cannot deny that the colonial scientific, economic, and military powers brought along Christian religion as another force at the service of the colonial rulers. Local people were not able to separate the white church with its European look from the white army with its "civilized" technology. Businessmen have taken the missionary roads and missionaries have taken businessmen's roads. Programs for social and cultural aid have often been carried out by religious organizations with economic help from the countries they represented.

The distribution of aid was so closely related to tasks of the churches that often adopting Christian faith and attending these churches were conditions for receiving help. This pattern produced many formal conversions to Christianity which lasted as long as the economic help continued and ended as soon as the rich partners left. Then Islam or "authentic" African animism took its place.

One example: As has been shown recently, ideological superpowers like the CIA have used religious institutions and missionaries to carry out programs and activities with clear political objectives. Perhaps the best-documented case is that of Belgian priest Roger Vekemans, director of the Center for Theological Research and editor of the monthly theological magazine *Tierra Nueva* in Bogota, Colombia.[1] The task of this Belgian priest and his competent team is to undermine systematically the work and publications of liberation theologians in South America.

One could say the same about many theologians and missionaries who are faithful first to their Marxist doctrine or revolutionary government. These people often want to identify with the poor in their fight against the injustices, corruption, and oppression of capitalism. But in the process of fighting the bad powers that be, these people are used by the new powers that come to replace the old. These people believe they are liberationists, but by their ideological prejudices they compromise the freedom and truth of the gospel.

Absence of ethics

Theologians and missionaries from right and left have one thing in common: They lack ethical criteria in their approach to missions and in the message they communicate. This is true of the theologies of liberation that put ideological faithfulness before ethical considerations. It is also the case with state church theologians who take their ethical norms not so much from the gospel as from the world. They do not believe that a Christian social ethic exists.[2] They believe we must borrow our ethical standard from society, since the law and the order of creation provide a moral foundation which believers and unbelievers can hold in common. They believe that the scope of the New Testament is too narrow to deal with the complexity of modern social problems. They bypass the fact that Christians, "in Christ," are no longer living under the order of creation but under the new order of redemption.

The gospel distinguishes between the kingdom of Satan, who still has the fallen world under his control, and the kingdom of God, who has brought a radical new liberation to those who follow Jesus and have his Holy Spirit. This new creation in Christ is characterized not so much by words as by deeds which reflect the holy nature of God and the redemptive love of Jesus.

Content of the message

The missionary message has also suffered from this lack of ethical content. One can hardly see the relationship between the message of salvation through Christ and missionary methods. Missionaries have forgotten that the gospel message has implicit methods of communication. "The *way* the gospel is communicated determines *what* is communicated, and vice versa."[3] The divorce between message and methods exists before the missionary reaches the field. Wilbert R. Shenk has written: "Missionaries have lacked a clear ethical vision. But they only brought with them what they had been given by the sending church."[4]

The main difficulty lay in the content of the message itself. Missionaries carried a message deeply rooted in the doctrines of the Protestant Reformation, particularly in the Reformation understanding of salvation by faith and grace alone, and not by works. The present polarizing debate on evangelism and social concern is the product of the same duality of faith and works. Those who want to "save souls" are seen as irresponsible by those who want to "minister to the whole person." The latter often means bringing aid to ameliorate social conditions. The intention is to prepare the soil for sowing the Word, but the method tends to reflect lack of faith and missionary motivation. Most often, the message of salvation never comes; the soil is never ready.

Theological weaknesses

The absence of ethical thrust in the missionary "gospel" is thus a product of the theological weakness of the message. Often the missionary is a better reflection of Protestant tradition than of the biblical challenge. The lack of biblical content is reflected in the missionary understandings of Jesus, discipleship, the church, and salvation.

Jesus. Today we still face the heretical understandings of Jesus evident in the early Christian era. The big question then was: "How can Jesus be both God and man?" To solve the problem most missionaries have chosen one or the other Jesus. The Jesus-only-man people talk about the incarnation as identification with people's material needs, while the Jesus-only-God people focus on people's spiritual needs and on seeking peace with God through Jesus. Both parties agree that the responsible person is not helped in social ethics by the God-or man-Jesus. One side sees Jesus as God and believes that what happened to him is not a pattern for us. Those who see Jesus only as man understand him in a cultural and sociopolitical environment which they believe is irrelevant for us.

What these people fail to see is that Jesus is at the same time the model for our human behavior *and* the means for our spiritual transformation. Both elements are inseparable aspects of the same reality. Jesus is the normative man, man as God would like him to be: Jesus, God-among-us and in us, by the power of the Holy Spirit. All that is in Jesus can also be in us when we are in Jesus and Jesus is in us. We have access to the same resources for living that he did: The same God who acted in him can act in us through him. In him we have the way, the truth, and the life, and no one can know God except by knowing him.

Often missionaries in their proclamation emphasize salvation through faith in the atoning death of Jesus. The emphasis in itself is not bad, but the broader meaning of Jesus' death is often diminished when only the once-and-for-all, sacrificial aspect predominates. It is true that Jesus died for us to take away our sins, that he paid the price of our rebellion against God. But it is also true that Jesus' death on the cross cannot be separated from his life and his resurrection. His death for us has a deep ethical meaning. Jesus died for us so that we can also die with him. In Jesus we die to the sin in us and around us and we are called to live a new life in the light of the kingdom's values. The cross is the way of our salvation and the shape of our life; it is the model of our love.

Jesus' death was the result of his faithful life, the normal treatment that the world offers to the Lord's obedient servant. Through Jesus' suffering he learned obedience (Heb. 5:8) and so models the kind of unconditional faithfulness to God we should have.

What Jesus lived and what he said of himself should also

hold for his followers. He has given us an example of what we
have to do and how we should do it (Jn. 13:15). If the full meaning of the cross penetrated our missionary methods and message
we would take more seriously the ethical demands of the life and
teachings of Jesus. This was the case with Paul, apostle of Jesus
and great missionary of the early Christian church. Paul learned
from Jesus that "suffering servanthood is God's strategy for mission. It is therefore natural," John Driver wrote, "that Paul's missionary stance should be characterized by weakness, by suffering
and by sacrifice" (2 Cor. 11:23-33).[5]

Discipleship. We must understand missions as the task of
making disciples, disciples sent (*apostéllo*) as apostles to be the salt
of the earth, to bring light to darkness as they go, empowered by
Jesus. Evangelism must not separate *kérygma* (preaching the
good news) and *didaché* (the teaching of Jesus and the apostles).[6]
Saving souls without making disciples is not faithful response to
the Great Commission (Mt. 28:19-20). The first-century church
used the Sermon on the Mount (Mt. 5—7) to teach those who
wanted to be baptized, so they would know what being a disciple
of Jesus meant.[7] Spreading the good news without calling people
to radical commitment has produced cheap, hollow Christian
faith.

Jim Wallis writes: "The great tragedy of modern evangelism
is in calling many to belief but few to obedience. The failure has
come in separating belief from obedience, which renders the
gospel message confusing and strips the evangelistic proclamation
of its power and authority. The evangelistic question has become
what do we believe *about* Christ rather than are we willing to
forsake all and follow Him."[8]

The life of discipleship has to find its roots in Jesus' call to
radical obedience. This is an urgent call to enter with absolute
faith into the new eon of God. This is the time of salvation, the
time of the gathering of the new Israel, the new people of God.
Jesus' demands of his disciples are the ones that God asked of his
people at Sinai: total obedience and sacrificial servanthood, participation in his life and destiny, being partakers of his mission

with all its suffering and glory. Only with this same understanding can we go as apostles, as missionaries. Missions today must be understood as moving ahead in the liberation movement of God, with the power of the Holy Spirit bringing freedom to those imprisoned in the darkness of sin. In the power of the Holy Spirit, groups of liberated people form whose words and deeds are the wonderful signs that a new creation is present, visible, alive, contagious. Every missionary should know that it is impossible to make disciples unless one is a disciple, and that one cannot act with divine power unless one is equipped with the tools and visions God gives through the fullness of his Holy Spirit (Lk. 4:18).[9]

The church. Many studies have been made on the theological meaning of various forms of the church. A close relationship exists between what one believes being Christian means and what one considers the marks of the church. Tell me what ecclesiology you have and I will tell you what kind of Christian you are. The challenge of our time relates to the life and shape of the church as distinct from the world. Christian ethics are useless unless the set of values which govern the church is radically different from those of the world. If the church is to be able to make its distinctive contribution, it must have a sound understanding of what the Bible means by the concept of the people of God and what Jesus wanted the corporate life of his disciples to be. Certainly he did not mean Sunday morning services or religious moments, special encounters, and the gathering of happy believers. He probably also did not mean the undefined, silent witness, lost in the air, unsullied in a dirty world.

He surely meant a different kind of group of people living close together in mutual dependence, sharing all they have and all they are, putting together their material, natural, and spiritual gifts for the building up of all and of each member. He surely meant a new kind of family, a model of society where truth and love can be seen in the eyes and the hands of those committed to each other, a group of people with an impressively different set of values which would put them at odds with a world of egoism and destruction. He meant a group of people who have thrown out their cherished idols in order to become attached to God in Jesus, to serve and suffer with joy for the liberaton of people still under the control of the prince of darkness.

Concern for statistics has made the missionary ecclesiology a question of superficial attachment to a religious group which at most offers social security and promotion. Christians are blinded to the wrongdoings of the world when the same wrongs are found in the church. Serious ethical concern will be absent where only numerical success matters. The faithful church will not exist unless people are taught consciously and practically that it is impossible to be at the same time a loyal citizen of the kingdom of God and subservient to the kingdom of this world.

Salvation. Life with God through Jesus in the context of the Spirit-filled community makes possible salvation, a saved life. Salvation is the hope of humanity, already possible and visible but not fully realized in the present world. Salvation is not an abstract ideal, a heavenly event outside daily life and decision-making. It is not the once-and-for-all guarantee of a free ticket to heaven. Rather salvation is heaven already here, the kingdom among us, the lordship of Jesus in our lives. Jesus cannot be Savior without being our Lord. The gospel is not correctly preached without concrete teaching about the meaning of Jesus' lordship in our ethical decision-making. We have been raised from the darkness of death so that we may walk in the light of the resurrection. The message of salvation through Jesus is a call to share the loving nature of God and his holiness.

This picture of salvation is true, but it is incomplete. We cannot live the teachings of Jesus, we cannot live salvation or walk in the resurrection without the power of the Holy Spirit in our lives. We cannot witness persuasively or progress in sanctification or be victorious over Satan and the power of darkness without the fire of Pentecost. As Paul wrote, missionaries have to go not so much with plausible words of wisdom, but in demonstration of the Spirit and power (1 Cor. 2:1-5).

This is another neglected dimension of the Christian message which could change everything from the meaning of

Jesus to the form of the church and the life of salvation. Jesus lived as he did because he was baptized and filled with the Holy Spirit. The church will also truly worship God and live the values of the kingdom in a hostile world when the gifts of the Spirit are present and are used in building up the body. Salvation will be clearly seen when the power of God through his Spirit transforms the lives of people and communities totally committed to Jesus. When people abandon the path of disobedience and turn away from sin through repentance and forgiveness, God gives them the same power Jesus had, so they can die to the flesh and walk in the Spirit (Gal. 5:24-25).

Clear teaching on the reality of Satan and evil spirits or demons is also connected with a better understanding and experience of the work of the Spirit. Too much psychology and anthropology without enough biblical teaching on the powers of evil can lead to failure in Christian missions. Without the biblical perspective, missionaries may appreciate other people's cultures and lifestyles but they will not help people to solve the problems of sin or be free from the bondage of Satan.

Biblical perspectives

The inseparable bond between ethics and missions can be understood only in biblical perspective.

The Old Testament. The Old Testament tells us the history of a people whose vocation was to be a blessing to all the families of the earth (Gen. 12:3). This people was a very weak people, but nevertheless God chose them and made a covenant with them. And God said, "Walk before me and be blameless" (Gen. 17:1). They lived in the midst of hostile nations and had trouble keeping their subsequent life unsoiled. But God promised that if they obeyed his voice and kept his covenant, they would be a kingdom of priests and a holy nation (Ex. 19:5-6). God called this people to share his ethical nature: "You shall therefore be holy, for I am holy." They could imitate God only by keeping his commandments, "by walking in his ways" (Deut. 8:6).

As it happened, this people often fell into temptation, going after other gods and imitating their neighbors. Yet their God used prophets and judges to call them again and again from the path of unfaithfulness. They were to be separated unto God, set apart from the injustice and violence of the rest of the world. God gave them hope for a new age with a wonderful messianic promise: "I will abolish the bow, the sword, and war from the land.... I will betroth you to me in righteousness and in justice, in steadfast love, and in mercy" (Hos. 2:18-19). This hope would be realized with the coming of the servant of the Lord, the prince of peace (Is. 9:6), the chosen one, the anointed one of the people of Israel. God had promised this people: "I will give you as a light to the nations, that my salvation may reach to the end of the earth" (Is. 49:6). All this would come to pass through the suffering love and capital punishment of the innocent Messiah at the hands of his enemies, whose iniquities he took upon himself so they could be healed and made righteous in the eyes of God (Is. 53).

The New Testament. The New Testament is the history of the new Israel of God, called to a new covenant not of law but of life. God demonstrated in Jesus his way of proclaiming the gospel. Jesus was God among us, redeeming his people so they could live in holiness and righteousness before him all the days of their lives. By forgiving their sins he brought salvation to his people and gave "Light to those who sit in darkness and in the shadow of death, to guide our feet into the way of peace" (Lk. 1:79).

When Jesus began his ministry he called people to repent, "for the kingdom of heaven is at hand" (Mt. 4:17). His words were like those of John the Baptist, who asked people to "bear fruits that befit repentance" by sharing clothing and food, by ceasing to be unjust, violent, deceitful (Lk. 3:8, 10-14). When he called his disciples, Jesus told them that the kingdom of God belonged only to the poor, the meek, the merciful, the pure in heart, those with hunger and thirst for righteousness, those persecuted for God's sake (Mt. 5:3-10).

In the Sermon on the Mount Jesus taught his disciples the ethical demands of the new kingdom order, concerning money, sex, violence, and religion (Mt. 5—7). Jesus showed his concern for truth and love, even in relation to enemies. Jesus' demands were so radical that his disciples thought he expected the impossible from them (Mk. 10:27). Jesus agreed, but assured the disciples that God makes the impossible possible for those who follow his way. But what is possible is still not easy. Jesus asked total obedience from his disciples; they would have their share in his suffering and mission. "If any man would come after me, let him deny himself and take up his cross and follow me" (Mt. 16:24). This verse is the center of Jesus' call to imitation and surrender. The rest follows from this. As the Father sent the Son, so Jesus sends his people (Jn. 20:21), that they may become in him "a chosen race, a royal priesthood, a holy nation" (1 Pet. 2:9), a people who imitate God in his mercy (Lk. 6:32-36). Paul also asked all Christians who have put off the sinful life and have put on the compassion of God and the peace of Christ (Col. 3:5-15) to be imitators of God, to walk in love, "as Christ loved us and gave himself up for us, a fragrant offering and sacrifice to God" (Eph. 5:1-2).

As Jesus "called the twelve together and gave them power and authority over all demons and . . . sent them out to preach the kingdom of God and to heal" (Lk. 9:1-2), as Jesus gave them the power of the Holy Spirit to be his witnesses to the end of the earth (Acts 1:8), so we are empowered and sent as witnesses, messengers, and partakers of the already present kingdom of God.

Church missionary history
The Constantinian heresy

Church history shows that the ethical and missionary dimensions of the Christian life correspond to the prevailing concept of the church and its relationship with society. Faithfulness and integrity in Christian behavior are related to the presence or absence of the discipleship concept as an integral part of the definition of what it means to be a Christian. Missionary activity has been related to the degree of compromise and connivance between the church and the state. The sociopolitical powers tend to claim a religious halo that does not properly belong to them.

This connection can be seen in the transition from the New Testament apostolic church to the Constantinian church of the fourth century. How can a minority, persecuted, disciplined, and missionary church become a persecuting, insipid, acceptable-to-anybody, and imperialistic mass church? When there is no moral distinction between church and society, then being a good Christian is the same as being a good citizen. And that happened through the unhappy marriage of church and state. Before, Christians died confessing that Christ—and not Caesar—was Lord; they refused to do military service because in Christ all enemies were objects of love and not of violence. After, non-Christians could not be soldiers; fight for Caesar was to fight for God. Before, Christians were considered enemies of the state and forced to deny their faith. After, even a pagan like Constantine was accepted as the armed defender of the Christian faith and as the head of the church. Before, people became Christians by the preaching of the gospel through sincere persuasion produced by the power of the Holy Spirit who acted with wonders and signs among the believers. After, people were forced to accept Christianity as the true religion through the power of the army with acts of violence and sociopolitical blackmail.

No wonder that when the Roman Empire proscribed the pagan cults, missionaries were sent with the support of the state and its army to convert the chiefs of other states. Thus the whole of Europe was evangelized and masses of people were baptized. The clergy sprinkled holy water on whole crowds of people, many of them soldiers. As K. S. Latourette puts it: "Kings furthered conversion through force, assisted by missionaries who carried on the work of instruction of the neophytes."[10] Thus, Europe soon became a *corpus christianum*; being a citizen of the state meant at the same time being a member of the Christian church.

Could a whole society live according to the ethical standards of the Sermon on the Mount? Of course not. Only disciples have the understanding and ability to live according to the teachings of Jesus. The only solution was to adapt the ethical demands of the gospel to the society at large by watering them down and creating a religious system in which everybody would be welcome. The hermits were the first movement of protest against this defection of the church. They left the world to live solitary, sanctified life in the wilderness. Monastic orders brought into communal life those who did not want to conform to the mass religion and longed for a life according to the fundamental teachings of Jesus.

But the church soon institutionalized, and two ethical standards became equally acceptable for Christians: "the counsels of perfection" for those who had a religious vocation, and the normal, commonsense behavior for the mass of secular believers, the laity. Theology was built on philosophical grounds; the great Augustine, even though a converted Christian, wrote his *Civitas Dei* to defend the state religion against the surrounding paganism. He justified the use of violence against the enemies of the state and the church, and thus opened the door to the Inquisition and forced conversions.

From darkness to Reformation

The popular Christianity of the Middle Ages with its horrifying crusades, its religious syncretism, and its moral blindness was the result of the deformation of Christian faith into cultural Christianity. The Christians answered the Arab invasion by imitating the Arabs' holy wars to help God gain political and religious control over holy and unholy lands. The influence of the crusade phenomenon continues to this day (e.g., in the Spanish civil war, Nazism—*Gott mit uns*, Vietnam, Lebanon, and Ireland, as well as in the Christian justification of modern wars and the theologies of revolution/liberation). Movements and models of church reform existed in the Middle Ages—the Waldensians, the Lollards, and the Hussites, although few if any stood for full separation of church and state or religious freedom, or even religious toleration. Religion was regarded as a territorial affair and church and state as ideally one.[11]

In the sixteenth century the Magisterial Reformation in Germany, Switzerland, and the northern countries made a dramatic change on the doctrinal level and with regard to the accep-

tance of the authority of the Scriptures in matters of faith and
Christian living. Yet the situation in Europe was not basically
changed.

> The principle of *cuius regio eius religio*, while adopted in a
> Germany fragmented politically and religiously, in effect was ap-
> plied elsewhere. Thus in Denmark, Norway, Sweden, and Fin-
> land, the state supported Lutheranism. The majority of Scotland
> became Presbyterian, and the monarchs in England and Wales
> and to a certain extent in Ireland endeavored to enforce con-
> formity to the Anglican establishment.[12]

The Anabaptist model

Only the pacifist Anabaptists and the Swiss Brethren, who
were forced to separate from the Zwinglian reformation, decided
at the price of their lives to obey God and his Word rather than
people. They were far more radical than the Protestants who soon
considered them enemies and collaborated with the Catholics in
persecuting them.

The Anabaptists did not accept the validity of the concept of
corpus christianum. They saw the nationalist reformations as
another form of Constantinianism. They insisted on holy life for
Christians and on separation from the world. By that they meant
taking seriously the ethical demands of the Sermon on the Mount,
seeing Christianity as discipleship (disciplined life and imitation of
Jesus Christ) and the healthy divorce between the church and the
state. They pioneered internal missions and traveled all over
Europe preaching the gospel of repentance and salvation to
nominal Christians, Catholic and Protestant. They baptized only
adults because they wanted believers to be disciples. Their zeal
and the power of the Holy Spirit were evident in their readiness to
suffer martyrdom because of their vision of Christian faith. They
refused to use violence to defeat their enemies, or to enforce
Christianity, or to defend themselves.

"The Anabaptists were the most missionary of all the
Protestant churches in the first generation," wrote J. C. Wenger.[13]
Church historian Franklin H. Littell gave us this view of
Anabaptist theology and strategy for missions:

(1) The Anabaptists rejected the territorial Church system and felt they were entitled to witness to all men everywhere, and those who voluntarily accepted the Gospel they baptized and received into fellowship. (2) They interpreted the missionary commission of Christ to be binding on all believers at all times. (3) The lay believer was the key in the rapid spread of Anabaptism. (4) The Anabaptist regarded the suffering of the martyr Church as its authentication.[14]

Menno Simons, the Catholic priest converted to Anabaptism who became the leader of the Mennonite movement in the Netherlands, wrote:

> We preach, as much as is possible, both by day and by night, in houses and fields, in forests and wastes, hither and yon, at home and abroad, in prison and in dungeons, in water and in fire, on the scaffold and on the wheel, before lords and princes, through mouth and pen, with possessions and blood, with life and death. We have done this these many years, and we are not ashamed of the Gospel of the glory of Christ.[15]

This movement spread throughout Europe so rapidly that it was considered public enemy number one for the state and the state churches. The Anabaptists were radical reformers, ecclesiological revolutionaries of the time, because of their radical understanding of Christian ethics and evangelism. But their only weapons were the word of God and spiritual power.

Mennonites as evangelical Protestants

What persecutions and martyrdom could not stop came to an end during times of peaceful settling. For most Mennonites of the eighteenth and nineteenth centuries the binding nature of Jesus' Great Commission (Mt. 28:19-20) was lost. Other denominations, from evangelical Protestants to Catholics, sent missionaries to faraway lands. John Eliot (1631), the Wesleys (1738), Zinzendorf (1740), William Carey (1792), Hudson Taylor (1852), David Livingstone (1857), and many others went forth "to preach the gospel among the heathen," in America, Asia, and Africa. It should be said that "the motives of those who made up the nineteenth-century missionary movement were mixed.

Missionary outreach went hand in hand with European, and especially British, imperialism."[16] Commercial and cultural imperialism accompanied political imperialism. Among the motiva-
tions, Theron F. Schlabach noted: "Another motivation surely
was romanticism, as would-be missionaries heard sudden calls to
far-off continents, distant sea islands, and exotic peoples."[17]

Mennonites lost their missionary zeal after the first-generation outreach. They became "the quiet in the land," an in-
troverted, ethnic people. Most of them were peasants who sought
privileges from the governments of the nations where they had
migrated to avoid persecution. Eventually many gave up their
pacifist conviction and further accommodated themselves to the
standards of this world. They became legalistic and forgot the call
to discipleship and mission. Their practice of ethnic and
geographic separation from the world resulted in deformed faith.

Only at the end of the nineteenth century did Mennonites
catch up with the modern missionary movement. But by that time
they had lost the Anabaptist vision of missions with its emphasis
on social ethics and discipleship. They were influenced more by
evangelical Protestants who understood the preaching of the
gospel in terms of "salvation through faith," in the style of Lutheran theology. They followed the patterns other Protestants had
set, and became one more evangelical denomination in the mission field, without Anabaptist specificity and peace witness. As
Robert L. Ramseyer put it: "Mennonite churches founded by
Mennonite missionaries as part of the modern missionary movement lack a distinctive peace witness. They are in almost all
essentials like churches founded by evangelical Protestant missionaries from Europe and North America."[18]

In the 1950s Mennonites in North America began to ask
questions about the ethical implicatons of missions, especially
with regard to nonresistance. Their questions were related to the
recovery of the Anabaptist vision as stated by Harold S. Bender,
John C. Wenger, John H. Yoder, Robert Friedmann, William
Klassen, John Miller, and other Mennonite scholars from North
America.[19]

A new group of Mennonite writers and leaders are taking seriously the meaning of specific aspects of the Anabaptist vision and applying them to the Christian life and the church and its mission. Colleges and seminaries are bringing into the learning experience the challenges of this particular accent. Many Christian groups are inspired by that vision, and on the missionary field people ask more questions about Mennonite uniquenesses, about what made us neither Catholic nor Protestant.

Let us hope that this distinctiveness is realized and not only discussed. Let us hope that it does not result in a new form of legalism. Let us see that the Spirit is present, that this vision is geared not so much at making us feel righteous but is an instrument of salvation aimed to reach those who are suffering the consequences of sin, those who need to hear and see the good news of God's redemptive act in Jesus.

Contemporary challenge

Today evangelicals are increasingly aware of the social and political implications of the message of Jesus. One clear example was the declaration at the World Evangelism Congress in Lausanne in 1974. Since then, many books and articles have been written and a lot of talking done on the subject. In a way this is the evangelical counterpart of the more liberal theologies of liberation. These theologies come as a reaction against the silence of Christian churches in the face of the flagrant injustices and corruption of most of the governments and ruling classes in the Third World. There the established churches had identified with and supported the status quo. Catholics and Protestants alike had been seen as part of the colonial forces, serving the interests of the rich.

The liberationists identify with the suffering of the poor and see no other way of loosening the chains of bondage except through changes in power structures and through improved social conditions via radical reforms and even peaceful or violent revolutions. They see the evangelical churches as "the refuge of the masses," where frustrated people without hope of changing their lot in life find other-worldly escape in religion.

Much is true in what the theologians of liberation say about the sins of society and the churches' compromises with the powers. Evangelicals must recognize that their ways of doing missions have often neglected the prophetic dimension of speaking out against the injustices of the state or of acting with concern for solving the social and economic problems of the poor. Often missionaries have lived in comfortable conditions. Some members of their churches looked at them with envy and contempt; others tried to benefit as much as possible from those riches. Some improved their economic situation because of contacts with missionaries and the moral standards of the church. Many accepted their poverty as a God-given situation.

Mennonites in mission fields have shared many of these traditional missionary patterns although they often demonstrated concern for social ills. The programs of Mennonite Central Committee (MCC) are a good example of this care "in the name of Christ." And yet, until recent times such a division of labor existed between MCC and the mission boards that missionaries considered involvment in peace concerns and social programs inappropriate to their task. Although at some points this separation was healthy, I welcome the more recent openness of mission boards to social projects as part of their missionary programs. The line which separated them from MCC is becoming less sharp.

One good example of the shift is the Mennonite missionary program in Bolivia. At first, it was an MCC relief, teachers abroad, agricultural, and development program. Through the witness of the Pax men and women a few small congregations have been growing with the combined effort of South and North American Mennonite churches and several mission boards as well as MCC. This demonstrates how a missionary program can grow out of a social concern.

The same could be said about the Spanish Mennonite Church in Brussels. The first program started with the help of Mennonite Board of Missions was social service for migrant workers. When some Christians from Spain arrived and asked for help, they found a place to meet for worship services and pastoral and teaching help. Soon this small group grew to be a good-sized congregation; now, after years of hard work, they are economically independent, have their own leaders, and are an intentional community which pioneers a mission program in Spain.

This program is very much related to peace and service concerns and tries to take into account all the specifics of the Anabaptist vision: discipleship as the heart of Christian commitment; an ecclesiology which emphasizes community, strong fellowship, and peoplehood; and service, suffering love, and peace as central to the life of salvation and the preaching of the gospel. How we function is as important as what we say; ethics are essential to the missionary methods and message, and to the life of the missionary community.

Mission is essential to the life of the church; the church is a missionary community. This community by its existence has a sociopolitical importance and witnesses to the new creation that God wants to make present through Jesus. It should be a model of radical commitment to God, an uncompromised voice of hope for the lost, a bridge of dialogue and reconciliation, a platform of real and concrete salvation, a model of a new society, a source for change in lives and structures. All aspects of life should be under the scrutiny of the Word of God, as that Word is understood by the prayerful community under the inspiration of the Holy Spirit. Obedience and good will are needed, but they are genuine only when the Spirit is at work and his fruits are seen as the confirmation of his therapeutic action.

Human relations are no longer a result of friendship, of biological or traditional ties, but of a common faith, a common discipline, a common mission, a common vision. Mutual care is no longer motivated by egoism in the flesh but by the love in the Spirit. The urgency of the task calls for a serious examination of past and present mistakes, for repentance and change. The fullness of Christ is manifested in the fruits of the Spirit and in the discernment and exercise of all of the spiritual gifts, for the building up of the community.

With the growing number of totalitarian states, the loss of

old values, and the birth of new religious ideologies and politically minded sects, the Christian churches need to be aware of the danger of compromise and confusion. Discernment and discipline, prayer and radical commitment to Christ the Lord, sound teaching and healthy practice, dependence on the Word of God and the fullness of the Holy Spirit: all of this is needed to live our missionary task according to the standards left by Jesus and the New Testament church. The church of tomorrow must be as much concerned about ethics as about mission and needs to be a living example of what God made known in Jesus when he sent him to bring salvation. Otherwise the world will not believe it.

We need new models of mission with a more careful accent on the ethical dimensions of the Christian message. Thus we ask with Robert L. Ramseyer:

> In our missionary message what do we say about capitalism, socialism, communism, about profit as a motive for economic activity, about international exploitation? What do missionaries say about the meaning of Christian love in economic relationships? Those who go as missionaries from North America to the countries of the so-called Third World need to be aware that they will be perceived as members of an exploiting society living among members of an exploited society. They will need to be conscious of the ways in which North American society, including its churches, does in fact participate in the exploitation of peoples.[20]

Also, with the change of behavior that the preaching of the gospel calls forth, confrontation with the powers, conflict with the state and society are going to be part of the missionaries' cross. In these circumstances we will need to remind ourselves that peace as *shalom* (harmony, justice, and mercy) is essential to the message of the gospel. And we agree with Marlin Miller:

> A renewed vision of the gospel of peace as an integral part of the Good News of Jesus Christ would have far-reaching consequences for missionary thought and practice. . . . It would mean an extension of the missionary proclamation in our time to include the messianic peace addressed to situations of enmity and injustice. It would mean giving priority to theological and missionary efforts which focus on points of conflict and reconciliation rather than

reinforcing or totally undergirding given social and economic conflicts and enmity. It would mean the renewal of the church as a
messianic community whose basis for existence derives not from
national, ethnic, or cultural givens, but from an ever new corporate identity in Christ. To all of this and more we are called and
freed by the "good news of peace through Jesus Christ."[21]

Because human behavior is the final object of Jesus' call to
salvation, radical obedience to God is the normal result of his redemptive work. To preach the gospel of Jesus is to call men and
women to a new life according to the standards of the kingdom as
lived and taught by Jesus. This is made possible through the
powerful and continuous action of the Holy Spirit in the believer.
Faith as faithful obedience to his will is what God calls people to
live by. Salvation is living for God, sharing his nature, his ways, his
mission. Jesus is Savior because he is the victor over evil so that we
can be witnesses to his lordship in our whole life.

Being a Christian involves being a witness of the lordship of
Jesus over the powers of this world. In all the levels of our life—
personal, familial, congregational, sociopolitical—we are witnesses of the presence or the absence of the power of God and the
reality of Christ's salvation. Mission means confronting the world
with God's call to salvation through Christ, with our words and
with our lives. Every faithful Christian is a missionary, and every
faithful congregation is a missionary community.

An examination of the ethics of missions helps us to see the
conditional character of the obedience that the Christian, the missionary, owes to the state and the ideological or economic powers
of this world. Our faithfulness is above all to God and his mission.
When the sociopolitical structures of this world call for falsehood
and violence we answer with truthful love, and in the face of oppression and wars we work for justice and peace. Always ready to
denounce and transform the multiple manifestations of sin in
people and structures, with the power of God, the power of the
cross, the power of love, we are ready to confront the evil powers
of this world, giving our lives to bring salvation to humanity. This
is our mission.

10
The "Great Century" Reconsidered

Wilbert R. Shenk

In a 1965 essay Paul Peachey took measure of "The New Ethical Possibility: The Task of Post-Christendom Ethics." Surveying the course of world history, including the impact of the West on other cultures since the sixteenth century, Peachey concluded: "In sum, thus, history has disowned the expectation that world society would be made in the image of Christendom."[1] While Peachey—the product of the free church/believers church tradition—might be expected to arrive at such a conclusion, he adduced his evidence from wide-ranging sources. None of those he called to the witness stand were representative of Peachey's own tradition.

In this essay I shall argue the thesis that the "Great Century" in missions was both a powerful last thrust of Christendom and an important instrument in bringing about the dissolution of Christendom. When we speak of the Great Century, we refer of course to that initiative in missionary action beginning roughly around 1800 and climaxing at the start of World War I in 1914.[2]

This movement, on the Protestant side, had its roots in Pietism and in the eighteenth-century Evangelical Revival. Although the formation of missionary societies occurred on a broad

---

Wilbert R. Shenk, Elkhart, Indiana, is vice-president of Overseas Ministries, Mennonite Board of Missions. He is editor of Mission Focus *and author of* Henry Venn—Missionary Statesman *(Orbis, 1983).*

front—in Europe, the British Isles, and North America—Great Britain quickly became the leader. The British dominated missions until around 1900. Coincidental with the World Missionary Conference at Edinburgh in 1910 the British relinquished the premier place they had held for a century. American Protestant missionaries now outnumbered the British.

The meaning of the Great Century is less in terms of the actual numbers of new adherents won to the Christian faith on the fields of Asia, Africa, and Latin America than in the formative impact the movement had on the Christian world. Steady geographical expansion shattered the geopolitical mold of Christendom. This growth outward changed the horizon of the churches' self-understanding. In the twentieth century far greater numbers of new believers have joined the Christian family in the non-Western world than during the Great Century, but the nineteenth century remains crucial as the formative period which gave shape to all that was to follow in the twentieth.

When we speak of Christendom we refer to that understanding of the Christian church which came to predominance following the Treaty of Milan in AD 313 between Constantine and Licinius. That treaty called for toleration for all religions, but the result was that Christianity soon became the religion of the emperor and thus of the empire. This marriage between church and state altered the character of the church. Rather than being the faith of those who voluntarily responded to the call to follow Jesus Christ as Lord, Christianity was now identified with the political power structures and struggles of the world.[3]

The church of Christendom was highly institutionalized, and the sacramental system provided the means of grace. While the Treaty of Milan initially promised religious toleration, Constantinianism soon came to signify religious intolerance. Europe would be Christianized through state-supported missionary action, often accompanied with force.

Despite the vicissitudes of one and a half millenia, much of the Christendom mentality remained intact in the nineteenth century. "In the sphere of mission to lands where the Gospel had not been preached," observes Ronald K. Orchard, "the task was conceived in a fashion which seems to owe a good deal to the medieval concept of Christendom."[4] It combined geographical and cultural elements in a realm that was counter-poised to "the heathen" in distant lands. "Christian nations" stood in contrast to the non-Christian peoples. In Christendom terms, "Christian" connoted geography, cultural forms and tastes, political structures, and legal systems—all without necessary reference to the church or any formal dependence on the church.

Viewed from the standpoint of cultural history, the course of Western culture was undergoing fundamental change during the nineteenth century. The Crystal Palace Exhibition held in London in 1851 serves as a convenient symbol for this transition into the world of modernity. Religion had lost its authority by mid-century, and modernism took over.[5] In Great Britain Evangelicals exerted a salutary influence on social policy through the leadership of the Wilberforces and Shaftesburys; but this movement had largely spent itself by mid-century. The church became increasingly preoccupied with defending itself against the assaults from science. At the two crucial points—the nature and calling of the church and the church's relation to the world—no fresh light broke through.

At nightfall of the Great Century, Walter Hobhouse, in the Bampton Lectures for 1909, asserted: "Long ago I came to believe that the great change in the relations between the Church and the World which began with the conversion of Constantine is not only a decisive turning-point in Church history but is also the key to many of the practical difficulties of the present day, and that the Church of the future is destined more and more to return to a condition of things somewhat like that which prevailed in the Ante-Nicene Church; that is to say, that instead of pretending to be co-extensive with the world, it will confess itself the Church of a minority, will accept a position involving a more conscious antagonism with the world, and will in return, regain in some measure its former coherence."[6] Hobhouse called for reform of the church along two lines: (1) honor Christ's primary intention to found a visible society on earth which would perpetuate his work; and (2) let this divine society be separate from, even antagonistic to, the world even though this made membership in it costly.[7]

This plea for the reform of the church along pre-Constantinian lines cannot be dismissed out of hand as the rantings of a Dissenting churchman. Hobhouse was a respected member of an established church speaking from a pastoral point of view.

Our task now is to examine the dynamics of the missionary movement in the nineteenth century in light of the forces which sought to perpetuate Christendom and the counterforces which contributed to its disintegration.

The Great Century: Discontinuity and continuity

Participants in the nineteenth-century missionary movement had a clear sense of its novelty. The first response to this fresh religious impulse was to create new structures to carry out mission goals. The formation of missionary societies, beginning with the Methodists in 1787 and the Baptists in 1792 in Great Britain, rose to a crescendo during the next three decades in Europe and the United States of America. The final quarter of the century saw an even greater organizing effort with many new missionary societies formed.[8]

Although patterned somewhat along lines of Roman Catholic orders, Protestant societies tapped the reservoir of voluntarism among the laity which enabled unprecedented growth in financial support and workers. The "faith mission" epitomized this development, drawing support from individuals in various denominations. Whether a missionary society was church-related or independent, it was sustained by individuals committed to world mission.

In *The Missionary Enterprise* Edwin Munsell Bliss repeatedly makes the point that missions mean voluntarism: "The keynote of modern missionary activity is the personal responsibility of the individual for the individual salvation of non-Christians." Then he adds, "To develop this individual responsibility and activity required first that men should learn to think for themselves; then act for themselves; then act together without losing the individual consciousness."[9] He insists that all initiatives originate with the individual. Bliss hails as the birthmark of the modern missionary movement, in contrast to earlier periods, "this sense of mutual, individual responsibility."[10] All of this is said without any effort to relate this action to the church theologically or ecclesiastically. In fact, the church seems to be viewed as a liability—an impediment to action. The solution was to move away from the church through voluntary and independent societies. The institutional church could not be taken to heart as an ally in the missionary cause.

Regardless of the ecclesiastical tradition, missionary societies found themselves in tension with the church. For an established church like the Church of England the existence of missionary societies which were not constitutionally linked to the hierarchy was a source of particular frustration. Yet the hierarchy was not at all organized to sponsor and administer a missionary program. One of the contributions made by the Tractarian Movement was to call for a more adequate ecclesiology, including its missionary dimension. As it was, however, even this challenge was largely lost because the Tractarians wanted to link their missionary strategy to a particular theory of the episcopate. This Anglo-Catholic view insisted that each mission must be headed by a bishop from the outset if it were to be a true mission. To the Evangelicals who distrusted prelacy and prized voluntarism, this theory was an anathema. Eventually Anglicans reached a *modus vivendi* ecclesiastically, but not theologically.

The sheer scale of the missionary movement in the nineteenth century finds no precedent in history. Although the Christian church was self-consciously missionary in its first decades, it was largely a spontaneous and organic movement outward. In the nineteenth century formal organization and conscious strategizing became hallmarks of this movement to reach the ends of the earth with the message of Jesus Christ. The vision which spurred mission supporters on was firmly grounded in the Old Testament prayer, "that thy way may be known upon earth, thy saving power among all nations" (Ps. 67:2). It was a vision renewed by Isaiah's promise that "the earth shall be full of the knowledge of the Lord as the waters cover the sea" (Is. 11:9b). Missionaries tended to believe that "knowledge of the Lord" came clothed in the language and forms of their own culture. Only gradually did they perceive their own provincialism and admit to the relativity of all cultures.

Even the most culturally isolated churches in the North Atlantic basin responded sooner or later to the missionary impulse. The churches which made up the sending base underwent profound change both in their self-understanding as well as their sense of responsibility for the world beyond their own national boundaries.

Although the movement began with all the assumptions about Christendom intact—effectively captured in the regnant slogan of the period: "Christianity, Civilization, and Commerce"—the movement outward into diverse cultures and climes soon taxed the old synthesis to the breaking point. The movement was fashioning a new empirical reality that stubbornly resisted being fitted into the old mold.

Until the nineteenth century it was expected that the state was a legitimate sponsor of missions. The roles of the Spanish and Portuguese crowns in missions in the fifteenth and sixteenth centuries was emulated by the other European powers through the charters granted to the trading companies and colonies being established from the sixteenth century on. By the nineteenth century the trading companies were increasingly wary of ties to the religious establishment, especially where this involved evangelizing activity among the indigenous peoples. Motivated by profit rather than altruism, these companies saw clearly that missionary work was not being greeted enthusiastically by local peoples. Their task of imposing rule from the outside and managing an economy for profit was bound to be immeasurably complicated by the presence of these religious interlopers. It had become patently clear to these quasi-state trading companies, in direct contrast to Constantine, that their interests were not going to be served by co-opting the church.

The history of the nineteenth century is replete with episodes where mission clashed with state or the one tried to use the other to advantage. The East India Trading Company long withstood pressures to allow missionaries to enter India. When by an act of the British Parliament in 1813 the Company charter was amended to open India to missionaries, it was a hard-won victory for mission supporters.[11] Behind it stood years of struggle on both sides. Pro-missionary forces had worked within the East India Company itself through sympathetic Company directors, in Parliament, and by a highly effective propaganda effort directed to the public to gain their end. Time after time William Wilberforce used his powerful oratory in behalf of the missionary cause. No one questioned the propriety of exerting political pressure to get a Christian nation to do what Christian governments ought to be concerned with—the Christianizing of the nations.

Even though no clear theory of church-state relations guided missionary leaders during the nineteenth century, they were mindful of abuses and misuses of political power in the service of evangelization in the past. In the nineteenth century no one defended the so-called Dutch method whereby the Dutch, having ousted the Portuguese from Ceylon (now Sri Lanka) in the seventeenth century, used coercion on Catholics to become Protestants and expropriated Catholic churches for Protestant worship. It was well known that such tactics had produced bitter fruit. Although missions did not always follow a consistent course where government was concerned, the trend was toward independence of the church from the state.[12]

As a corollary to the growing separation of church/mission and state, missions became increasingly involved in the quest for religious liberty and human rights. Despite the witness of the Radical Reformers of the sixteenth century—which laid the foundation for the free church tradition—the notion of religious liberty remained only a faint hope.[13] Indeed, the Reformation inspired renewed persecution.[14] Far from being an experiment in religious liberty, the first two centuries of American history was of a piece with Europe's.[15] The nineteenth century marks progress on this front.

One cannot overestimate the importance of the campaign for the abolition of the slave trade in Great Britain—won in 1807— and the outlawing of slavery itself—in 1833—in creating a conscience on human rights.[16] The movement was aided by the wider intellectual and cultural currents, to be sure, but the missionary was often found at the storm center of clashes between indigenous peoples and Western traders or colonial administrators, especially in the first half of the century. The flowering of imperialism after 1850 blunted the movement until after World War I.

Mission leaders in the nineteenth century saw themselves as being pioneers in discovering missionary principles and action. The foremost American missions leader in the nineteenth century was Rufus Anderson of the American Board of Commissioners for Foreign Missions (Congregationalist). In his book, *Foreign Missions: Their Relations and Claims*, Anderson devotes a chapter to "Principles and Methods of Modern Missions." After summarizing the main features of St. Paul's missionary approach, which Anderson takes to be the model for all subsequent efforts, he calls attention to "a discovery of recent date."[17] This discovery is that an indigenous church must be led by an indigenous pastor. Anderson's insight, which he did not credit to himself alone, became the chief cornerstone for the foundation of indigenous churches wherever missions went. As much as any one thing the emergence of this principle assured the end of Christendom, for it freed the church politically and culturally to find suitable forms in particular contexts.

Anderson's fellow pioneer on the other side of the Atlantic, Henry Venn, shared in the search for principles. In a letter he wrote to Anderson in September 1854, Venn wryly observed "that while the present era is one for the development of Missionary principles in action, it is also one of incompetent theorizing and with a tinge of Missionary romance."[18] Both felt the urgency of

wanted a disciplined believers' church in Asia and Africa while the church at home was inclusive. This was not simply a problem of the double standard. It encouraged the missionary to fall into the trap of being arbiter of right and wrong in ethical matters in a foreign culture, the very thing Venn had cautioned against in his 1868 statement. It reinforced the notion that Christendom was normative for other peoples in other lands. It did not call for historical perspective—the fact that the Western church was itself the product of a long nurturing process—nor sufficient cultural sensitivity.

This tendency was intensified by renewal movements such as Keswick. As a result of the Keswick movement, fresh missionary volunteers began to offer themselves in the late 1800s. One such group joined the Church Missionary Society Niger Mission in 1890. Samuel Ajayi Crowther had led the mission from its founding in 1857. After he was consecrated bishop in 1864 he continued to give oversight to the Niger Mission. Bishop Crowther was a saintly man but less effective as an administrator. When the new missionaries arrived in 1890 he was in his mid-80s and in poor health. What the missionaries found in the Niger church distressed them, and they proceeded to act with dispatch. The result was that Crowther died in disgrace, the Nigerians were summarily displaced from positions of effective leadership, and the missionaries took firm control. Undoubtedly, the aged bishop had not been able to maintain adequate discipline in all his congregations, but what proved so hurtful in the long run was the puritanical zeal with which the young missionaries did their house-cleaning. They alienated and embittered relations with Nigerian minister colleagues for many years thereafter.[22]

The missionary movement during the Great Century was more than a religious movement, though this was its driving force. The missionary pioneered in creating educational, medical, and other social service systems in many countries. The idea of development which came into vogue following World War II had its precedent in missionary practice in the nineteenth century. For example, as a part of the effort to combat the slave trade in Africa, missionaries and their collaborators introduced numerous schemes to provide legitimate economic opportunities which would make the illicit trade in slaves economically unattractive. Their slogan was, "The Bible and the Plow." The goal was to drive out bad trade with the good.

Some missionary leaders concerned themselves with an overall strategy for the development of Africa. Taking their cue from Great Britain's experience in the Industrial Revolution, they gave priority to preparing a middle class which would provide leadership in Africa's own eventual "Industrial Revolution." Such steps had impact far beyond the immediate goals of a mission. In the judgment of Nigerian historian, E. A. Ayandele, "If any individual is to be credited with originating Nigerian nationalism, ideologically, then that individual is unquestionably the Rev. Henry Venn.... Singlehanded and deliberately, he urged Africans to be prepared to assume the leadership of their countries."[23] It was a task to which Venn gave some of his more dedicated and creative energy. The same story can be told through other biographies in other parts of the world.

Each of these innovations contributed to the transformation of Christendom by realigning relationships between church and world and driving Christian leaders back to first principles of Christian discipleship. But this is by no means the whole story. The impulse to maintain and even strengthen Christendom was strong and continued to influence missionary action. The appeal to extend the Christian commonwealth throughout the world by the conquest of "heathen" lands remained strong until well into the twentieth century.

In the popular mind missions in the Great Century sailed under the flag of "Christianity, Commerce, and Civilization." The Three C's did not originate in 1800. Already in the 1600s when Eliot and Mayhew began their missions among the Native Americans of Massachusetts and Martha's Vineyard, mission leaders introduced the notion that in order for a people to be Christianized they first had to be civilized. This involved full induction into the culture of Christendom; and this was prerequisite to being received into the church. In time it was observed that peoples of other cultures were not necessarily eager to shed their culture for a new one. Furthermore, those individuals who submitted to this "conversion" sometimes did so for ulterior motives.

In the nineteenth century voices began to be raised against the original formulation which placed civilization prior. Leaders such as Rufus Anderson and Henry Venn found it necessary from time to time to protest against the old formula. Instead they called for conversion as the priority. In his book, Anderson lamented that modern missions labor under a burden which the early apostles did not face. He took the position that "the higher civilization of the Christian Church" is not what we are to propagate even though that is what many Christians assume.[24] He urged that attention be focused rather on the "simple form of the gospel as a converting agency." But in the end Anderson described the missionary challenge of the day in Christendom terms: "The greater part of the globe, and nearly all the great nations, are open and ready for us; and we are to go for the early and complete conquest of every nation."[25]

Anderson could not rid himself of his ambivalence. He wished to concentrate missionary resources on evangelization, but he acknowledged that other services were required to sustain the growing church. Anderson and Venn took refuge in conversion as the priority. They argued that the individual, once converted, would be motivated to improve culturally, economically, and socially. Venn in particular had growing doubts about the desirability of the Asian or African taking on Western ways, but he continued to believe that the peoples of other lands needed the scientific and economic advantages that Western culture offered. Thus, he did not repudiate the Three C's slogan. He simply emphasized the priority of Christianization.

Venn died in 1873 and Anderson in 1880. However, even before these missionary statesmen passed from the scene the mood in Christendom began changing. The age of the "humanitarians" who felt a responsibility to be guardians of the "weaker" peoples of the world suffered eclipse by 1850, and the winds of the new imperialism began to pick up force. John Robert Seeley, professor of history at Cambridge, was the chosen vessel to give voice to these incipient longings for empire. His book, *The Expansion of England,* published in 1883, offered "a dream of empire without conflict or coercion."[26] Seeley's phrase quickly entered common parlance. Bishop Alfred Barry reflected this heightened sense of identity between national mission and church mission when he entitled his Hulsean Lectures, *The Ecclesiastical Expansion of England in the Growth of the Anglican Communion.*[27]

On the western side of the Atlantic Josiah Strong, secretary of the American Home Missionary Society, published a tract in 1886: *Our Country: Its Possible Future and its Present Crisis.* Strong appealed for the United States, as a part of the Anglo-Saxon world, to take seriously its larger mission. The book proved to be an immediate success. Unfortunately, Strong's liberal and compassionate vision, in the hands of others, soon provided reinforcement for a spirit of manifest destiny which ran counter to Strong's own intention. United States Senator Albert J. Beveridge, in the vanguard of those urging the expansion of the United States into the Caribbean and the Philippines, helped awaken this new quest. "The dominant notes in American history thus far have been self-government and internal improvement," said Beveridge. "The dominant notes in American life henceforth will be not only self-government and internal improvement, but also administration and world improvement.... It is ours to govern in the name of civilized liberty. It is ours to administer order and law in the name of human progress."[28] Within this historical and political context mission leaders did their strategizing.

A. T. Pierson was a leading missions strategist who thought globally. In the January 1889 *Missionary Review of the World,* Pierson challenged the churches to take as their resolution: *The Whole World to Be Evangelized in the Present Generation.*[29] He sketched out a scheme for reaching the one billion non-Christian inhabitants of the world through the thirty million Protestants by the turn of the century.

Robert E. Speer (1867-1947) served nearly fifty years as a missions executive and leading exponent of missions. He ably articulated the Christendom position to his generation. In his book, *Missionary Principles and Practice*, he devotes a chapter on "The Civilizing Influence of Missions." Speer offered a sturdy defense of the investment in missions in terms of their social and political impact. He claimed that "The missionaries are the greatest pioneer agencies opening the world and bringing the knowledge of it to the civilized nations."[30] He pointed to the ways in which missions have aided governments in establishing order and improving the common weal.

In the Duff Lectures for 1910 delivered in Scotland, Speer discussed at length the relationship of politics to missions. He spoke approvingly of the responsibility the powerful nations carry for the weaker ones and described the necessarily close coopera- tion called for between the Western nations and missions. So inti- mate is this relationship that "just as the missionary inevitably has a political message wrapped up in his mission and his Gospel, so the statesman or the merchant has a religious message, which he delivers in spite of himself, for or against Christ and the aim which the missionary serves."[31] Yet he did admit that the image of "mis- sions and governments" remained ambiguous in the eyes of the peoples of other nations. He appealed for more fully Christianized governments to insure they would act in a manner compatible with missionary aims and Christian ideals.

Following the first World War, The Committee on the War and the Religious Outlook prepared a report which was published as *The Missionary Outlook in the Light of the War* (1920). What is striking about the report as a whole is the absence of any serious ethical reflection on the fact of war itself. In his introduction to the report, Robert E. Speer congratulates the missionary movement for the way its goals and ideals were adopted by the United States government "as its moral aims in the conflict."[32] These aims were fivefold: (1) establish permanent peace, (2) safeguard democracy and human freedom, (3) assure the application of the law of righteousness to both nations and individuals, (4) offer service to humanity, (5) and secure a social order based on brotherhood. For Speer this is merely a political statement of the goals of the missionary enterprise. He suggested that missions had "been doing peacefuly, constructively, unselfishly, quietly, for a hundred years the things that, in a great outburst of titanic and necessarily destructive struggle, we tried to do by war."[33] The missionary movement is thus inextricably linked to national purpose.

The report interprets the missionary contribution in terms of its role in creating a new internationalism. Shades of President Woodrow Wilson's hopes for the League of Nations linger in the background. The report asserts, "The missionary has held before the nations—is holding before them today—the ideal of a Christian national life, insisting that it must be built on righteousness and presenting Christianity as the power without which the highest nationhood cannot be realized."[34] A new international order would assure peace and prosperity.

Despite the gathering momentum of nationalist movements in Asia and Africa, beginning in India and Indonesia toward the end of the nineteenth century, the Christendom vision remained a force in missionary thought until after World War II. Walter Marshall Horton wrote, "In an age when world peace, world citizenship, world fellowship, are the goals after which popular imagination reaches out, the only objective big enough to define the comprehensive aims of the Christian world mission is the creation of a world Christian civilization."[35] Horton suggested that the first part of the Great Commission had been fulfilled. The next stage should be devoted to the second half: "teaching them to observe all things." The opportunity before the church now was to offer a religious center around which nations and peoples might unite.

Christendom depended on a close integration of the political, religious, and cultural. The tide of "rising expectations" of the peoples of the non-Western world, especially from the late 1800s onward, was for freedom to restore their *corpus Islamianum* or *corpus Hinduianum* rather than continue under the sway of a hated foreign *corpus Christianum*. Furthermore, the vision of freedom for the individual, learned at the hands of missionary teachers in mission schools or in European universities, was set within a framework of a democratic political system which guaranteed the right of private conscience. The Western colonial powers were increasingly caught in an untenable contradiction. In the end an expansionist Christendom could be maintained only by coercion. Even the peoples of the West had tired of the constraints of the old order; the other peoples of the world were increasingly unwilling to submit to this yoke of bondage.

Indonesia declared its independence from the Netherlands in 1945; Great Britain peacefully—after long opposition to the independence movement—transferred sovereignty to India and Pakistan in 1947. China closed its doors to Christian influence in 1949, decisively rejecting what the missionary had tried to bring. These were harbingers of the continued movement toward political independence of Asia and Africa in the 1950s and 1960s.

Although not recognized as such until recently, the mission-founded churches of Asia and Africa spawned their own independence movement. Religious independency was a complex combination of political, religious, and social drives which issued in the emergence of a new genre of church, combining indigenous elements of ethos, form, and symbol with what had been learned from the Western church. But it was independent of all Western control or support.[36]

That part of the missionary movement most closely identified with the Christendom thrust of the Great Century rapidly lost momentum after 1945 while independent and free church groups surged forward. The latter often seemed to act as if they were still living in the nineteenth century. They treated sociopolitical issues simplistically and interpreted the missionary call as the simple and unambiguous action of saving souls.

The church

In the previous section we have described the Great Century in terms of the dialectic between continuity and discontinuity. The drive to extend Christendom worldwide and maintain Western

hegemony carried the seeds of its own destruction. And the dis-
continuities unleashed their own disintegrating impact. In the
process the church was being freed from the burden of a compromise made one and a half millenia earlier. Indeed it was being
forced to rediscover its true identity. However, this transformation
came at a time when the church as a whole was ill-prepared to
understand it.

The missionary movement in the nineteenth century found
its theological dynamic in soteriology. Ecclesiology played no significant role in the development of mission theology, except for
Tractarian influence in Great Britain. Only in the twentieth
century under the stimulus of missiologists such as Hendrik
Kraemer and theologians such as Karl Barth has the challenge of
reconstructing ecclesiology from the standpoint of the apostolate
begun to be taken seriously.[37] To put the issue too simply, in the
nineteenth century the doctrine of the church functioned primarily in defense of the church as institution. Earlier renewal
movements such as Pietism and the Evangelical Revival had
skirted the issue by concentrating on the salvation of the individual, and this mentality continued to dominate evangelical
thought. Mainstream Protestantism also lacked a dynamic ecclesiology.

The genius of John Wesley's contribution was his intuition
concerning the need of the individual to find a disciplined community as a means of personal nurture, growth, and service. Since
the church-as-institution could not provide this, Wesley
proceeded to organize his converts into cell groups, all the while
protesting his loyalty to the established church. Thus, even
Wesley's insight failed to make an impact on the understanding of
ecclesiology in the eighteenth and nineteenth centuries. The doctrine of the church was not high priority in theological thinking.

The situation was no better in terms of pastoral theology.
One of the outstanding British pastoral figures of the Great
Century was Charles Simeon (1759-1836), for fifty-four years vicar
of Holy Trinity Church, Cambridge. He burned with missionary
passion and played a major role in founding the Church

Missionary Society in 1799. Simeon was more self-conscious about the church than most Evangelicals in his generation. Yet in his voluminous writings the church emerges as little more than a collection of individuals and discipleship is construed as the individual's duties before God without reference to the community. Evangelicals moved even more strongly toward individualism after Simeon's time.[38]

A classic formulation appears in the basis for membership in the Evangelical Alliance adopted at its formation in 1846. Although the Alliance understandably tried to chart a course which avoided conflict with the organized churches, and consequently makes no explicit reference to the church as such, its leaders were equally intent on ensuring doctrinal correctness on the part of its members. The second of the statement's nine points affirms "The right and duty of private judgement in the interpretation of the Holy Scriptures."[39] The thrust of the statement is on the individual.

In his history of the Second Evangelical Awakening in Great Britain in 1859, J. Edwin Orr devotes a chapter of a scant four pages to "Revival Theology."[40] He concludes that the Revival contributed nothing new theologically or doctrinally. It made its impact in the awakening to life of nominal church members and those outside the pale of the church.

This was the theological womb of the modern missionary movement: missionary theory based on soteriology as personal experience. Stephen Neill concluded that "Protestant missionaries have gone out with the earnest desire to win souls for Christ, but with very little idea of what is to happen to the souls when they have been won."[41] As a result, the emphasis in missionary practice fell largely on the ecclesiastical and sociological aspects of the church—its organization, growth toward independence of foreign sponsorship, numerical expansion, affiliations with other church bodies—rather than its ecclesiological dimension.

There is poignancy in a Henry Venn's despair over nominalism in the Church of England and his dread of this watered-down standard spreading to the young churches of Africa and

Asia. Yet he never raised the question of how to develop a church with a functional discipline. At crucial points he continued to look to the state—both at home and abroad—to be disciplinarian.

All of the newly planted churches in non-Western lands had to begin, by definition, as believers' churches. They are the product of primary evangelization whereby men and women have voluntarily declared their allegiance to Jesus Christ and his body. They have existed from the beginning independent of political control. Many of these churches have been able to survive only by continued evangelization. Even after several generations they have retained some of this character. But this is largely the result of circumstances, not conscious design on the part of the parent missions. The possibilities this posed for developing *in loco* an ecclesiology at once biblically and theologically responsive were passed by.

Such a development should have proceeded along two lines: (1) the church local, and (2) the church universal. The church is more than a collection of saved individuals. The body of Christ is a corporate expression of the living Christ. It comes to concretion in particular cultures and among particular peoples. It is a worshiping, serving fellowship which witnesses to the world of God's righteousness now become manifest in its midst. But no local fellowship, no association of churches, no national church is complete in itself. The church universal embraces each local fellowship, bringing it to the completeness of which it is incapable so long as it remains alone. The church universal is both empirical reality and eschatological hope. It ever stands in a tension with the sociopolitical order. One strand of the missionary dynamic is that the body of Christ is not yet complete. Christ as head of the church impels his body to continue working to complete the body. This clearly calls for the witness to be carried to the four corners of the world.

Such an ecclesiology has immediate implications for the church as a disciplined community living under the lordship of Christ, a community of ethical discernment. The church as a missionary community is always aware of its pilgrim character, and its first loyalty is to Christ and his body in both its universal and local manifestation, rather than to the kingdoms of this world. Anything which might compromise its missionary task must be rejected. It witnesses to a kingdom which is of a different order from that of this world.

The Great Century produced a church which rather imperfectly understood its nature, mission, and relationships. That church was a faithful replica of the church in the West. When the challenge of two world wars and numerous lesser ones came in the twentieth century, the church universal had no prophetic word for the world.[42] This is the challenge facing the body of Christ as it enters the twenty-first century: to regain its integrity.

11

The Anabaptist Vision and Our World Mission (I)

Robert L. Ramseyer

A half century of concentrated study of the Anabaptist-Mennonite heritage has left us with a variety of statements defining the essential core of the original Anabaptist vision.

The Anabaptist vision was the vision of people who believed that the Christian is called to be a faithful follower of Jesus Christ; that being a faithful follower means living according to guidelines which have come both from the teachings and example of Jesus himself and from the teachings and examples of those who were active in the church during the apostolic age; that the only reliable source of these guidelines is the Scriptures; and that the Christian life is normally to be lived through participation in a community of similarly committed people who constitute the true church. This is a vision, a goal, and no claim is made that any or all of the Anabaptists were totally faithful to this vision, any more

Robert L. Ramseyer, Elkhart, Indiana, is director of the Mission Training Center and professor of Missions and Anthropology at Associated Mennonite Biblical Seminaries. He served as a missionary to Japan with the Commission on Overseas Mission of the General Conference Mennonite Church, Newton, Kansas, from 1954 to 1972 and 1978 to 1982. This chapter was originally presented to the expanded Mennonite World Conference Presidium in San Juan, Puerto Rico, in July 1975 and was printed in Mission-Focus *in March 1976.*

than the original apostles perfectly embodied in their lives their own understandings of what being faithful to Jesus should mean.

Faithfulness and the first generation[1]

This chapter deals primarily with one essential element in the Anabaptist vision, an element which is often overlooked, perhaps because as a sociological element it appears to be unimportant in what may be thought of as an essentially theological vision. The original Anabaptists were all first-generation people—people who in becoming Anabaptists consciously rejected their backgrounds, including their religious heritage, as being part of the "world." The thesis of this chapter is that this simple sociological fact of coming from a non-Anabaptist background to the Anabaptist faith is an essential part of that faith. This "first generationness" is at the root of the difference between Anabaptists and Mennonites.

When Anabaptists joined the movement, they were conscious of the fact that their new faith had separated them both from their own heritage and from those around them who did not share in that faith. They were new persons, sure of their relationship to God and sure that this new way was God's way. Everything which was not part of this new way was worthless. Thus the Anabaptists were free. When they made decisions, they were unencumbered by practical considerations about what might happen to the heritage, to the church, to church institutions. As persons with no heritage except the New Testament, they needed only to be concerned about the will of God as the new people of God understood it. Such radical faithfulness is never possible for us in later generations regardless of the genuineness or depth of our faith. We recognize a faith and institutional heritage which has been handed down to us as coming from God and worthy of preservation. With this concern for preservation has come also a tendency to minimize separation from others, a tendency to play down the uniqueness of our faith and to demonstrate that we also are good citizens playing a useful role in the world.

When Anabaptists joined the movement, the only things which separated them from outsiders were things related directly to their faith. The Anabaptists were conscious of being a people, the people of God; but the marks of that peoplehood came from their relationship to God. Ethnic lines never corresponded to nor reinforced lines of faith. Because we are not a first-generation people, this has not been possible for us as Mennonites. Many things which have nothing to do with faith set us apart from others.

Because we are not a first-generation people, we have neither the radical separateness of faith on the one hand nor the lack of ethnic separateness on the other hand which nurtured and made possible the Anabaptist vision and movement.

This shift in the basis of our peoplehood, from being the people of God to becoming an ethnic group, this loss of what I have called first-generation radicalness, is true not only of the biological and cultural descendants of those first Anabaptists in Europe. These same attitudes also seem characteristic of many of the Mennonite churches in Asia, Africa, and Latin America. Here too is a concern for preservation. We want to be part of society rather than separate; we feel a need to demonstrate that we are good citizens and that our faith will make a positive contribution to national development; we want to show that our church is a useful institution in society; we strive to prove that we are as authentic in our society as are any of our fellow citizens. Rather than demonstrating a radical difference between the people of God and this world, we try to gloss over it, making that difference as small as possible.

Part of our problem may be a genuine misunderstanding about the role of a follower of Jesus Christ in human society. Part of our problem comes from a concern for the welfare and preservation of the church. No way can we be followers of Jesus Christ, at least as the Anabaptists understood what it means to be a follower, if our primary concern is for the welfare and preservation of any institution. If in the process of decision-making we qualify the radicalness of a step we might take by a concern for the survival of the church, we have left Jesus' way. Jesus' words about seeking to save our life and losing it apply just as much to the church as to the life of the individual disciple.

Recovery of original radicalness

If this shift from Anabaptism to Mennonitism, from radicalness to accommodation to the world, from a concern to follow Christ alone to a concern for the preservation of a church and a heritage, is inevitable after the first generation, where does that leave us?

The thesis of this chapter is that the only way in which we can share in the Anabaptist vision is to share in the experience of first-generation Christians. The only way to be genuine disciples of Jesus Christ is to be part of a group which is sociologically, ideologically, and attitudinally first generation. One might work at this two ways. We could say to our children, "This church is for us. You must go off and do your own thing. Begin your own church as you feel God's Spirit leading you." This would force our children to be first-generation Christians. But this we cannot do because we believe that what we have is vital for all people, including our own children. How could we say to them, "We will accept people from our generation who are out in the world, but we will not accept you, nor will we train you in the faith. You must do this on your own"?

A second possibility is to become so vitally engaged in mission that a large proportion of our group will always in fact be first-generation Christians. It means becoming so open in listening for God to speak to us through our brothers and sisters, regardless of how long they have been committed to following Christ, that our group decision-making will always reflect the consciousness of having moved from the world to the people of God. It requires becoming so vitally and radically committed to Christ in our group life that none of our biological children will want to be part of the group unless they fully share this commitment. Such a group would strive consciously to be so open and fluid, so radically committed to Jesus Christ as we find him in the New Testament, that it would never develop a static institutional heri-

tage which would need to be defended. Without this orientation
the church will inevitably become an end in itself, something to
be preserved rather than a means to the end of being faithful. For
faithfulness includes the mission of bringing others to faithfulness
to Jesus Christ. An effort to preserve always brings accommodation to the world.

Thus the Anabaptist vision, the New Testament vision, can
be recovered only in a group whose conscious orientation is to the
first generation, to those who have made the radical step from the
world to the people of God, to those whose allegiance has shifted
from allegiance to the institutions of human society to faithfulness
to Jesus Christ. Such a group is truly a people, the people of God;
but the only marks of its peoplehood, the only cultural traits
which its members have in common and which distinguish them
from those who are not part of this people, are the marks which
come directly from following Christ.

From this we should see that no Anabaptist vision can exist
apart from mission, apart from sharing this vision with others as
the way of being faithful to Jesus Christ.

Anabaptists in mission

If the Anabaptist vision, a vision which we assume to be the New
Testament vision, can be recovered only in mission, we need to
think yet about what this vision says to the nature of mission.
What differences does the vision bring to mission itself? We are
familiar with the so-called modern missionary movement and the
spread of the Christian church around the world in the nineteenth
and twentieth centuries. We also know of the participation of
Mennonites in this general missionary endeavor; Mennonite
World Conference illustrates graphically the presence of Mennonites around the world.

But we are also painfully aware that neither participation in
mission nor being a newly formed church is guarantee that a New
Testament church, a church of people committed to Jesus Christ,
will result. Mennonite participation in the modern missionary
movement has not been a recovery of the Anabaptist vision. The

churches which have grown out of this missionary activity have in most cases shown as little of that radical commitment to Jesus Christ which we have termed the Anabaptist vision as have the older Mennonite churches of the West.

Part of the problem is that we who have gone out as Western Mennonite missionaries have not really understood what it means to be the people of God, that is, aliens and pilgrims as far as the societies of this world are concerned. When we have been less enlightened, we have identified the Christian faith with the ethnic characteristics of the Mennonite churches from which we have come. We have tried to found churches which were like the churches of Gronau or Lancaster or Saskatoon. And these churches have grown up as little islands separated from the people around them. They have been separated, however, not on the basis of what faithfulness to Jesus Christ demands, but on ethnic characteristics brought from another country.

When we have been more enlightened as missionaries, we have realized the danger of bringing along our own cultural characteristics with the gospel and have tried to help indigenous churches come into being. Unfortunately these churches became truly indigenous, at home in their world, not seeing that faithfulness to Jesus Christ demands a critical look at their world and their cultural traditions, not seeing that loyalty to him inevitably cuts across loyalty to one's nation and one's people, no matter what that nation and people are. We fell into the trap of seeing the church as somehow serving as a replacement for previous religious institutions so that without realizing it the Christian faith came to be interpreted as a new and superior civil religion.

The Anabaptist vision says that to be a Christian one can have only one Lord, Jesus Christ, and that being a Christian means being his disciple. The Anabaptists understood that being a disciple meant being called out of the world, whatever that world was—North American, Latin American, African, European, or Asian. Whether it is an Eastern or a Western world makes no difference. Christian disciples live in a state of constant alienation from the natural human societies in which they find themselves.

One of the practical consequences of this understanding of discipleship for Christian mission is that the Anabaptist takes seriously Jesus' talk about the narrow gate and the real difficulty of passing through it. The Anabaptist would have no part in trying to broaden that gate so that people could pass through it in greater numbers more easily. But at the same time the Anabaptist will try to be sure that the gate really is Christ's gate and that it is not narrowed because of other things which have nothing to do with loyalty to Jesus Christ. Thus Anabaptist missionaries will try to make clear from the beginning that the message includes a call to loyalty to Jesus Christ and to him alone. They will try to spell out as clearly as possible what this may mean. This model comes from Jesus himself who called people to him and promised rest and release, but who also told them sharply and in some detail of the conflict and persecution which would come if they followed him. Anabaptist missioners can never say, "These people are too new to be faced with this all at once. Let us simply present the promises of Jesus and bring them into the church. After they are in, we can gradually talk about commitment and loyalty to Jesus Christ and what these will mean in daily life." Rather, Anabaptist missioners emphasize the sharpness, the radicalnes of the step from the natural society in which people live into the people of God.

To the Anabaptist the call of Jesus Christ is a call to radical, fully committed discipleship from the very beginning. Obviously, only gradually and throughout our lives do we understand the implications of what this commitment means for the way in which we live. However the commitment itself is never gradual; it is sharp, radical, complete from the beginning. The sharpness of this commitment stands out most clearly when the company of disciples is full of those who have made this decision consciously as they moved from the world to discipleship in the people of God.

Since Anabaptists do not separate faith from life and doctrine from ethics, commitment and discipleship will make a difference in the concrete ways in which they live day by day. Their commitment will be something which people can see. Anabaptists have no possibility of being either secret Christians or an invisible church.

One of the most apparent distinctives of a church with the Anabaptist vision will be the quality of fellowship and mutual concern which it displays. Within the fellowship will be nothing of the distinctions between groups which may be found in the natural society from which its members have come. Within the Christian fellowship, class, caste, clan, nation, and family distinctions have no relevance. The church will be the one fellowship in which people can come together without reference to the society in which they were born. Here social boundaries have no meaning.

This quality of fellowship has special relevance to the condition in which most human beings find themselves today. On the one hand our world is divided among social groups which demand contradicting loyalties and set people against each other in a multiplicity of settings. People are more open than ever to the reconciling force which can be released within a group where all members share a common commitment to Jesus Christ.

On the other hand our world is also experiencing the rapid breakdown of what for many people have been their traditional primary reference groups. Rapid social change in the face of urbanization and industrialization has left many people feeling isolated in a confusing mass of humanity. They are isolated individuals with no one to turn to for help and counsel, no one to care whether they live or die. Here the Anabaptist fellowship with its care and concern for individual people, a fellowship in which people are committed to each other because of their common commitment to Jesus Christ, comes as the answer to an urgent need. The church becomes the new family for its members, the family of God. As Jesus said, "Here are my mother and my brothers."

Coming from this background, Anabaptist disciples are also uniquely equipped to speak to the work of reconciliation in the larger human society. Disciples are peacemakers who work at the reconciliation of human groups through the abolition of social injustices which bring conflict between persons or between groups because of their own firm rooting in the Anabaptist fellowship.

Closely related to this is the Anabaptist emphasis on love and nonresistance in all relationships. Obviously this goes far beyond the refusal of Christians to take part in their country's military activities, although it will certainly include such a refusal. Because Anabaptists are clear in their giving of primary loyalty to Jesus Christ, they will be able to resist all efforts of their states to make them take sides for their nation against the peoples of other nations. They will see clearly that loyalty to a government which would make them regard people of another nation as less worthy of concrete acts of love than the people of their own nation is in direct conflict with their loyalty to Jesus Christ.

Obviously, in many situations this will cause Anabaptists to be regarded as enemies of the people, as traitors to their class or to their nation, as disreputable members of their society. But Anabaptists know that just as God's love is not limited by any human boundaries, love which springs from commitment to Jesus Christ also cannot be limited by the boundaries which human beings may choose to erect. Priorities are clear: I am first of all a disciple of Jesus Christ and only secondarily an American or Zairian or Japanese or Canadian or Brazilian or German. I know that in every case will come conflict between what my commitment to Christ requires and what my natural human groupings demand of me. I can never satisfy both.

Finally, the church with the Anabaptist vision is distinguished by the active and full-time participation of all of its members. The Anabaptist fellowship does not leave mission to experts. All members are fully and actively engaged in its mission.

This is the role of the Anabaptist vision in our world mission as I understand it. In its very essence it is irresponsible and unrealistic by the standards of any natural human society. It maintains that as disciples of Jesus Christ, as the people of God, we are in our first loyalty members of a different society which has its own standards of evaluation.

This is only a vision; it is not a program. The challenge which comes to us is to keep this vision clearly before us as we make program decisions, to make all of our decisions in mission in the clear light of this vision.

12

The Anabaptist Vision and Our World Mission (II)

Takashi Yamada

In trying to understand the Anabaptist movement and vision, we cannot ignore already existing definitions and concepts. These are important and helpful. Yet to develop our mission thought on that basis may limit our ideas to a certain fixed framework and mold our thought by what already exists.

On the other hand, any approach or system of thought can grasp only a part of the whole. So whenever we try to approach any living reality, we inevitably grasp it in some distorted ways. Even so, our sincere efforts to seek for the reality or the truth can deepen and enlarge our thoughts further. Repeating this patiently, we may come closer to the truth.

Another thing we need to consider as we approach the subject of world mission is that we nonethnic Mennonites should not accept without question what our Western brethren have

Takashi Yamada, Kobayashi, Japan, has been a pastor since 1956. He has also served as chairman of the Kyushu Mennonite Christian Church Conference, Japan Mennonite Fellowship, member of Asian Mennonite Conference Executive Committee and Mennonite World Conference Presidium. In addition to various articles, he was coauthor of Experiments in Church Growth *(Japan Church Growth Research Association, 1968). This chapter was originally presented to the expanded Mennonite World Conference Presidium in San Juan, Puerto Rico, July 1975, and was printed in* Mission-Focus, March 1976.

inherited and developed in the course of their history. I feel keenly that we need to create our own unique visions in the particular cultural backgrounds of our own lands and nations, uniquely inspired by the original experiences of the early Anabaptists. This is true in many other fields of study and discussion, and especially so when we deal with the Anabaptist vision, which challenges us to make voluntary and responsible choices and commitments before God based on the strength of our own identities in Christ.

The Anabaptist Vision

When I read H. S. Bender's well-known definition of the Anabaptist vision for the first time many years ago, it inspired me. I understood it as a beautiful doctrinal expression of our Mennonite position. I wanted to know what it really meant in the context of my own life and ministry. I struggled with it for years after that as I continued to minister to a local congregation, trying to find our Mennonite identity.

One problem I had with definitions such as Bender's was that I often felt as if I had been trying to find my loved one through a frosted glass. Bender's sword just didn't clash with mine. Something kept me from perceiving it in a real way. The problem may have been in finding in present reality what was described historically.

Then several years ago, I thought of trying to grasp the Anabaptist vision from two angles: through living relationships of creative tension within the fellowship of disciples of Christ and an outer confronting tension between the fellowship and the outside world.

An intense attitude of confrontation

I understand that the Anabaptist vision is neither something which can be grasped as a package of doctrines, nor a spiritual heritage wrapped up with some specific abstract or worn-out theological terms that can be superficially transmitted to people in later ages. It may be understood as a certain striking force that captures and drives some people and directs them into a unique and creative way of living.

If we dare to try to describe it, it is an attitude of dynamic living. Ordinary people of the world may regard it as a peculiar way of living. It is a particular attitude which comes out of a certain religious conviction. Finally, we can say that it is an attitude of confrontation. It is a confrontation with demonic power which tries to control and oppress people and distort and destroy their society.

Essentially, this attitude may be created within and among us when we are confronted with Jesus, his life, and his attitude of living in a unique and dynamic way. Once I read that Mennonite men used to grow beards to show that they were different from others, that their way of living was different from that of ordinary people of the world. The attitude of confrontation is seen in this kind of radicalness.

The sixteenth-century Anabaptists confronted the Reformers and their churches, which promoted their reformation work by compromising with the secular political powers. It was a confrontation with the European tradition of *corpus christianum*, which by then had lasted for more than a thousand years.

When we think about political powers we tend to distinguish between evil ones and good ones. It may not always be wrong to do this, but at least we need to recognize that any political power or human government basically has power to control people for its own purposes. It is important to distinguish the radicalism of mainstream Anabaptists from that of those who resorted to violence.

The structure of the attitude of confrontation

To view the Anabaptist vision as a confronting attitude is not sufficient. We need to look into its inner structure and see how it functions. The attitude has its inner structure of living integrity in Christ. It means that we see the attitude being taken in a field of certain personal relationships in dynamic spiritual tension. There is a creative tension between Christ and those who are following after him, and among the followers themselves, as well as a confronting tension between the world and the fellowship of Christ's followers.

As fish can live only in water, this confronting attitude may exist only in a certain field of spiritual tensions caused by the living Christ. When this attitude is taken, we find some specific expressions of spiritual tension in the actual historical setting. If we try to systematize and formulate them into some traditional doctrinal terms, they may be defined best as discipleship, believers' church, and an ethic of love and nonresistance.

From an ideological point of view, we may describe this inner dynamic structure as follows:

1. Deepening individual self-finding and establishing one's self-identity in Christ (discipleship).
2. Extension of the liberated life—forming a voluntary fellowship of believers (believers' church).
3. Maturity of the liberated life—developing the solidarity and the integrity of the people's society in Christ (love and nonresistance).

These aspects are vitally and inseparably related to and overlap with each other. They coexist, forming the attitude of confrontation. This is the dynamic of the Anabaptist vision. If the spiritual tension loosens, the whole attitude gets out of shape. If either one of those aspects of the inner structure becomes weak or disappears, the attitude becomes weak and collapses.

The confronting attitude as antithesis to reality of fallen people and society

The Anabaptist vision, grasped in the way described above, encourages us to see that the vision was something possible, and it is still possible even today. I was struck by the forceful witness of the Anabaptist vision when I began to understand it in this way.

We see this confronting attitude and the structure of its inner dynamic exemplified and working in a perfect way in the life of Jesus. We also see the same thing happening in the life of the group of early disciples, in spite of their human weaknesses and failures. It was actually the work of the living Christ in them.

Jesus stood on the side of the common people of his day, especially those who were considered to be religiously and socially alienated and unqualified to belong to the Jewish society. They were suffering severely under the double oppression and exploitation of both the Roman government and the Jewish religio-political power structures of the day. Standing on the side of these people, Jesus proclaimed the coming of the kingdom of God and its blessing being extended even to these people.

By doing that, Jesus assumed an intense attitude of confrontation with the existing power structures. He lived the life of genuine love and nonresistance and finally ended up in the suffering death on the cross, being punished as a political criminal by the Roman government. It was the most powerful confrontation that has ever appeared in human history. It gave a fatal blow to the demonic powers of the world.

Through the coming of the Spirit of Jesus Christ, the fellowship of those who were willing to follow Jesus' steps was formed. They took the same confronting attitude with the world powers and at the same time expanded their fellowship, witnessing God's mighty saving power to the people outside of the church.

In the sixteenth-century Anabaptist movements, we see the inevitable confrontation between *corpus christianum* and *corpus Christi*. The intention of the Anabaptists to form *corpus Christi* as well as their lives of love and nonresistance instead of domination by force and violence over their neighbors declares this confrontation.

Most of the Reformers of those days seemed to have run away into the realms of the concept and theory of their reformation. They tried to build up their religion and churches on those concepts and theologies. They started with a certain confronting attitude, but later they compromised and shook hands with the existing worldly powers, endorsing the use of force to suppress the movements of Anabaptists and the common people. They lost their balance in keeping up a confronting attitude. The Anabaptists went right on with their confronting attitude. In this way they became an antithesis to the Reformers.

Some negative aspects of the Anabaptist vision

As sixteenth-century Anabaptists lived in the actual context of history, they and their movements were of course limited and influenced by their environments and conditions as well as their weaknesses. To be an antithesis to the fallen reality of the world is significant. But the antithesis itself has some weaknesses as antithesis.

While the Anabaptists relativized the authority of the religious and political power structures, their nonconformity with the world seemed often to have given up the possibilities and persistent efforts to bring changes in the existing social systems. Later Mennonites came to have a sort of "pure church" idea and became closed religious groups isolated from the world. It is right to say that the "church is not of the world," but that does not mean that we can disregard the fact that the church is in the world. If the antithesis comes out of its context and begins to walk by itself, it becomes a fixed tradition such as that which later Mennonites tried hard to preserve for themselves.

Progessive succession of the vision

The Anabapist vision should be recovered and reinterpreted as its living context continues to change. The Anabaptist vision cannot be simply defined as one of the reformation movements or the movement of restitution to the primitive church. We are not to go back to the past. We need to catch the vision anew constantly in our given situations. The Anabaptist vision makes us open to our future.

Often our confronting attitude seems to come to a deadlock and experiences many failures because of its own nature as a confrontation. The vision may go on fulfilling something even if we suffer setbacks and defeats. It is not something we can discuss on the level of success or nonsuccess, victory or defeat.

Our world mission

The following are some of my basic ideas as to our world mission today.

Antithesis to our own reality

If we want to recover the Anabaptist vision, we must know, first of all, that the vision is an antithesis to our own reality. Here we need to be very specific, dealing with each actual situation and reality in Asia, Africa, and other parts of the world.

Total involvement in our total life

The Anabaptist vision challenges us to follow Christ, not only in the realms of personal life and the life of a religious group, but also in the midst of today's social, economic, and political situations of the secular world. The fact that the Anabaptists rejected infant baptism and boldly took radical action by performing adult baptism by themselves was taken up by the establishment as a serious issue directly related to the politics of those days. Consciously and inevitably they challenged the political realm, motivated by their genuine and thoroughgoing obedience to Jesus.

Anti-Western thought as characteristic of Anabaptism

Anabaptism, which was born in a certain period of Western history, is an antithesis to the stream of thought and history of the medieval and modern West. If the Anabaptist movement was a confrontation with traditional Western Christianity and Constantinianism, it must be an antithesis and a judgment on modern Western Christian society which, as a whole, has not been able to overcome essentially that Constantinianism. (The Christian West, however, has broken down, and passed into the post-Christian era, as modern secularization has progressed rapidly.)

Anabaptism is a judgment on scientific rationalism. Western scientific rationalism depends greatly upon scientific technology developed from human knowledge and power. It is devoted to the promotion of efficiency-centered ideas and practices, placing a lopsided value on development and progress. It tends to disregard the importance of the nonrational and that which cannot be quantified.

Western civilization in due course has found its outlets to the East and other parts of the world. It has made a great impact upon the peoples in those parts of the world. Against this historical background of the expansion of Western civilization into other parts of the world, the worldwide extension of Western Christianity through the modern missionary movements occurred.

This movement should be highly regarded, but also rightly evaluated. We should not overlook the fact that sometimes it has resulted in westernization or Western Christianization of the people in the non-Western world. Here the critical function of the Anabaptist vision comes in. The Anabaptist vision encourages and inspires world mission in its true sense, but it also discourages and denies modern Constantinianism on a worldwide scale, or worldwide Christianization as something like "Coca-Colization."

Creativity of the Anabaptist vision

The Anabaptist vision functions not only as an antithesis but also as a dynamic creative power to bring the individual and society into true integrity in Christ. Sixteenth-century Anabaptists unconsciously played a role which gave rise within Western culture to modern civil freedom.

Unfortunately the Anabapists themselves could hardly develop this aspect of their vision because of the severe persecution and unpeaceful situations in which they were placed. Among the later Mennonites we see much energy and many efforts being spent in preserving their tradition within ethnic communities. (We can be appreciative and grateful, however, for their sincere efforts to preserve the Anabaptist vision. Without it, we would likely not be discussing the Anabaptist vision and our world mission today.)

Some practical concerns in our world mission
Reexamination of the old philosophy of mission

When we look at the situation of the Third World after World War II, we note the sweeping waves of the rise of nationalism among those who had suffered under the old Western colonialism.

In spite of the fact that many of those nations in the Third

World have achieved their independence, they are still suffering greatly from various leftover phenomena of the old colonialism. They are struggling with diverse and difficult domestic problems such as their economic difficulty caused by mono-culturization and deformed economic conditions, as well as other social problems. They have also faced critical international problems since their independence.

The remaining influences of the old colonialism are not easily overcome, even by political independence and changes brought about in political and social systems. These nations need to make tremendous self-improvement efforts for many years to come. Even here in the very process of this self-improvement and development, the overwhelming power of the advanced nations constantly intervenes in their strenuous effort of building up their own nations. Here I am not only referring to the neocolonialism of the West but also the recent economic invasions by Japan.

We have to consider seriously the weight of this historical background when we look at overseas missions. Foreign missions in the Western Christian churches have not always played their part as antitheses to the colonialism of their own countries. Overseas mission work has not always been carried out through vicarious suffering of missionaries on behalf of their own nations' domination of the peoples in the mission fields. We scarcely notice a strong sense of grief and the spirit of redeeming the past wrongs of colonialism on the side of the sending churches. Sometimes overseas mission is carried out with a feeling of the rich giving to the poor. (I personally dislike saying this, for I know so many excellent and faithful missionairies who are devoting their lives for the sake of other people.)

With regard to Mennonite overseas missions in the past years, we "younger" Mennonites must express our deep appreciation and praise God for many blessings he has given to the work. Yet Mennonite overseas missions, as far as I know, have not always been done with a thorough understanding and expression of the Anabaptist vision on the side of the older churches. It is not appropriate, therefore, for Western Mennonites to grieve over the products of such mission work, the younger churches, lacking in Anabaptist vision and its practices.

The Anabaptist vision must not simply and naively be tied up with our world mission in a short-circuit way. Those who say that world mission should be carried out in order to recover our Anabaptist vision are wrong. This is the reverse of the direction we ought to move.

Toward finding a new philosophy of our world mission

As the Swiss Brethren once transcended the nationalism of Zwingli, both the Western Mennonites and the Third World Mennonites today have to overcome their racial and nationalistic egos as well as their group egos so that they may establish their own Mennonite identity. Then they may build up worldwide solidarity from which real concern for world mission may come naturally. This has rich implications and applications on the practical level.

Our world mission as nonresistant Mennonites

We have already seen that the Anabaptists' nonresistant position was vitally related to their attitude of confrontation. The confronting attitude expresses itself paradoxically in the ethics of love and nonresistance as it seeks to build up true solidarity among people in Christ. The autonomous self who is liberated in Christ is at the same time the one who appreciates and enjoys peace and tries to produce peace. The Anabaptist vision conflicts with a world mission without pacifism.

In the stream of modern Western history since the Middle Ages, Western religion, thought, and culture have produced or taken an active part in the rise of capitalism and modern scientific technology. These things have encouraged Western nations to attempt to conquer nature and dominate the world by power. This domination by power has finally led to the production of nuclear weapons and all kinds of pollution. (Japan has adopted Western technology and taken part in the attempt to dominate Asia by power.)

Ever since Western civilization with its tremendous economic and military power encountered Oriental civilization, colonialistic domination and tragic distortion of people and Eastern societies has been occurring. Now modern Western civilization itself has come to a deadlock and is facing serious crisis today. Sixteenth-century Anabaptist vision has stood as an antithesis in the stream of the history of domination by power. It may have more possibilities to contribute to the modern world than it had in the sixteenth-century world.

Our world has been changing rapidly. We know that since 1965, or even before, the Catholic Church has proclaimed the end of the "Constantinian period." In Asia just some thirty years ago most of the nations were under colonial or semicolonial domination of the West and Japan. Since then various religions have played their roles in bringing modernization to Asia. In Vietnam the amazing energy of the Vietnamese Buddhists has led and supported the people to stand up and fight against the colonial domination by France, Japan, and then America. Recently in South Korea Christians, both Catholic and Protestant, have been bold enough to stand up against the government which is threatening the freedom of the people. In the large area of Southwest Asia, Islamic religion has been the spiritual ground of many nations who have suffered from Western domination, although in Indonesia the situation seems to have been different from those of other countries.

In the midst of these situations in the East, what unique roles will our Anabaptist vision play? And how?

Finding the Anabaptist vision anew in the
midst of modernization today
The coming of modernization into the Third World is an irresistible tide. In many Asian and African countries modernization is being strongly promoted and progressing rapidly. As it comes, it changes the whole picture of people's society.

Modernization can be characterized by secularization and urbanization. In "advanced" countries, the so-called information society and mobi-centric society have appeared. Such ideas as post-industrial society or even post-civilized society have become popular among some people. At the same time several phenomena of the computerized society have begun to appear. The possibility of unifying and controlling people and their society by huge computerized systems is becoming greater.

Here again we need to pay attention to the twofold unique functions of the Anabaptist vision: the secularizing function to relativize human-made systems and the creative function to reconcile people and build up new societies. The mobility of the early Anabaptists and their single lifestyle may have something to say to people in urbanized modern society.

Our world mission in evangelism

I take up evangelism at the end of this chapter not because I regard it as less important, but I do this in order that we may take up this important task in its right context, maintaining the proper balance in the whole of our world mission.

If we grasp the Anabaptist vision as an attitude of confrontation and try to understand its inner structure in the way described before, evangelism covers every aspect of the confronting attitude, and it is also comprehended in each aspect of the inner structure of the attitude.

Here the dichotomy of evangelism and social action—quantitative growth and qualitative growth—is transcended by taking up evangelism and church planting on a deeper level. Such a dichotomy may have arisen as the church became fixed and institutionalized and as the work of the church became divided and program centered. In the early Anabaptist movement we do not find such a dichotomy.

Let me state briefly the three basic keys to Mennonite evangelism and church planting:

1. Establish Mennonite identity.
2. Encourage as much participation of church members as possible.
3. Permeate deeper into the world and enlarge contacts with people of the world.

Voluntary participation of Third World Mennonites in the world mission should be encouraged. The fixed traditional idea that overseas mission is the work of the Western churches needs to be corrected. The present one-way direction of mission work—from older churches in the West to the "mission field" in the Third World—must be changed. Joint mission attempts are to be expected in many parts of the world in coming years.

Present patterns and structures of churches, conferences, and overseas missions administration, as well as the larger Mennonite fellowships, should be more flexible and ready to be reshaped as we are stimulated and inspired by catching the Anabaptist vision on the grassroots level.

This may take a long time and undergo some painful surgical operations. The relation between life and its outward forms or patterns must be carefully studied and considered. More "adhocratic" systems of administration need to be developed instead of bureaucratic ones in order to cope with the rapid changes and diverse needs of world situations.

The invention of nuclear weapons and pollution of the natural environment as well as many aspects of human life and the possibility of worldwide food shortage have caused people to face a serious world crisis today. Indeed, people in the world are now in the same boat, sharing a common fate. The attitude of confrontation in its eschatological tension urges us to have a sympathetic view of the world so that we may actively participate in God's mission in the modern world today.

Living the Anabaptist vision

How do we actually renew and refresh our Anabaptist vision and make it live today? It will depend much on our encountering Jesus in striking ways in our lives in this modern age. We must face the words of Jesus from an entirely unique and dynamic point of view in their actual historical contexts and see him living and moving with his confronting attitude toward humanity's fallen reality.

However, I feel that the order of this question and answer

should be reversed. We can say that if we encounter Jesus in striking ways today, we may forget about our Anabaptist vision. We will then find ourselves being in reality the Anabaptist vision.

13

Anabaptists and Mission

David A. Shank

This chapter grows out of my missionary commitment and ministry in Belgium from 1950 to 1973 in what has been called a post-Christian culture; significantly, Anabaptists had been particularly active in that area four hundred years earlier. A post-Christian culture contrasts sharply with pre-Christian areas of missionary endeavor, as it does also with a so-called Christian culture in which the Anabaptists flourished, or with a similar phenomenon in North America in the middle of this century. My own reflection on this subject is done from within a religious tradition which has emerged from the Anabaptist breakthrough of the sixteenth century. Further, I recognize the influence that Anabaptist studies have had upon my own thinking; yet I am not an Anabaptist scholar, and must necessarily do much of my reflection with the aid of secondary sources.

David A. Shank has served African independent churches in Ivory Coast and surrounding countries since 1976 under assignment with Mennonite Board of Missions. He previously served with MBM in Belgium from 1950 to 1973. He has written Who Will Answer? *(Herald Press, 1969),* His Spirit First *(Herald Press, 1972), an unpublished thesis on West African Prophet William Wadé Harris (1980), and articles for* Mission Focus, Journal of Religion in Africa, *and* Perspectives Missionnaires. *This chapter was presented in résumé form at an Anabaptist Seminar at Goshen College, Goshen, Indiana, on January 28, 1975, on the occasion of the 450th anniversary of the beginning of Zürich Anabaptism.*

At the outset, I must readily admit the importance for me of hearing Franklin Littell's chapter on the missionary motif within Anabaptism, when he presented it to Mennonite Central Committee staff and workers in the spring of 1946,[1] six years prior to its publication in what was later to become the classic, *The Origins of Sectarian Protestantism*.[2] At that particular moment in my personal pilgrimage, a clear statement of the missionary roots of my tradition (with which I was not then certain that I could identify) indeed helped me to make the decision to remain with the Mennonite Church.

My use of the word Anabaptist in this chapter is not limited to what have sometimes been called the evangelical Anabaptists. Instead, I tend to include the whole gamut of pluralism within the early movement of the radical left wing of the sixteenth-century Reformation and observe it evolving toward a consensus into evangelical Anabaptism around 1550. The great diversity in the earlier years is significant, as George Williams[3] and J. M. Stayer[4] have indicated. But even Littell's presentation, particularly concerning mission, appears also to take that much broader and diverse expression of Anabaptism as the source of his study.

My use of Anabaptism here refers to an evolving Christian movement of spiritual breakthrough; it will be seen first as a historical phenomenon, second as a typical stance within Christian history and ecclesiology, and finally as a source for defining the contemporary task in the last quarter century of the twentieth century. But before looking at those three relationships of Anabaptism to mission, we must first provide an understanding of the latter.

How shall we understand mission?
Historical approaches

In English-speaking Christian circles, the word mission usually refers to the organized, institutionalized sending out of spiritually and professionally qualified workers. These workers go from a Christian church, community, and people to a non-Christian religious context such as Buddhism, Hinduism, Shintoism,

Confucianism, Islam, or the so-called animism of primal societies. On the European continent in Christian circles, mission most often denotes much more the idea of the essential task of a person or group, or church. These differences in usage have sometimes resulted in a lack of clear communication.

R. Pierce Beaver, the dean of American missiologists, sees mission as an apostolate beyond the congregation and home locality, involving commissioning and sending representatives to witness on behalf of the sending church and its disciples.[5] This he contrasts to the local apostolate of the church which is called evangelism. Mennonite theologian John H. Yoder has indicated that when stripped to its root, mission does refer to someone being sent from a geographical or cultural home with a mandate to testify in some other home.[6] Ray Gingerich, an interpreter of Anabaptist missionary understandings, suggests that mission must extend beyond the etymological meaning to include the witness of the church outside its social perimeters, and to include the forming of new communities.[7]

These are all helpful guides to understanding mission, yet none of these definitions picks up the full implication of what might also be called mission consciousness or the sense of mission. This was particularly evident among Anabaptists of the sixteenth century; the historian C. J. Dyck has described their particular pattern of zeal growing out of a sense of "sent-ness" as *Sendungsbewusstsein*.[8] This was clearly distinct from the simple witness of piety and life.

In a different direction, mission as an obedient fulfillment of Christ's Great Commission has been a major missionary dynamic for the past two centuries, at least since the time of William Carey. This was also, according to Littell, a major part of the Anabaptist thrust of the sixteenth century; it was indeed my own understanding of mission in 1946 as crystallized by Littell's presentation.

In another direction, the Roman Catholicism of pre-Vatican II times understood mission as planting the (Roman) Church in every region where it was not fully established.[9] But the post-

Vatican II stance sees mission rather as the "duty to spread the faith and the saving work of Christ *in virtue of the express command* [of Christ] ... and in virtue of that life which flows from Christ into his members.... The mission of the Church is therefore fulfilled by that activity which makes her fully present to all men and nations" as compared to missions which "is the term usually given to those particular understandings by which heralds of the gospel are sent out by the church and go forth into the whole world to carry out the task of preaching the gospel and planting the church among peoples or groups who do not believe in Christ."[10] The importance of the mandate of Christ can clearly be perceived in both mission and missions as understood by present-day Roman Catholicism.

Lesslie Newbigin concluded more simply that mission is the crossing of a frontier of strangeness between faith in Christ as Lord and unbelief in order "to make Christ known and obeyed as Lord among those who do not know and obey him."[11] Here the crossing of the frontier is accentuated and not Christ's mandate nor the missioner's obedience to it; the resulting church-as-community is implicit only in the expression, "obeyed as Lord."

Mission of the Church: The Great Commission

This diversity of understanding of mission calls for clarification. I will use the word mission in the sense of fulfilling the Great Commission of Christ (in Matthew 28 and Mark 16). This understanding of mission gives the other definitions and understandings their proper perspective. But in so doing, I have personally come full circle in my own thinking. My own decision and commitment included a clear sense of obedient response to Christ's Commission. I had a clear awareness that this obedience was not an option but was, on the contrary, central to an understanding of the gospel, and indeed was central to my own tradition's roots in its earliest and most dynamic years. Over the years, however, the use of the expression, "obedience to the Great Commission," seemed to me to evoke and conjure up a wooden literalism on the one hand, and an unbiblical romanticism on the other hand. The

Great Commission seemed to deal more with mission activity—mission boards, fund-raising, going abroad, foreign fields—than with the real mission to which the Great Commission calls. William R. Hogg has pointed out how this happened within Protestant missions in general.[12] Since the Bible was seen as the Word of God, and the Scripture text said "Go!" missionary obedience meant going. So people went to be obedient, and missionary activism has often been the result.

Much of the literalistic obedience, the superficial activism, and unwise enthusiasm of the past two centuries merited the critique of Harry Boer, who has written that the Great Commissions's "meaning for and place in the life of the missionary community must . . . be differently construed than is customarily done [since it] derives its meaning and power wholly and exclusively from the Pentecost event."[13] I too have experienced and insisted upon the importance of the Holy Spirit in the fulfillment of Christ's mission and thus for the whole missionary enterprise.[14] Yet the work of the Holy Spirit in suspending obedience to the letter, superficialism, and the carnality of missionary activism does not remove the fact that that Commission is fundamental and central for the existence of the church. In reality, as one reads the account of Luke, it becomes apparent that the command and the promise of the Great Commission came fully alive when the Holy Spirit was received by the Jerusalem community. It is so reported by Peter in his much-later meeting with Cornelius: "He commanded us to preach unto the people, and to testify that it is he which was ordained of God to be the Judge of quick and dead" (Acts 10:42). Christ's prior command gave clear structure and order to the experienced power of the Holy Spirit.

The significance of this prior order of Christ has been effectively pointed out in an exegesis of Matthew 28:16-20 by Karl Barth:

> The Kingly ministry of the Messiah is here entrusted to the first disciples constituting the king's troops. . . . As recapitulation and anticipation revealing the hidden reality of the eschatological community, the Great Commission is truly the most genuine utterance

of Jesus.... The command to baptize is ... the transferral of the messianic power of Jesus the priest of all men ... [and] as baptism constitutes the existence and nature of all discipleship, teaching constitutes the ways and works of the disciples.... They are to live within the earthly confines of the Kingdom of God and to submit to the order of life established there.... All baptized become *eo ipso* subservient to this order of service, the foundation of the Christian community [which] exists only where the things commanded by Jesus are "observed".... Because of Jesus' presence the Great Commission of the risen Lord to baptize and evangelize is valid throughout the days of this "last age."[15]

The importance of the Great Commission is also indicated by *Lumen Gentium,* Vatican II's Dogmatic Constitution on the Church, which begins by citing Mark 16:15: "Go ye into all the world and preach the Gospel to every creature." This recent Roman Catholic declaration reaffirms that the Great Commission is central to the definition and existence of the church.

The personal and corporate experience of the power of the Holy Spirit must mark the ongoing life and history of the church; such will intensify the social and communal character of the church, making its presence an effective witness to God's purposes. However, both the Spirit and the community can tend— for a moment—to eclipse the Great Commission. But such an eclipse does not remove the all-encompassing mandate-with-promise of the resurrected Lord of heaven and earth; it is indeed operative until the "close of the age." The mission of the church is not only defined and created by that Commission, but response to it must be a major criterion of the church's fidelity. The effectiveness of the church in giving continuity to the carrying out of that mandate—itself an essential part of "all I have commanded you"—becomes a major determinant of the future of the church. The present study of Anabaptists and mission is done with that understanding of mission.

Anabaptism and mission as a historical phenomenon
As a movement evolving from 1520 to the middle of the century, Anabaptism had its genesis in a context of rapid cultural, social,

and political change. The "return to the Scriptures" which had begun before the turn of the century meant that new spiritual and ethical understandings were being fed into that rapidly changing human scene. The development of those understandings was taking place in a situation where the authority of Scripture was set alongside other authorities, both ecclesiastical and political. Differing patterns of reformation developed in Germany, Switzerland, and France; yet out of a great diversity of experiences, affirmations, hesitancies, and oscillations a Protestant consensus emerged. Lutherans and Zwinglians never came to complete unity. Later developments in England and Scotland underscore the pluralism within that growing consensus. But this diversity within Protestantism makes the diversity within Anabaptism all the more understandable. Stayer's[16] examination of the early diverse positions on the use of the sword among Anabaptists justifies his rejection of the facile categorizing by the first generation of American Mennonite historians of Anabaptism.

Indeed, early Anabaptism included the revolutionary and the moderate, the chiliast and the ethicist, the charismatic and the weird, libertinism and legalism. Such divergences within the movement did lead to mutual non-recognition and mutual rejection even among adherents who were then closer to each other than they were to the Protestant consensus or the Magisterial Reformation. The major difference between the latter and the Anabaptist movement is to be seen in the relationship of each to the society at large. Where the Protestant Reformers consciously and intentionally assumed responsibility for the mainstream of society, the Anabaptists were clearly a marginal movement. This distinction between mainstream and marginal soon became the difference between legality and illegality. At the same time, the marginal and illegal character of the movement must not give the impression that the *impact* of the movement was unimportant; on the contrary, that impact was felt by the whole society.

In that period of rapid change, all of society was caught up in an eschatological excitement. When Michelangelo's *Last Judgement* was unveiled in the Sistine Chapel on October 13, 1541, all

Rome is said to have flocked to "gape at the spectacle ... the most urgent in advertising the perpetual imminence of the Last Day. The city shuddered in awe and stupefied admiration."[17] Martin Luther's own expectation of the imminent return of Jesus Christ was such that from today's perspective he would appear to be like the *Schwärmer*, a term which he reserved for those he judged to be irresponsible enthusiasts. Against that backdrop, the intense eschatological expectation which lay behind the Anabaptists' sense of mission is not surprising. But it was not the eschatological intensity which marginalized them; it was rather the ethical, social, and political content of their hope which created their marginality and their impact on society.

Thomas Müntzer's social radicalism, related also to his belief that God's kingdom was coming soon, directly influenced Anabaptism, and particularly through one of its greatest evangelists, Hans Hut. The impact of the chiliast Melchior Hofmann on the pre-Mennist covenanters in the Netherlands, and the outbreak of the Münsterite kingdom in Westphalia have left a permanent mark on the Anabaptist stream, even when—following Menno Simons—it was in reaction. The later Hutterian eschatology and the sense of mission it engendered is also a part of a greater stream. None of these tendencies began a new movement of eschatological anticipation; they responded *differently* to the eschatological urgency characteristic of their times.

Obedience to the command of Christ

Here we must note that one of the major differences between Anabaptists and the Magisterial Reformers was the centrality of the Great Commission. This was true of all of the tendencies.

> No texts appear more frequently [than Matthew 28, Mark 16, Psalm 24] in the confessions of faith and court testimonies of the Anabaptists and none show more clearly the degree to which Anabaptism was different in conviction and type from the intact and stable ways of Magisterial Protestantism.... No words of the Master were given more serious attention by his Anabaptist

> followers than the Great Commission.... The form of the Com-
> mission seemed to sum up His whole teaching in a glorious
> program comprehending the whole world.... It was fundamental
> to individual witness and to the ordered community of believers as
> well.... [It was] not only obeyed most seriously, but it was given
> sweeping application. It applied to all Christians at all times....
> The Anabaptists were among the first to make the Commission
> binding upon all members.[18]

These words from Littell are confirmed by the research of
Schäufele, with the exception that baptism was carried out only
by "Anabaptist office-bearers" since "apart from the very beginning of the movement, no ordinary member was authorized to
baptize."[19] "The missionary activity of the ordinary members of
the brotherhood was limited to oral proclamation of the
Anabaptist message of repentance and salvation which they
themselves had accepted, and to which they conformed their own
lives."[20]

This was true not only for the working man who testified to
his fellow-laborers, according to Schäufele, but was true also for a
remarkable number of women. "The woman in Anabaptism
emerges as a fully emancipated person in religious matters, and as
the independent bearer of Christian convictions. The gospel was
carried aggressively and emphatically into everyday life. The
'sacred area inside the church buildings' disappeared as the only
place where salvation is mediated."[21]

Karl Barth has written in his exegetical study of Matthew 28:
"The existence of the new community consists not only in the
apostles' preaching of the Gospel and of their fellow men's listening. It is constantly renewed as the listeners themselves become
'apostolic' and as new disciples begin to proclaim the good
news."[22] There is no doubt about this being the exegesis of the
Anabaptists; this was indeed the dynamic which was produced
among them in a time of opposition and persecution.

The content of discipleship—"observe all things that I have
commanded you"—that was to grow out of obedience to the
Great Commission was observable within a month after a community formed in Zollikon near Zürich. In his February 18, 1525,

letter to the Zürich Council, Felix Manz wrote with clear reference to Matthew 28:

> [God] has sent his Son with all power in heaven and on earth so that whoever calls upon him and trusts him would have eternal life. In like manner, Christ sent His disciples commanding them that they should go to all peoples to teach, giving them such power from God His Father and through his death, so that all who would call upon His name might have forgiveness of sins and to baptize with the outer sign. So as he was teaching in this way, certain came to him with tears asking that he baptize them—and he didn't refuse them, but *first taught them love, and unity, and communion of all things, as the apostles also in Acts 2*, and to think on the death of Christ and not to forget his shed blood, finally the meaning of the breaking of the bread, and the drinking of the wine, *how we are all saved by one body and all washed with one blood and are become a union the ones of the others*, brothers and sisters in Christ our Lord[23] (my emphasis).

A month earlier, Manz had written his Protestation to the Zürich Council; on two occasions before the Council he clearly stated the centrality of the Great Commission in the preaching, baptizing, and teaching ministries. In the first week after the Zollikon congregation was formed, George Blaurock went into the parish church there and asked the priest what he was planning to do. "Preach God's Word," was the answer. But Blaurock spoke out: "Not you, but *I am sent* to preach"[24] (my emphasis). Here is indeed the *Sendungbewusstsein* which Dyck has underscored. This same Blaurock, along with Stumpf, "pressed Zwingli most consistently to gather a purified 'community of all things as also the apostles [had it] in Acts 2.' "[25] The community intention of both Manz and Blaurock was an expression of more than "simply Christian charity."[26] Indeed the appeal to Acts 2 is found over and over again.

The other elements of the "all things" which Christ commanded, as reported by Manz, were love and unity. These had been carefully defined by the Zürich brethren in the months that preceded the January 21, 1525, founding of the congregation. An intense study of the Scriptures was the basis for those understandings. The faith commitment which those understandings had engendered involved a stance like "sheep in the midst of wolves" where violent coercion in matters of faith was excluded. War and violence as method and stance in the word were also excluded on the basis of the lamb of God himself and his overcoming strategy. Grebel's letters to Müntzer in the fall of 1524 and to Andreas Castleberger in May 1525 are good expositions of that understanding.

Finally, Blanke's *Brüder in Christo*[27] describes the way in which baptism gave coherence to a revival in Zollikon; conviction of sin, repentance, and faith were all elements which took on congregational shape through baptismal commitments. It was on the day following the founding of the congregation in Zürich; the pattern was the same.

All of the elements of the Great Commission were clearly present in those early days: an awareness of being sent; preaching the gospel; faith, repentance, forgiveness of sins; baptizing into the body; teaching what Christ commanded—love, unity, community, and the Great Commission itself. The final command of Christ became the ordinance of life; it offered a mandate and an explicit strategy which became the center and organizing principle of a whole movement.

Emerging mission strategy

A large gathering—later called the Martyrs' Synod—was held in August 1527 at Augsburg to work out a clear missionary strategy. One of the major missioners at this synod was Hans Hut, who had been responsible for baptizing hundreds of Anabaptists. We learn again something of how Anabaptists saw mission work from what he taught those whom he sent out. One of them, a Georg Nespitzer from Passau, described the baptismal covenant thus: "to abstain from sins and where one sees his brother sin, shall he punish him; also where there is need, to help so far as body and life reaches; but whosoever wishes not to do this, he should abstain from baptism and zealously stick to that decision."[28]

Another of Hut's converts, Leonard Schiemer—a former Franciscan friar—was sent to Bavaria, Salzburg, and the Tyrol.

He described the "Fellowship of the Saints" in his own articles of faith, where he used the term from the Apostles' Creed. Citing Acts 2, 4, and 5, he wrote that the baptized "must keep love and fellowship with the congregation." This was further defined as "holding with his congregation all the gifts received from God, whether teaching, skill, goods, money, or other.... [These] he must invest in the congregation's needs."[29]

According to Christian Hege and H. S. Bender, more than sixty leaders and representatives from South Germany, Switzerland, and Austria were present at this important Missionary Synod. Hans Hut's presence in this assembly was crucial, since as the leading evangelist he had won and baptized more people in the previous two years than all the other leaders had done together. But his chiliasm with its clear prediction of events prior to the return of Christ—expected in 1528—did not have the approval of everyone present. In fact, his views apparently were at the center of the discussions in council, along with the issues of the use of violence and the community of goods.

All the questions were resolved even if in ways unacceptable to Hubmaier in later discussions. An apparent consensus was obtained, for "in spite of the cruel persecution, no Anabaptist took recourse to violent resistance nor was there evidence of a planned attack against the government in all the cross-examinations even on the rack."[30] There were indeed variations on the theme of the use of violence: Hubmaier accepted the notion of a regenerate magistracy; Hut felt that violence should be put aside *until* the return of Christ; Müntzerite ideas were revived in Esslingen yet in 1527; and in the North, the Münster debacle was still to come.

But these can be seen as variant fringes of a central thrust that put an accent on a community of brotherhood, peace, and unity in discipleship. This inner consensus was to be spelled out again at Schlatten in 1527, in what is known as the Schleitheim Confession; the need for the definition was again the existence of the fringe tendencies. The central thrust has always had to struggle with a pull in the direction of a spiritualism on the one hand and the magisterial tendencies toward theocracy on the other hand. Each has had its own forms of deviation from what was perceived by many to be the consensus. For that, the major pull appears to be the coming kingdom of Christ and its manifestation in the life of Jesus.

Thus in a climate of strong eschatological hope, Anabaptist end-time obedience to the Great Commission carried a universality which became particular as baptism created local communities of committed disciples. The forms of economic sharing differed, but the exigency was there; the same was true for the rejection of coercion in faith and social relationships. These dimensions seemed to be essential to the gospel that was preached, to the teaching of what Christ commanded, to the covenant of baptism. The communities developed a three-pronged protest: ecclesiastical, social and economic, and political.[31] The amazing thing is not that fringe deviations were present, but that the central thrust remained functional in spite of the strong pulls.

One major deviation can be linked to Melchior Hofmann with his distorted dualism, deformed Christology, and his belief that he was the promised Elijah preparing the final advent of Jesus. He apparently built on earlier sacramentarian influences in the Netherlands and stimulated the movement which at one pole ended in the Münsterite theocracy with its tragic end.[32] But his ministry also provided the groundwork for an emerging consensus in the North as it was later formulated by Menno Simons and Dirk Philips, both in constant dialogue with deviant fringes.

With Hofmann, it is important to understand the place of the Great Commission in his thought. In his *Ordonnantie* of 1530 he makes it clear that the Great Commission is the ordinance of the Lord which orders all else. This thrust deeply influenced Menno Simons, whose use of the Great Commission often appears to be a simple defense of the practice of "faith first, baptism second." But a closer reading of Menno's writings makes it clear that it is Christ the King who has given his great command, order, or ordinance which now orders life in new spiritual, social, and political relationships. That his understanding was strongly flavored by what C. J. Dyck[33] calls a flesh-spirit ontological dualism justifies to some extent E. Bloch's[34] critique of Menno as favoring social and political withdrawal, when compared to the earlier thrust of Thomas Müntzer. But this spiritualist revolutionary, if indeed pulled by an eschatological hope, was not structured by the Great Commission; baptism, construed to be inner, was in the spirit, and spiritual leading superseded the written Word. This constituted a major pull away from the central Anabaptist core; the real question is not how Menno compares with Müntzer—the Marxist philosopher's hero—but whether there is another norm for both: the fulfillment of the mission made explicit by the Great Commission of Christ.

The specific Hutterite community model was another derivative of the basic pattern of a missionary community of mutual and total commitment to the leader Christ, carrying out his Great Commission in a confrontation with a *getäufte Heidentum.*

The "Christ as leader" motif appears to be a major one among the Anabaptists; it needs much more careful study than it has yet received. Erasmus' *Enchiridion* had set a model for the Christian as the "knight under orders" which could understandably lead to relativizing all earthly authorities. For example, nine days after the Zürich baptismal fellowship of January 21, 1525, which Williams calls the birthday of Anabaptism, twenty-five members of the Zollikon congregation—including Manz and Blaurock—were arrested; one of their number declared that he "had enrolled under the *Dux* Jesus Christ and would go with Him to death."[35] The image of the knight in service to his lord was used later by Menno Simons as well. A reading of Anabaptist texts, with that relationship in mind, can give the impression that the use of the pair, "disciple-Lord"—or the milder "disciple-Master"—to describe the Anabaptist understanding is probably a weak expression of the sixteenth-century ethos in which Christ was seen to be the new Lord and King in contrast to the contemporary dukes, lords, and kings. The Anabaptists saw themselves much more as subjects of Christ than as disciples. As Christ's subjects they obeyed the first ordinance—the Great Commission—of the ruler of the realm.

The existence of a mobile community of commitment subject to a universally commanding Lord of the realm created a
whole new sociopolitical configuration. It was not, indeed,
dissimilar to A. D. Nock's description of the primitive Christian
church: "a holistic reality—a new life in a new people."[36] Indeed
the binding character of the Great Commission for all members
meant a new exploitation of all of the gifts within the community
for the sake of the gospel. Early in the movement, in what would
today be called charismatic outbursts, the formerly nonvocal and
passively receptive people, both men and women, became a
responding and responsible people of God. J. Lawrence
Burkholder has gone so far as to suggest that the outstanding fea-
ture of their discipleship was their obedient response to the Great
Commission.[37]

The manner in which that new sociopolitical reality related
to the states and magistracies has only been suggested in passing.
Stayer has indicated several tendencies, and even an overlapping
of tendencies in adaptation to varying circumstances. My suggestion is that these divergent emerging patterns may be more
clearly seen and understood in the light of a model of a typical
messianic movement. The phenomenon of messianism and its dynamics can be effectively employed for perhaps a better understanding of the movement than heretofore.

Anabaptism, as a type: Messianic resurgence

Three types of mission understandings in the sixteenth century
can be observed. The first is that expressed by the Roman
Catholic and Magisterial Protestant dictum of *cuius regio eius religio.* In Protestant countries everyone was Protestant, and in
Catholic countries everyone was to be Catholic; the population
was Christianized, people believed the gospel, and mission was
fulfilled. Particularly among the Protestant Reformers, the Great
Commission was regarded as binding only for the early apostles;
the apostles had fulfilled the mandate, and the contemporary
Protestant state was the beneficiary.

Within Catholicism, this type carried on mission by colonial expansion; the *corpus christianum* extended itself by annexing foreign territories and claiming them for the church as well as the monarch. Christopher Columbus saw himself as explorer and missionary, and his royal backers shared his perception. Here the Great Commission was binding, but understood as involving the exportation of a total religious, social, cultural, and political complex. It was a new sacral reality imposed on the inhabitants of territories which were to be incorporated.

A second type was that illustrated by the Jesuit order in the 1540s; it is the foreign missionary sent by the missionary order into lands which—if they were not politically annexed through colonial ties—were, nevertheless, often under the impact of, for example, Portuguese commerce. Francis Xavier, active in the Far East, typified the approach which often involved hasty instruction followed by baptism of the masses. A large population was integrated into the church via baptism rather than through strict political expropriation. The missionary specialist was sent by a specialized order to gather in the masses. In Latin America— Mexico and Peru—a missionary in 1536 estimated the baptized at between four and nine million; in reality the missionary was often in the forefront of later political annexation. But the work of a Matteo Ricci in China at the end of the sixteenth century indicates how attempts were made to introduce Christianity within a cultural pattern and a sociopolitical structure without annexation. It was a work accomplished by remarkable experts sent by a highly expert missionary order.

The third type, as we have seen, was that which made the Great Commission binding on all church members; the mission was to those who were of the Christian religion by simple acculturation within a so-called Christian civilization. There, as we have seen, it was a call to become freely subject to the Lord Christ within a disciplined congregation practicing brotherhood and peace, and whose essential nature was to be "for the world."[38] It was a rejection of the ecclesiasticism which blessed the existing political, social, economic, and cultural patterns. It called for a congregation of those voluntarily responding to Christ's call, and who then confronted the violence, the greed, and domination of that society; the congregation was created by a free response of obedience to Christ.

Free-church tradition

The implications of this type for missionary history are significant for the period starting in the eighteenth century and going well into the nineteenth century, the period Latourette called "the age of the most extensive geographic spread of Christianity." A majority of the missionaries spreading the gospel in other lands in this period were influenced by this free-church type. Because of that influence, parallels between sixteenth-century Anabaptism and nineteenth-century missions are noticeable. Quite often a critique of the colonial regimes was inherent in the missionary presence; active assistance by governments in the nineteenth century was minimal; the missionary movement was a people's movement; women played an important part in this century of expansion. Missionaries set high standards for admission into the congregations which constituted the newly forming "younger church."

According to Latourette,[39] in the thousand years prior to this period, mission work involved group movements and mass baptisms. In nineteenth-century missionary practice, entrance into the church came by individual decision rather than by collective movement. The result: At the end of the century in the areas of missionary effort, Christians were a small disciplined minority with an extraordinary effect upon the non-Christian populations.

However, important differences exist between the free-church type of mission in the nineteenth century and the earlier phenomenon of Anabaptism in the sixteenth century. In the latter case, the missioners were full participants in the history and culture of the people whom they addressed; in the nineteenth century, the missioners were foreigners working in new languages in exotic cultures among peoples whose history was unknown. Missionaries went from a literate, so-called industrial society to preindustrial societies conditioned often by orality. The sixteenth-century Anabaptist mission was within a common religious heritage and tradition; the nineteenth-century missionary went from one religious tradition—Christianity—to another, and serious confrontation with a new religious system and tradition took place for the first time. In the sixteenth century, generally the underprivileged people protested in faith against the ecclesiastical and sociopolitical domination to which they were submitted.[40]

The nineteenth-century missionary impact was parallel with colonial developments, and the missionaries were identified with those developments even if they in fact were in opposition to certain colonial policies. In the sixteenth century, leadership appeared to emerge spontaneously and charismatically with the development of the movement; this pattern indeed served as a critique of the established church leadership patterns which were not geared to the Great Commission but to established parishes. In contrast to the free-church type of leadership, the nineteenth-century missionary carefully supervised newly planted churches, and leadership models were provided according to established Western patterns. These differences are important.

What can we say about these various types in our contemporary missionary context? First of all, the free-church type has now become the majority position of contemporary Western Christianity. Littell has pointed out how, within the American understanding of separation between political and religious covenants, all American churches have become the first modern manifestations of so-called "younger churches," religious communities gathered out of a context of unfaith.[41] From this perspective, most modern Western missions have, for all practical purposes, planted "free churches." Even the Roman Church, since Vatican II, declares itself to be a free church in this sense; in a striking manner, *Dignitatis Humanae* early refers to the carrying out of the Great Commission as the way to establish religious liberty. *Ad Gentes* begins with the Isaiah messianic text about the "light to the nations" and then immediately quotes the Markan Great Commission. Further, in *Lumen Gentium* the dominating notion of "people of God" (as compared with "body of Christ") situates the church in a stance not at all unlike the Anabaptists' missionary stance in the sixteenth century.

Much of the sixteenth-century uniqueness of the free-church type has now been dissipated with the breakup of Constantinian patterns. We can rejoice indeed that the old state-church patterns have broken up; but the increasing universality of free-church patterns is not as such a subject for rejoicing when we discover free churches, both in the West and in what were formerly seen as mission fields, functioning in unconscious or voluntary liaisons with governments, in societies and cultures, as uncritical supporters of socioeconomic and political patterns. This is not the same phenomenon as the oppressive state church of the Constantinian synthesis; but the fact that it is freely accepted dare not hide the fact that it is also a far cry from the Anabaptist fulfillment of mission. A modern free church is not necessarily a continuity of the Anabaptist vision.

Believers' church tradition

The language of "free church" to describe the Anabaptist-type mission and church has thus shifted in recent years to that of "believers' church." A conscious effort to develop the concept of a believers' church as a church type, perhaps best illustrated by the sixteenth-century Anabaptists, was made in 1967 at the Conference on the Concept of the Believers' Church (Louisville, Kentucky).[42] Since then, the typology has become better known through Donald F. Durnbaugh's history which appeared the following year.[43] The conference of 1967 recognized both the limitations of the free-church type and the fact that believers' church as type "has not been commonly used in the expanding ecclesiological vocabulary of twentieth-century Christians."[44] Nevertheless, since that time, the use of the typology has become (at least in Mennonite circles) commonplace. It is an attempt to accentuate, even in a free democratic society, the difference between a mass church—a culture religion, a popular church of popular religious acculturation—and the congregations of committed believers.

Within the conference itself, the new language—not yet thoroughly defined—was not always helpful to all participants. Dr. Duncan suggested that people from believers' church traditions should function more ecumenically "if for no other reason than to discover whether there is any longer any distinction between believers' churches and others."[45] Yet in the same conference, after process, such distinctions were clearly affirmed. Reflecting the Anabaptist experience, the believers' church type was thus defined in relation to mission: "The congregation is called out of the wider society for a communal existence within and for, yet distinct from, the structures and values of the rest of the world. This distinctness from the world is the presupposition of a missionary and servant ministry to the world. At times it demands costly opposition to the world."[46]

Elsewhere, as a part of that definition, the missionary stance is perceived as working out "the church's being as a covenant community in the midst of the world."[47] Indeed, the Anabaptists did this latter in fulfillment of the Great Commission; we have seen how the economic, social, and political protest was indeed an inherent consequence of the obedience to the "all things" of the effective sovereign over the community: the Christ. One senses that in the shift from history to type, it is possible that the centrality of the Great Commission of the Sovereign may subtly be shifted introvertly to the self-realization of the community. Part of the shift is due to the nature of the typology itself: As with the free-church type, it is comparing types of ecclesiastical communities, and—by definition—in Western experience it is in contrast to the fallen church, the state-church, the official-national church, or the acculturated church. It is a type still based on the Troeltschian church/sect distinction of Constantinian times.

The fact that the believers' church type is, as such, a Western type, growing out of Western developments, could indeed alert us to the problems of its potential irrelevance to the context of world mission, where many situations are clearly similar to pre-Constantinian times in the West. At the same time, in its attempt to recover a pre-Constantinian Christian community, Anabaptism

as perceived in the believers' church type cannot be wholly irrelevant, even in pre-Constantinian situations. Yet, I have heard
Mennonite missionaries speak of the irrelevance of the Anabaptist
vision to their particular missionary assignments. That vision, the
church/sect typology, the free church, and the believers' church
are all models which help an American church to understand itself
and to refocus its calling in the midst of freedoms and pressures
peculiar to its life. The implications of those typologies, however,
extend much beyond a denomination or even Western Christianity, even if the typologies often do not apply universally.

At the same time, sociologist of religion A. W. Eister has indicated how the Troeltschian model was "valid for the setting of
cuius regio eius religio" but that there was no valid reason for
"transporting it across the Atlantic."[48] Thus Eister finds it not always helpful in understanding the dynamics of numerous
American sects, which have developed in a context of separation
of church and state. But he even finds it less helpful for understanding the millenarian, messianic, and nativistic movements of
the Third World, with its cargo cults and separatist churches.
Indeed some of these movements may be seen developing in
contexts where the free-church type of Western Christianity was
involved in missionary endeavor.

Messianic community

For those who believe that the Anabaptist historical
manifestation was indeed one which has Spirit-given lessons for
the whole church of Christ—"all that in every place call upon the
name of Jesus Christ our Lord, both theirs and ours" (1 Cor.
1:2)—I should like to suggest that there is indeed in it a
manifestation of another type, more universal and more in line
with the missionary mandate. It is the *messianic community*
type.

The French sociologist of religion, Henri Desroche, in a
lengthy introduction to his dictionary of messianisms gives a helpful and suggestive typology which he calls the messianic cycle.
This typology has grown out of his study with a team of collabora-

tors from several continents; it covers the manifestations of messianism within the Christian era.[49] According to Desroche, following the impact of a messiah upon a socially, politically, economically, and religiously oppressive human context, a three-directional explosive movement tends to appear as followers believe and follow in the promise of a new holistic humanity, or a new kingdom. The first direction points to that promised coming reality and works already at its creation. But from that direction two major deviations generally appear, resulting from a loss of faith in the coming kingdom, due to its nonappearance.

Both directions tend to justify the previous movement, but in different ways. One deviation emphasizes the religious aspect of the message, and of the kingdom which has not appeared; it then reinterprets the messiah in religious terms, forgetting the social, economic, and political dimensions of the hope that person had created. On the other hand, a second deviation emphasizes the sociopolitical aspects of the message, and reinterprets the messiah in political terms. This deviation minimizes the whole dimension of inner life and faith and authenticity which appears to be religious and alien to structural aspects of society which make social and economic changes possible.

Significantly, Desroche points out how from the perspective of the deviations, a messianic resurgence becomes possible as the over-religious again reorients to the holistic messianic community of the original vision. Similarly the resurgence can come from the political deviation as it again reorients to a holistic religio-socio-politico-economic intention, reflecting the messianic promise.

For Desroche, this is a pattern of hundreds of messianic movements, each with its own variation of the typology which he develops in detail. In this sense, he is not describing Christianity as such, but a universal phenomenon which recurs when conditions in a society appear to engender a messiah. I would differ from Desroche in my use of his typology in affirming, on other grounds, the universal and crucial character of the messianic movement which has grown out of the impact of Jesus of Nazareth whom we confess as *the* Messiah, and whose birth, life,

224 Anabaptism and Mission

death, resurrection, and *parousia* constitute a context of history within which other movements occur, whether in relation to him or whether in apparent indifference to him and his impact.

But within this typology, Anabaptism itself is seen as a messianic resurgence, a part of a greater resurgence created by the rediscovery of the Word of Scripture in a context of rapid change. That resurgence deviated in the revolutionary spiritualism of a Müntzer as well as in the Magisterial Protestantism of Luther and Calvin, all of which were seen as a revolt against the sacral *corpus christianum*, so far afield from the obvious commands and intent of Jesus of Nazareth. The spiritualizing of Schwenckfeld and the theocracy of Münster are further deviations from the central consensus of the Anabaptists, apparently shared by both Luther and Zwingli, before their "realism" led them to deviate from the community of faith, love, unity, brotherhood, and peace which the coming kingdom of Christ announced.

In this typology, the sacral oppressive society of Judaism under Rome is simply replaced by the sacral oppressive society of Constantinianism. This latter has been effectively described by Leonard Verduin,[50] who points out the parallels between the Donatists of the time of Augustine and the Anabaptists of the sixteenth century. Both, indeed, were forms of messianic resurgence from out of that sacralism.

John H. Yoder, in his paper at the 1967 Believers' Church Conference, gave a description much fuller than the Troeltsch polarization, in delineating—following a suggestion from the latter—four specific ecclesiological and religious models at the time of the breakup of the Constantinian sacral reality in the sixteenth century.[51] These four models were those of the *corpus christianum,* the *theocratic* type, the *spiritualist* type, and the *believers' church* type. Although important, in my judgment, the model did not receive the merited attention in the conference because it was presented the last day. However, Yoder, in his description of what he calls the classical options seen in the sixteenth-century reformation, writes: "The same demonstration could be derived elsewhere as well; it seems that the same possibilities spring forth in every age."[52] Indeed, following the Desroche typology, within Christianity they spring forth from within a context of the universal messianism fulfilled in Jesus Christ and the kingdom of God. The messianic typology situates the believers' church in an eschatological tension and indicates how it can move away from its intended vision, how indeed resurgences can spring forth in every time. Elsewhere Yoder has written effectively of a *messianic* ethic, and a *messianic* community.[53] They are much better perceived in the typology of a messianic cycle, their inherent context.

From the perspective of our concern here, as illustrated by the Anabaptists, the Great Commission appears as the vanguard thrust of a universal messianic movement. To understand the history of Christianity as a messianic movement places ecclesiastical realities in much better perspective. But it also suggests a canonical direction for the critique of movements, and not simply four ecclesiastical options, equally valid in its inner consistency; indeed it illustrates the New Testament language of apostasy. Most of all it best illustrates the world kingdom opposition inherent in the biblical data and which is said by Littell to be a basic element in the concept of the belivers' church,[54] as illustrated by Anabaptism. Further, the messianic model helps to understand better and interpret the challenge presented by non-Christian messianic movements in the world today, themselves a critique of established Christianity.[55]

Anabaptism and missions today

We have already observed how the Anabaptist missionary thrust within sixteenth-century Christendom differed from the free-church-inspired missionary thrust of the nineteenth century in a non-European context. We may appropriately ask what that historical movement can contribute to our modern understanding of the missionary task, even though the context in the last two decades of the twentieth century is again different from both of those periods. The idea of the irrelevance of the Anabaptists' experience for today is based on the assumption that theirs was a response to an unfaithful church in sixteenth-century Europe which in no way parallels the task of missions in a context where the church has emerged from a non-Christian past. This is, of course, true. But once one has understood the dynamics of Christian messianism and its expression in Anabaptism, one can find important parallels and analogies for today's missionary task.

The way in which the life of the community was ordered by the worldwide missionary task in obedience to the coming Messiah is exemplary. Since the Lord is bringing in his kingdom, it is incumbent upon his disciples already to prepare others for the unity, love, brotherhood, peace, and justice of that kingdom in a community of faith where those fruits of his presence are operative in the power of the Spirit of the Lord.

The sacralism out of which such a breakthrough occurs may no longer be the *corpus christianum;* it may rather be that of some primal society, or of a techtronic society of the West. In many places of the Third World, one may in fact find layers of each of these superimposed. In each context, in any case, an essential part of the missionary task is to discern those oppressive, destructive, life-denying human patterns which religion tends to sacralize and which the Spirit of Christ denounces as in the biblical world of 1 John 2. This reminds us that the contexts of mission differ greatly even if the messianic thrust remains the same. It also means that the spin-offs of a messianic thrust may not always be identical in different contexts, but that they are recognizable; they should be recognized for what they are—deviations—and not just as pluralism in missionary expression.

The fact that Anabaptism emerged as a messianic resurgence reminds us of the latent possibilities within non-messianic and establishment forms of Christian religiosity. These indeed are within the historical context of the Christian messianic cycle which contains its own potential, given the right conditions, for a resurgence oriented by the coming kingdom of Christ.

The Anabaptists with their simple grasp of the universal nature and call of the Great Commission never allowed that to hinder them from local, specific commitments as expressions of their obedience (which others often interpreted as legalism). The hesitancy due to sophisticated knowledge of "inevitable sect cycles" must not interfere with the freedom which sees messianic resurgency as God's own strategy for giving continuity to his purposes in the world. The "weight of sin that so easily besets us" must not receive the bias of favor; that rather must go to the newly created cells of enthusiastic obedience to the sovereign Lord of the coming kingdom.

The Anabaptist identification with the human suffering of Christ, the rejection of the then-current triumphalism of Christendom, and the awareness that espousal of violence was a refusal of Christ all point to the specific messianism oriented by the suffering servant of Isaiah 53 as fulfilled in Jesus' life. This model of discernment in answering "Who is the Lord?" remains absolutely urgent in our time. M. M. Thomas has written:

> The call to . : . threefold liberation leading to freedom as mastery over nature, as search for identity and justice in society, and as openness to the future, clearly has arisen within the cultural and spiritual climate created by what has been called "messianic religions" with their historical consciousness, though it has risen in protest against them; and this messianism has been maintained even in the secular ideologies of the modern period. In fact, with the forces of modernity making inroads into all cultures and societies, they are all absorbing the messianic consciousness.... Therefore the spiritual question modernity poses for mankind is the discerning of the character of the messiah and the messianic community and the nature of the hope of eschatological unity which will make freedom a promise of mature humanity to men and women universally, and that of distinguishing them from messianisms which betray that promise and dehumanize men and women.[56]

Finally, the eschatological kingdom orientation of the Anabaptists remains the essential mainspring of mission—of Christian messianism. Neither sixteenth-century deviations nor twentieth-century spiritualisms, Mormon nor Moonie, dare function to reduce the driving hope that the history of all nations shall be fulfilled in a "new heaven and a new earth" when "every knee shall bow and confess that Jesus the Messiah is Lord."

Until that time the classic Anabaptist consensus remains perhaps the most important missionary mentor that God has given the church of Christ, except for their servant Lord and the first church that grew out of the obedience of those whom he sent, when he said, "All power is given me in heaven and on earth. Go, therefore, and make disciples of all nations, baptizing them . . . teaching them to observe all that I have commanded you; and lo, I am with you always, to the close of the age."

Notes

Chapter 1

1. Robert Friedmann, "Conception of the Anabaptists," *Church History* IX (1940), pp. 341-65, 362. "Anabaptist" was a name given by their enemies, to make them liable to the old Roman death penalty for re-baptizers. "They repudiated the name, insisting that infant baptism did not constitute true baptism and that they were not in reality re-baptizers. Their argument was of no avail. The name was so conveniently elastic that it came to be applied to all those who stood out against authoritative state religion." Austin Patterson Evans, *An Episode in the Struggle for Religious Freedom: The Sectaries of Nuremberg, 1524-1528* (Columbia University Press, N.Y., 1924), pp. 14-15. Roland H. Bainton has introduced a terminology which efficiently groups the Anabaptists and other radical dissenters from dominant Protestantism, and indicates the heterogeneous character of their protest; "The Left Wing of the Reformation," *The Journal of Religion* XXI (1941), pp. 124-34. For precision, it is better to refer to different groupings: Swiss/South German, Hutterite, Dutch.

2. Kenneth Scott Latourette, "A Historian Looks Ahead; The Future of Christianity in the Light of its Past," *Church History* XV (1946), pp. 3-16, 12, 14.

3. Kenneth Scott Latourette, "New Perspectives in Church History," *The Journal of Religion* XXI (1941), pp. 432-43, 438.

4. Joseph I. Parker (ed.), *An Interpretative Statistical Survey of the World Mission of the Christian Church* (International Missionary Council, N.Y., 1938), pp. 83-159.

5. In John Baillie's rethinking of the concept of the church implied by the idea of a Christian civilization, he abandons the older, coercive pattern. John Baillie, *What Is Christian Civilization?* (Charles Scribner's Sons, N.Y, 1945). "Such a recovered civilization would clearly be of the open type which alone I am prepared to defend, and in it the older conscriptive idea of the church's authority would have completely given place to the idea of religious freedom ..." (p. 41). Significant to our present study is Dr. Baillie's word on infant baptism: "The question ultimately turns on the measure in which we believe the Church to have been justified in the principles governing its admission to baptism in the various periods.... It has long seemed to me that the element of truth to which too little weight is given by the protesting movements is that contained in the Christian doctrine and practice of the baptism of families.... The insight enshrined in this doctrine and practice is that the most likely way to bring men to an individual decision for Christ is to nurture them within a Christian community. This community is in the first place the family, and hence the controversy has always revolved around the baptism of infants born to Christian parents. But it is necessary that something of the same principle should be extended also to ... larger social units.... I believe it wrong to hold as of no account the Christianity which pervades the life of a community before it is confirmed in the personal decision of every individual citizen" (pp. 34-35).

6. A renowned authority on the Reformation has concluded that the present religious problem in Germany may be due in part to the fact that sectarian Protestantism, which flowered in England and America, was there early destroyed. Roland H. Bainton, loc. cit., p. 134. It is interesting to note that some contemporary leaders are raising again the old issue of the immobility of the state church. Pastor Martin Niemöller was reported to the effect that he "was raised a Lutheran and did not realize that the traditional Lutheran theology regarding the state was wrong. He now believes that the Church must exercise stronger influence on political life, as in England and America, where the church 'acts as the conscience of the state,' " reported in *The Lutheran* XXVIII (September 26, 1945), 52:4.

7. The conflict over the parish system is excellently discussed in Karl Ecke, *Schwenckefeld, Luther und der Gedanke einer apostolischen Reformation* (Berlin, 1911), pp. 70ff.

8. M. Searle Bates, *Religious Liberty: An Inquiry* (N.Y., 1945), p. 151. On the Reformation era, see pp. 148ff. See also Roland H. Bainton, "The Struggle for Religious Liberty," *Church History* X (1941), pp. 95-124.

9. Hugh Vernon White, *A Theology for Christian Missions* (Chicago, 1937), p. 4.

10. In such works as E. Belfort Bax, *Rise and Fall of the Anabaptists* (London: Swan Sonnenschein & Co., Ltd., 1903); Karl Kautsky, *Communism in Central Europe in the Time of the Reformation* (London, 1897).

11. Ernst Troeltsch, relying upon Alfred Hegler's *Geist und Schrift bei Sebastian Franck* (Freiburg i. B., 1892) has given somewhat popular circulation to the important distinction between the Anabaptists proper (whom he calls *Täufer*) and the prophetic leaders who arose beside them *(spiritualisten)*. *The Social Teaching of the Christian Churches* (New York, 1931), footnote 440, p. 949. See also his "Die Täufer und Spiritualisten," in "Protestantisches Christentum und Kirche in der Neuzeit," in P. Hinneberg's *Geschichte der Christlichen Religion: Die Kultur der Gegenwart* (Leipzig & Berlin, 1922).

12. In spite of the charges of their enemies, the records show that the mainline Anabaptists repudiated revolution and chiliasm. The Swiss early distinguished between themselves and Thomas Müntzer on this issue; see the letter of Conrad Grebel and associates to Müntzer, September 4, 1524, printed in Christian Neff, ed., *Gedenkschrift zum 400 jährigen Jubiläum der Mennoniten oder Taufgesinnten 1525-1925* (Konferenz der Süddeutschen Mennoniten E.V., 1925), (Ludwigshafen am Rh., 1925) pp. 89-99. The Hutterian condemnation is found, among other places, in Josef Beck, ed., *Die Geschichts-Bücher der Wiedertäufer in Osterreich-Ungarn* (Wien, 1883): XLIII *Fontes Rerum Austriacarum* (Hist. Comm. Kaiserl. Akad. der Wiss. in Wien), 2te Abth., p. 73. Also, A. J. F. Zieglshmid (ed.), *Die älteste Chronik der Hutterischen Brüder* (Carl Schurz Memorial Foundation, Cayuga Press, Inc., Ithaca, N.Y. 1943) p. 144. On Menno and the Dutch wing: " . . . as before God who knows our hearts, we are clear of all their abominable doctrine, uproar, mutiny, blood-shed, plurality of wives and the like abominations. Yea we hate and from all our heart oppose them as acknowledged heresies, as snares to the conscience and deceit, as deception of souls and pestilential doctrine . . . ." Quoted in John Horsch, "Menno Simons' Attitude toward the Anabaptists of Münster," *The Mennonite Quarterly Review* X (1936), pp. 55-72, 57. There is ample evidence that the authorities distinguished between the Taüfer and the revolutionaries in court, however their polemicists blurred the distinctions in free writing; see Gustav Bossert, ed., *Quellen zur Geschichte der Wiedertäufer: Herzogtum Württemberg* (Leipzig, 1930), *Quellen und Forschungen zur Reformationsgeschichte* XIII, Numbers 69, 79, 190, 287, etc.

13. Karl Holl, "Luther und die Schwärmer," in *Gesammelte Aufsätze zur Kirchengeschichte* (Tübingen I, 1923), p. 466.

14. Gustav Warneck, *Evangelische Missionslehre* (Gotha, 1892-97), 2 1/2 volumes; *Zimmers Handbibliothek der praktischen Theologie* XVI, III, pp. 2,3.

15. This proof-text also appears frequently in the Anabaptist writings. See Jakob Hutter's "Brief an den Landeshauptmann in Mähren," in Lydia Müller (ed.), *Glaubenszeugnisse oberdeutscher Taufgesinnten* (Leipzig, 1938); *Quellen und Forschungen zur Reformationsgeschichte* XX, p. 163. Pilgram Marpeck criticized the state-church men who wouldn't go unless protected, "and not freely under the cross of Christ"; John Horsch, *Mennonites in Europe* (Scottdale, Pa., Herald Press, 1942), p. 315.

16. See Ethelbert Stauffer, "The Anabaptist Theology of Missions" in *The Mennonite Quarterly Review* XIX (1945), pp. 179-214, translated from "Märtyrertheologie und Täuferbewegung" in *Zeitschrift für Kirchengeschichte* LII (1933), pp. 545-98.

17. On the frequency of the theme, "restitutio," see Roland H. Bainton, "Changing Ideas and Ideals in the Sixteenth Century," *The Journal of Modern History* VIII (1936) pp. 417-43, footnote on p. 428.

18. Lydia Müller (ed.), op. cit., p. xxi.

19. Ethelbert Stauffer, "Märtyrertheologie und Täuferbewegung," *Zeitschrift für Kirchengeschichte* (1933) LII, pp. 545-98, 549.

20. Well discussed in Fritz Heyer, "Der Kirchenbegriff der Schwärmer," *Schriften des vereins für Reformationsgeschichte* 56 (1939), 156:1-108. pp. 13-15. On the changing periodization of history see Rudolph Stadelmann, *Vom Geist des ausgehenden Mittelalters* (Halle, 1929); *Deutsche Vierteljahrschrift für Literaturwissenschaft und Geistesgeschichte* XV, p. 223. Also, Wallace K. Ferguson, "Humanist Views of the Renaissance," *The American Historical Review* (1939) XLV, reprint, pp. 3f.

21. On the point of origin of Anabaptism: If we narrow the term to those leaders and congregations who established a continuing and disciplined church life, Zürich is plainly the point of origin—and was accepted as such by the Swiss/South Germans, Hutterites, and Dutch. In the period before the primary sources were available the judgment of the Lutheran polemicists was accepted; the point of departure was, therefore, Wittenberg. Thus, Joh. Henrich Otte, *Annales Anabaptistici* (Basel, 1672), p. 8. He said the Swiss movement stemmed from Müntzer and Nicholas Storch, and from the work of Martin Borrhaus (Cellarius), who went from Wittenberg to join Oecolampadius, serving as professor of theology at the University of Basel until his death in 1564 (p.15). This point of view is still nursed along by those who wish to show that Luther's idea of the origin and significance of "Anabaptism" was sound; see Robert Friedmann on Heinrich Böhmer's Seminar, loc. cit., p. 344. Gottfried Arnold, with habitual liberality, stated that Anabaptism had its origins in two different groups: first, Storch, Stuebner, Cellarius, Müntzer; further *Hubmeyern, Mantzern, Grebeln,* Blaurock. *Kirchen- und Ketzer-Historie* (Frankfort am Mayn, 1700), 2 volumes. Volume II; XVI XXI, p. 262f. Both are to be strongly distinguished from Münster; p. 264a. During the summer of 1523 Stumpf and Grebel came to Zwingli and Jud and suggested a separate church; the Reformer said that he would have nothing to do with a "Donatist" church and answered with "he who is not against us is for us" and the parable of the tares. From that point separation was assured between those desiring to restore New Testament life and the Reformation party. Emil Egli, *Die Züricher Wiedertäufer zur Reformationszeit* (Zürich, 1878), pp. 14-17. Also No. 692 (April ?, 1525) in Emil Egli, ed., *Actensammlung zur Geschichte der Zürcher Reformation in den Jahren 1519-1533* (Zürich, 1879). 2 volumes. I, pp. 308-14.

22. R. Christoffel, *Zwingli; or, the Rise of the Reformation in Switzerland* (Edinburg, 1858), pp. 160-61. Jakob Kreutzer, "Zwinglis Lehre von der Obrigkeit," *Kirchenrechtliche Abhandlungen* 57 (1909), 1-100, p. 64.

23. Emil Egli (ed.), op. cit., No. 674 (March 16-25, 1525), I, p. 299: One testified that he slept at home during the services; and besides he had read in his testament "who believes and is baptized. . . ." See also No. 1631 (December 26, 1529), I, p. 692: Here the Great Commission (Mk. 16) and the Ban (Mt. 18) are linked together as basic ordinances.

"Rechenschaft und bekanntnus des glaubens . . ." (Trieste, 1539) stressed Mark 16; Lydia Müller (ed.), op. cit., p. 193. When Hanns Schlaffer was called up before the authorities at Schwatz in 1528, he answered them on Matthew 28, Mark 16; van Bracht, *A Martyrology of the Churches of Christ Commonly Called Baptist* (Hanserd Knollys Society, London, 1850-53), I, p. 50. The central authority in Hübmaier's "Von dem christl. Tauff der Gläubigen" is Matthew 28:19; see Carl D. Sachsse, *Balthasar Hübmaier als Theologe* (Berlin, 1914), *Neuen Studien zur Geschichte der Theologie und der Kirche*, XX, pp. 19-20. Karl Schornbaum (ed.), *Quellen zur Geschichte der Wiedertäufer: Markgraftum Brandenburg* (Leipzig, 1934), *Quellen und Forschungen zur Reformationsgeschichte*, XVI:2, No. 260 (May 1531), pp. 236-37: Questions prepared for the Windesheim *Wiedertäufer* indicate the authorities' expectation of testimony based on the Great Commission and the Acts. A. J. F. Zeiglschmid (ed.), op. cit., p. 31.

24. Josef Beck (ed.), op. cit., pp. 62, 64 (Hanss Schlaffer).

25. Lydia Müller (ed.), op. cit., p. 15 (Hans Hut), p. 92 (Hanss Schlaffer), p. 112. B. Hubmaier wrote to the authorities that he knew of no other order but preach, believe, baptize; Emil Egli (ed.), op. cit., I, p. 449. When at St. Gall Uolimann was summoned before the Council, April 25, 1525, for going on his own authority with baptism and the Supper, he said the original order was teaching, believing, baptizing; and this lasted to the time of Tertullian and Cyprian when they began to baptize sick children. See Richard Heath, *Anabaptism From Its Rise at Zwickau to Its Fall at Münster* (London, 1895), p. 39. (Contains interesting material in spite of an erroneous thesis.)

26. Karl Schornbaum (ed.), op. cit., No. 44 (September 20, 1527), p. 34 (Hans Spitelmair).

27. Justus Menius, *Von dem Geist der Widerteuffer* (Wittemberg, 1544), folio Liij.

28. Ibid., no pagination.

29. Heinrich Bullinger, *Der Widerteuffern ursprung/fürgang/secten/wäsen/usw.* (Zürich, 1560), 148b.

30. An Anabaptist examined by Joh. Brenz; Gustav Bossert (ed.), op. cit., No. 169 (April 9, 1557), p. 146.

31. Lydia Müller (ed.), op. cit., p. 214 (Ulrich Stadler).

32. The gathering of a community with New Testament discipline (spiritual government according to Matthew 18:15-17) was the ground of the Anabaptists' running controversy with Schwenckfeld. Pilgram Marpeck and his associates held to a vigorously covenantal teaching, and repudiated Schwenckfeld for refusing to use believer's baptism which the latter termed a new captivity of the conscience. He was moved to study the question by Menius' book and urged suspension of infant baptism. On the other hand he opposed the Anabaptists' insistence upon becoming children of God by faith baptism. "The Spirit moveth where it listeth. . ." (Jn. 3:8). "Von dem Kindertauf," in *Corpus Schwenckfeldianorum* (Elmer E. S. Johnson [ed.] for the Bd. of Publ. of the Schwenckfelder Church and Hartford Theological Seminary, 1907ff.), III, pp. 812-24, 816. Also, X, p. 932. The Anabaptists replied that he would not have been satisfied with Christ's church if contemporary with him and that believer's baptism and the ban were biblical ordinances given by Christ for the maintenance of his church. Johann Loserth, "Studien zu Pilgram Marpeck" in Christian Neff (ed.), op. cit., pp. 134f., 150. See VII CS pp. 161ff. for bibliography on the relation of the Anabaptists and Schwenckfeld.

33. A. J. F. Zieglschmid (ed.), op. cit., pp. 269ff. See also p. 60: Baptism stands on Mark 16, Matthew 28 (Hanss Schlaffer, 1528). And on pp. 250f., a statement by Gabrielites who joined the Hutterians in 1545 begins with baptism, based on Matthew 28 and Mark 16. See Lydia Müller (ed.), op. cit., p. 236f. At an examination of various people at Erlangen, 1527, Hans Ritter the Nodler said: (1) the Lord commanded "go ye . . ."; (2) man must submit under God as animals under man; (3) they went to flowing water, filled a hat, and poured; Karl Schornbaum (ed.), op. cit., No. 16. p. 16. In the Confession of an

Anabaptist at Antwerp, 1551: "Question. 'What do you hold concerning infant baptism?' Answer. 'I consider it nothing else than a human institution.' Qu. 'By what then will you prove, or establish your baptism?' Ans. 'By Mark xvi,' " T. J. van Braght, op. cit., I, pp. 436-37.

34. Karl Schornbaum (ed.), op. cit., No. 353 (April 27, 1534), p.338.

35. "Urgicht . . . 16. September 1527," in Christian Meyer, "Zur Geschichte der Wiedertäufer in Oberschwaben: 1. Die Anfänge des Wiedertäuferthums in Augsburg," Zeitschrift des Historischen Vereins für Schwaben und Neuberg (1874) I, pp. 207-56, 223.

36. So one writer concluded, referring to the excellent example of the Master, baptized by John in his thirtieth year; Lydia Müller (ed.), op. cit., p. 93.

37. See article by Hege, "Augsburger Täufergemeinde," in *Mennonitisches Lexikon* I (ed., Christian Hege and Christian Neff), Frankfurt und Weierhof (Pfalz), 1913-, I, pp. 92-96; also Hege's article "Märtyrersynode," *Mennonitisches Lexikon III* (1938), pp. 53-56.

38. Robert Friedmann, "The Epistles of the Hutterian Brethren," *Mennonite Quarterly Review* XX (1946), pp. 147-77, 153.

39. Ibid., pp. 160-61.

40. A. J. F. Zieglschmid (ed.), op. cit., p. 183.

41. In the Five Articles (c. 1547); Lydia Müller (ed.), op. cit., p. 252.

42. On the relation of their missionary power to willingness to suffer, note Fritz Heyer, loc. cit., pp. 20-21.

43. Lydia Müller (ed.), op. cit., p. 249.

44. On the threefold baptism see Leonhard Schiemer in Lydia Müller (ed.), op. cit., p. 77f.

Chapter 2

1. Roland H. Bainton, "The Left Wing of the Reformation," *Studies in the Reformation* (Boston: Beacon Press, 1963), pp. 119ff.

2. Franklin H. Littell, *The Free Church* (Boston: Starr King Press, 1957).

3. Donald F. Durnbaugh, *The Believers' Church: The History and Character of Radical Protestantism* (New York: Macmillan, 1968), p. 33.

4. James Leo Garrett (ed.), *The Concept of the Believers' Church* (Scottdale, Pa.: Herald Press, 1969).

5. John Howard Yoder in ibid., pp. 250ff.

6. Martin Luther, *Works* St Louis edition, Vol. X, col. 229. Quoted in Leonard Verduin *The Reformers and Their Stepchildren* (Grand Rapids: Eerdmans, 1964), p. 127.

7. Ibid. Vol. V, col. 747. Quoted in Verduin, p. 126.

8. Martin Bucer, *Quellen Hesse* pp. 238-39. Quoted in Verduin, p. 111.

9. Ibid., p. 270. Quoted in Verduin, p. 111.

10. Menno Simons, *The Complete Works of Menno Simons c. 1496-1561* (hereafter *CWMS*), J. C. Wenger (ed.), Leonard Verduin (tran.), (Scottdale, Pa.: Herald Press, 1956), p. 91.

11. Ibid., p. 92

12. Dirk Philips in *Bibliotheca Reformatoria Neerlandica* X, (The Hague: Martinus Nijhoff, 1914), p. 389.

13. *CWMS*, p. 337.

14. Pilgram Marpeck, quoted in Alvin J. Beachy, *The Concept of Grace in the Radical Reformation* (unpublished PhD dissertation, Harvard Divinity School, 1960), p. 40; or (Nieuwkoop: B. De Graaf, 1977), p. 23.

15. Hans Denck, quoted in Alvin J. Beachy, p. 37; (p. 21).

16. *CWMS*, p. 334.

17. Dirk Philips, quoted in Alvin J. Beachy, p. 140; (p. 75).

18. *CWMS*, pp. 409-10.

19. Ibid., p. 402.

20. Ibid., pp. 109-10.

21. Conrad Grebel, in "Letters to Thomas Müntzer by Conrad Grebel and Friends," George H. Williams (ed.), *Spiritual and Anabaptist Writers*, Vol. 25, *Library of Christian Classics* (Philadelphia: Westminster Press, 1957), p. 80.

22. *CWMS*, pp. 175, 198.

23. Günther Franz, et al. (ed.), *Urkundliche Quellen zur hessischen Reformationsgeschichte IV. Band. Wiedertäuferakten, 1527-1626* (Marburg, Elwertsche Verlagsbuchhandlung, 1951), p. 174.

24. Quoted in Peter James Klassen, *The Economics of Anabaptism, 1525-1560* (The Hague: Mouten & Co., 1964), p. 31.

25. Ibid., p. 30.

26. Balthasar Hubmaier, quoted in ibid., p. 32.

27. Hans Hut, in Lydia Müller (ed.), *Glaubenszeugnisse Oberdeutscher Taufgesinnter* (Leipzig, 1938), p. 13.

28. Jacob Hutter, in A. J. F. Ziegelschmid, "Unpublished Sixteenth-Century Letters of the Hutterian Brethren," *Mennonite Quarterly Review* (Hereafter *MQR*) XV, 2 (April, 1941), p. 138.

29. Hans Schmidt, in Wilhelm Wiswedel, "Die alten Taufergemeinden und ihr missionarisches Wirken," *Archiv für Reformationsgeschichte* 40 (1943), p. 197.

30. *CWMS*, p. 298.

31. Ibid., p. 633.

32. Ibid., p. 743.

33. J. C. Wenger (tran. and ed.), "The Schleitheim Confession of Faith," *MQR* XIX, 4 (October 1945), p. 248.

34. *CWMS*, p. 97.

35. Conrad Grebel, op. cit. p. 79.

36. *CWMS*, p. 338.

37. Hans Umlauft, in Franklin H. Littell, *The Anabaptist View of the Church* (Boston: Starr King Press, 1958), p. 93.

38. *CWMS*, p. 65.

Chapter 3

1. Gustav Warneck, *Outline of the History of Protestant Missions*, translated from the second German edition of 1882 by Thomas Smith; (Edinburg: James Gemmell, 1884), pp. 11-23.

2. For the bulk of this review, following the literature it surveys, I shall be accepting the quasi-equation of Reformation with the Lutheran wing of that movement. It must be recognized at the outset, however, that this simplification is unfair to the originality of Calvinism. We shall return to this topic in note 15 below.

3. Kenneth Scott Latourette, *A History of the Expansion of Christianity*, Vol. 3, *Three Centuries of Advance* (New York: Harper and Row, 1939), p. 25ff.

4. Putting kings and traders in the same category is slightly anachronistic. Sixteenth-century colonialism was more a search for gold than for trade. The British and Dutch trading empires really began only in the next century.

5. Kurt Dietrich Schmidt and Ernst Wolf, eds., *Die Kirche in iherer Geschichte*, vol. 4, fascicle T, *Missionsgeschichte der neueren Zeit*, by Hans-Werner Gensichen (Göttingen: Vandenhoeck and Ruprecht, 1961) pp. T5ff.; Gensichen, "Were the Reformers Indifferent to Missions?" *Student World* 1,2, (1960), pp. 119ff.; John Warwick Montgomery, "Luther and Missions," *Evangelical Missions Quarterly* 3 (1967), pp. 193-202 (expanded from

Christianity Today 10 (1966), p. 802. Montgomery made his critique of Warneck easier by using an encyclopedia article rather than Warneck's book and related articles. Both Gensichen and Montgomery relied largely on Werner Elert, *The Structure of Lutheranism*, trans. Walter Hansen (St. Louis: Concordia, 1962), vol. 1, pp. 385ff.

6. Francis Xavier did not learn the local languages either, and missionary Catholicism kept its Latin cultic patterns; yet the Catholic missionary settlements did study and communicate with indigenous culture whether in Asia or the Americas.

7. "Yet, when everything favorable has been said that can be said, and when all possible evidences from the writings of the Reformers have been collected, it all amounts to exceedingly little." Stephen Neill, *A History of Christian Missions* (Harmondsworth: Penguin Books, 1964), p. 222, citing Gensichen, *Missionsgeschichte*.

8. Both Montgomery and Elert gathered such expressions of what Warneck called the Reformer's "witnessing spirit."

9. Gensichen, *Missionsgeschichte*, T6.

10. Gensichen, *Missionsgeschichte*, T6.

11. Gensichen, *Missionsgeschichte*, p. 391. Nikolai's erudition was enormous for the time, but his survey has some limits for the apologetic purpose for which Elert has appealed to it:

   a. Much of the Christian presence around the world which he documented represents the results of Catholic missions of the sixteenth century, and thus does not describe the geographic awareness of Luther's own time.

   b. Most of Africa and North America, which Nikolai knew about, are missing from the list. Thus Nikolai demonstrated that there are unchurched parts of the world. Elert admitted that Luther also knew this (p. 387).

   c. This presence around the world existed, and was known about, only by virtue of the Jesuits who, according to Nikolai, were preaching the Protestant message of justification by faith, but were doing it and reporting on it through a specific institution, beside the ordered congregational preaching office, which Elert, arguing in Luther's behalf, said was not necessary.

12. "Walter Holsten, "*Reformation und Mission,*"*Archiv für Reformationsgeschichte* 44, (1953), p. 9.

13. Ibid., p. 31.

14. From this perspective it is a sign of theological immaturity to care about the historically concrete. Elert wrote that concern for institutional mission belongs in the business administration offerings of engineering schools, and he sarcastically asked if Warneck thought Luther should have gone to Mexico. We do not add to the list of reasons a fifteenth, that mission to the heathen was "strictly impossible," as was argued by Hans Hillerbrand, "Ein Täuferisches Missionszeugnis aus dem 16. Jahrhundert, "*Zeitschrift für Kirchengeschichte* 71, (1960), p. 323. It is not clear what Hillerbrand meant. He wrote that this impossibility applied to the Anabaptists as well, so it seems he meant an empirical and not a theological impossibility. He cited Elert but misinterpreted him, since Elert spoke of theological reasons against missions, not of empirical impossibility.

15. As indicated in note 2 above, we are speaking of Lutheranism. Later we shall note wherein Calvinism was significantly different. Yet Calvinism also has its superficial apologetes in the style of Elert and Montgomery. C. George Fry has presented an argument similar to that of Montgomery: "John Calvin: Theologian and Evangelist, "*Christianity Today*, October 23, 1970, p. 59f. Fry described evangelism as the effort, directed to baptized Europe, to establish Protestant state churches where Catholicism had been before and to impose ethics by legislation. He counted on the benevolence of a Reformation Day audience not to notice that what is usually called evangelism by *Christianity Today* readers and editors, namely a challenge to individuals to make a first decisive commitment to Christ, was not included.

16. The reference here is to an ecclesiology, not to one particular denomination. Cf. Donald Durnbaugh, *The Believers' Church* (New York: Macmillan, 1968) and James Leo Garrett, ed., *The Concept of the Believers' Church* (Scottdale: Herald Press, 1970).

17. The term "state church" has had different meanings in different centuries and is held by some Reformation historians, who give it an eighteenth-century definition, not to be a correct description of the Reformation pattern. George H. Williams has given currency to the term "magisterial" as recognition that both government (magistracy) and university theology (magisterium) had normative roles. I have come to prefer "official" as a more translatable equivalent of Williams' point.

18. All the more surprising is Latourette's omission in view of his being a Baptist and his treatment of the other wings of the Reformation in his church history text. The third volume of his seven volume survey, *A History of the Expansion of Christianity*, deals with the period in question: *Three Centuries of Advance: 1500 A.D. to 1800 A.D.* (New York: Harper and Row, 1939). See especially chapter 2.

19. Gensichen's chapter is entitled "The Reformation Century," but deals exclusively with the official, continental Reformation. Walter Holsten and Karl Holl do refer in this connection to the *Schwärmer* as sharing to an even worse degree the humanism of the Zwinglians.

20. Wilhelm Wiswedel, "Die alten Täufergemeinden und ihr missionarisches Wirken," *Archiv für Reformationsgeschichte* 40, (1943), pp. 183ff.

21. Franklin H. Littell, "Protestantism and the Great Commission," *Southwestern Journal of Theology* 2, (1959), pp. 26ff; "The Anabaptist Theology of Missions," *Mennonite Quarterly Review*, 21, (1947), 5ff; also chapter 4 in his *Origins of Sectarian Protestantism* (New York: Macmillan, 1964), pp. 109-137.

22. *Das missionarische Bewusstsein und Wirken der Täufer*, Neukirchener Verlag, 1966, Vol. 21 in *Beitrage zur Geschichte und Lehre der reformierten Kirche*. Some of the same ground was covered in an unpublished study of "Early Anabaptist *Sendungsbewusstsein*" done by Cornelius J. Dyck for Professor R. Pierce Beaver of the University of Chicago in 1957.

23. Leonhard von Muralt and Walter Schmid (eds.), *Quellen zur Geschichte der Täufer in der Schweiz, Erster Band, Zürich* (Zürich: S. Hirzel Verlag, 1952), p. 178. This may have been meant as a joke, or as seeking political refuge. In any case it shows an awareness of the non-Christian world to which one might travel. If Hillerbrand (note 13 above) meant by "impossibility" that travel was somehow physically unthinkable for Protestants, this must be challenged. The Anabaptists in Moravia were visited twice by sectarians from Macedonia. They sent emissaries to Lisbon to see about colonization possibilities in the West Indies and to Amsterdam with the same question about the East Indies. If, on the other hand, Hillerbrand meant that mission to pagans without the protection of a colonial military umbrella would have been illegal and risked loss of life, then he was quite right, but the Anabaptists would not have regarded this as a reason for not going.

24. Having identified the basic issue as ecclesiology, it is possible to return to the originality of Calvinism within the official Reformation. Calvin moved in a direction different from that of Zwingli, Bibliander, Bullinger and Erasmus. This movement was not unrelated to his and Martin Bucer's contacts with Anabaptists in Strasbourg, Marburg, and Geneva. While Calvin regarded church and state as ideally mutually supportive and having the same membership, the church has its own theologically important structure (whereas for Luther ecclesiastical structure was *adiaphoron*) with a discipline which, though presupposing membership of all in the covenant, could at least exclude apostate adults. When pietism later led Calvinism to make confirmation a meaningful, adult, uncoerced profession of faith, this was another mediating step toward a believers' church ecclesiology. So was the training at Geneva and Lausanne of ministers for Spain, France, Italy, or Poland, to the extent to which such people served in churches which accepted their calling to

function without support of government. Thus in numerous ways Calvinism stands between the "purer types" represented in the literature we have been surveying. Comments by Dr. Sidney Rooy have been helpful in clarifying this point.

Chapter 4

1. Gunnar Westin, *The Free Church Through the Ages*. From the Swedish by Virgil A. Olson (Nashville: Broadman Press, 1958), pp. 2-8.
2. Hans Kasdorf, "The Reformation and Mission: A Survey of Secondary Literature," *Occasional Bulletin of Missionary Research* 6:4 (October 1980). The section on the Anabaptist mission involvement affords significant references for in-depth studies.
3. Franklin H. Littell, "Protestantism and the Great Commission," *Southwestern Journal of Theology* 2:1 (1959), p. 30. Cf. Franklin H. Littell, *The Origins of Sectarian Protestantism: A Study of the Anabaptist View of the Church*, third printing (New York: Macmillan, 1972), pp. 109-37; notes on pp. 195-206.
4. J. D. Douglas, ed., *Let the Earth Hear His Voice* (Minneapolis: World-Wide Publications, 1975), p. 8.
5. Cf. Franklin H. Littell, "The Anabaptist Theology of Mission," *Mennonite Quarterly Review* 21:1 (1947), p. 13. Also chapter 1 in this book.
6. Harold S. Bender, "The Anabaptist Vision," *The Recovery of the Anabaptist Vision*, ed. by Guy F. Hershberger (Scottdale, Pa.: Herald Press, 1962), pp. 42-43.
7. Cf. Donald A. McGavran, *Understanding Church Growth* (Grand Rapids: Eerdmans, 1970), p. 85f. The HUP (homogeneous unit principle) is a much-debated concept in missiological circles. Those interested in studying the subject may want to consult the following: *Global Church Growth Bulletin* 17:1 (January-February 1980) and 17:2 (March-April 1980). Both issues are devoted to that debate. Several years ago the Lausanne Continuation Committee sponsored a consultation on the HUP. The conclusions were published in "The Pasadena Consultation—Homogeneous Unit," *Lausanne Occasional Papers No. 1* (Wheaton, Ill.: The Lausanne Committee for World Evangelization, 1978).
8. Wilhelm Wiswedel, "Die alten Täufergemeinden und ihr missionarisches Wirken," *Archiv für Reformationsgeschichte* 40 (Part I, 1943); 41 (Part II, 1948). The quotation is from Part II, p. 124. Translation mine.
9. Littell, 1972, p. 120.
10. Fritz Blanke, *Brothers in Christ*, translated from German by Joseph Nordenhaug (Scottdale, Pa.: Herald Press, 1961), pp. 32-33.
11. Ibid., pp. 34-38.
12. Wolfgang Schäufele, *Das missionarische Bewusstsein und Wirken der Täufer* (Hamburg: Neukirchener Berlag des Erziehungsvereins, 1964), pp. 121-23.
13. Littell, 1959, pp. 15-16.
14. The full title of this hymnbook reads, *Auss Bundt, das ist: etliche schöne Christenliche Lieder, wie die in der Gefängnuss zu Passau in dem Schloss von den Schweizer-Brüdern und andern rechtgläubigen Christen hin und her gedichtet worden*. Reprinted edition (Basel: Jak. Heinr. von Mechel, 1838).
15. Donald F. Durnbaugh, *The Believers' Church: The History and Character of Radical Protestantism* (New York: Macmillan, 1968), pp. 231-32.
16. Horst Penner, *Weltweite Bruderschaft* (Karlsruhe: Verlag Heinrich Schneider, 1960), p. 20.
17. Littell, 1959, pp. 38-39.
18. John Allen Moore, *Der Starke Joerg: Die Geschichte Georg Blaurocks, des Täuferführers und Missionars* (Kassel: Oncken Verlag, 1955), p. 35. John C. Wenger, *Even Unto Death* (Richmond: John Knox, 1961), p. 24.
19. Wolfgang Schäufele, "The Missionary Vision and Activity of the Anabaptist

Laity," *Mennonite Quarterly Review* 36:2 (1962), p. 100. Also chapter 5 in this book.

20. Durnbaugh, op. cit., p. 232.

21. Schäufele, 1962, p. 99.

22. Ibid., pp. 104-105.

23. Durnbaugh, op. cit., p. 233.

24. Schäufele, 1962, pp. 106-109.

25. Littell, 1972, p. 112. Cf. Wiswedel, op. cit., Part II, p. 123.

26. Schäufele, 1964, p. 117.

27. Wiswedel, op. cit., Part I, p. 196.

28. Schäufele, 1964, pp. 122-23.

29. Cf. Wiswedel, op. cit., Part II, p. 119ff.

30. Ibid., pp. 121-22.

31. Schäufele, 1964, pp. 165-72.

32. John A. Toews, "The Anabaptist Involvement in Mission," *The Church in Mission: A Sixtieth Anniversary Tribute to J. B. Toews*, ed. by A. J. Klassen (Fresno: Board of Christian Literature, Mennonite Brethren Church, 1967), p. 95.

33. Schäufele, 1964, p. 62.

34. Ibid., p. 167f.

35. Ibid., p. 185. Modern examples of tentmaking ministry are described by Professor J. Christy Wilson of Gordon Cromwell Theological Seminary in *Todays' Tentmakers* (Wheaton, Ill.: Tyndale House, 1981).

36. Cf. ibid., pp. 238-46. Ernst Crous, "Anabaptism, Pietism, Rationalism and German Mennonites," *Recovery of the Anabaptist Vision*, ed. by Guy F. Hershberger (Scottdale, Pa.: Herald Press, 1962), pp. 237-38.

37. Schäufele, 1964, p. 245.

38. Ernst Troeltsch, *The Social Teachings of the Christian Churches*, two volumes, tran. from the German by Olive Wyon (London: George Allen and Unwin, 1950), Vol. II, p. 704.

39. Moore, op. cit., p. 29.

40. Schäufele, 1964, p. 34.

41. Roland Bainton, *The Reformation of the Sixteenth Century* (Boston: Beacon Press, 1970), pp. 101-102.

42. Robert Friedmann, *A Theology of Anabaptism* (Scottdale, Pa.: Herald Press, 1973), p. 44.

43. Harold S. Bender, "The Anabaptist Theology of Discipleship," *Mennonite Quarterly Review* 24:1 (1950), pp. 27-29.

Chapter 5

1. This is the position of the modern historiographers of Zürich Anabaptism, See Fritz Blanke, *Brothers in Christ* (Scottdale, Pa., Herald Press, 1961), pp. 35ff.; Heinrich Bornkamm, *Historische Zeitschrift*, Vol. 182 (1956), p. 387; Gunnar Westin, *Geschichte des Freikirchentums*, 2nd ed. (Kassel, 1958), p. 79, calls it a "weitverzweigte volkstümliche Erweckung." Unfortunately this phrase is omitted in the English translation, *The Free Church Through the Ages* (Nashville: Broadman Press, 1958), p. 87. Westin applies the concept to later areas of the Anabaptist expansion also, for instance, in the region around Nürnberg.

2. H. S. Bender, "The Anabaptist Vision," *Mennonite Quarterly Review* (herafter cited as *MQR*), XVIII (1944), pp. 67ff.; idem, "The Anabaptist Theology of Discipleship," *MQR*, XXIV (1950), pp. 25ff.

3. Karl Schornbaum, *Quellen zur Geschichte der Täufer* (hereafter cited as *TQ: Bayern, II*) (Gütersloh, 1951), p. 27.

4. Karl Schornbaum, *Quellen zur Geschichte der Täufer* (hereafter *TQ: Bayern, I*) (Leipzig, 1934), p. 61. In Thuringia the newly baptized were told explicitly: "Welicher einin order mere, er sei ime gefreundt oder nit, zu ime in diese punctus bringen kann, der solle es tun." Paul Wappler, *Die Täuferbewegung in Thüringen* (Jena, 1913), p. 231; Fritz Heyer, *Der Kirchenbegriff der Schärmer* (Leipzig, 1939), p. 72.

5. Jacob Hutter in his "Epistel an die Gefangenen zu Hohenwart" (1534), published by A. J. F. Zieglschmid, *MQR*, XV (1941), p. 126.

6. Letter of Michael Sattler to the Anabaptist congregation at Horb (1527), in the unpublished *Täuferakten* of the Swabian Imperial Cities (hereafter cited as *TQ; Württemberg, II.*), section "Hohenberg." See also *Mennonitische Geschichtsblätter*, n.s., 9 (1957), p. 28.

7. With this limitation Franklin H. Littell's sentence is valid: "The Anabaptists were among the first to make the Commission binding upon all church members." Littell, *The Anabaptist View of the Church* (2nd ed., Boston: Star King Press, 1958), p. 112.

8. *TQ: Bayern, I*, No. 367.

9. Friedrich Roth, "Zur Geschichte Eitelhans Langenmantels von Augsburg," *Zeitschrift des Historischen Vereins für Schwaben und Neuburg* (hereafter *Schwaben und Neuburg*), XXVII (1900), pp. 13f.

10. *TQ: Württemberg, II*, section "Hohenlohe," Urgicht of Sept. 16, 1535.

11. *TQ: Württemberg, II*, section "Heilbronn," testimony concerning Endris Wertz.

12. See *TQ: Württemberg, II*, section "Ulm" (Michel Herzog, examination of March 10, 1572).

13. A. Nicolandoni, *Johannes Bünderlin von Linz* (Berlin, 1893), pp. 197-98.

14. In the house meetings at Zollikon all read who could read. L. v. Muralt-Schmid, *Quellen zur Geschichte der Taüfer in der Schweiz, I* (Zürich, 1952) (hereafter *TQ: Zürich*), No. 56, p. 65 (1525). See further *TQ: Württemberg, II*, section "Esslingen," Ludwig Scheurer, March 26, 1528; Jörg Fry, June 16, 1528.

15. See Beatrice Jenny, *Das Schleitheimer Täuferbekenntnis*, 1527 (Thayngen, 1951), pp. 12, 61, Horst Quiring, "Das Schleitheimer Täuferbekenntnis von 1527," *Mennonitische Geschichtsblätter*, n.s. 9 (1957), p. 36.

16. *TQ: Württemberg, II*, section "Esslingen," examination of Dec. 16, 1529.

17. The exceptional situation of the Anabaptists in Moravia will be treated later.

18. Paul Peachey, *Die soziale Herkunft der Schweizer Täufer* (Karlsruhe, 1954), pp. 57, 89.

19. Fr. Roth, "Der Höhepunkt der wiedertäuferischen Bewegung in Augsburg und ihr Niedergang im Jahre 1528," *Schwaben und Neuburg*, XXVIII (1901), p. 97.

20. Fr. Roth, op. cit., p. 99. See also op. cit., pp. 56, 69, 74, 83, 84, 100.

21. *TQ: Zürich*, p. 303 (Grosshans Keüffeler, 1529).

22. Gustav Bossert, *Quellen zur Geschichte der Täufer* (hereafter *TQ: Württemberg, I*), p. 265; see also p. 267.

23. Roth, "Eitelhans Langenmantel," p. 22. See also Blanke, op. cit., p. 60; M. Krebs, *Quellen zur Geschichte der Täufer: Baden und Pfalz* (Gütersloh, 1951), (hereafter *TQ: Baden-Pfalz*), p. 79 (1582), p. 316. Since this case concerns a statement handed in to the government, the declaration by the woman that she had been "compelled" by her husband to accept Anabaptism should be received with some skepticism.

24. See *TQ: Zürich*, No. 341, p. 359 (1532); *TQ: Württemberg, I*, 491 (1577). See also Roth, "Höhepunkt," p. 54. A good example of one spouse blaming the other one for seduction to Anabaptism, when it came to the ultimate confession to the authorities, may be seen in *TQ: Baden-Pfalz*, No. 552 (1538).

25. Influence of the father, *TQ: Baden-Pfalz*, pp. 353, 355 (1555), 77 (1582); *TQ: Württemberg, I*, pp. 251 (1569), 463 (1575). Influence of the mother, *TQ: Baden-Pfalz* pp. 310, 330 (1597 and 1609); see also *TQ: Württemberg, I*, p. 495 (1577).

26. See K. Sinzinger, *Das Täufertum in Pustertal* (dissertation, Innsbruck, 1950), p. 227 (ca. 1534); ibid., pp. 210 f. (1533 or 1534).

27. *TQ: Zürich*, p. 162 and Peachey, op. cit., p. 89 (1525; Heinrich Aberli, of Zürich, who baptized his brother-in-law, a convert to Anabaptism).

28. Sinzinger, op. cit., p. 160 (1531); Samuel Geiser, *Die Taufgesinnten-Gemeinden* (Karlsruhe, 1931), pp. 190-91 (Canton Bern, 1566).

29. *TQ: Bayern, II*, p. 149 (Kaufbeuren, 1545).

30. *TQ: Bayern, II*, Nos. 14, 15, 18, 19, 22.

31. *TQ: Zürich*, No. 58, p. 67 (1525).

32. *TQ: Württemberg, II*, section "Esslingen," examination of Jan. 15, 1529. See also Roth, "Höhepunkt," p. 56 (testimony of Caspar Schlosser, 1528); *TQ: Württemberg, I*, p. 727 (influencing a neighbor through Anabaptist literature, 1598).

33. Sinzinger, op. cit., p. 310. *TQ: Zürich*, No. 391 (1525? or 1529; school acquaintance as a point of contact). *TQ: Württemberg, I*, p. 855 (1614; won by a friend of his youth).

34. *TQ: Württemberg, I*, p. 705 (ca. 1578). See also Sinzinger, op. cit., p. 336 (before 1535).

35. *TQ: Bayern, I*, p. 177 (1530). See also *TQ: Württemberg, I*, No. 99 (1539); ibid., p. 542 (1582).

36. Sinzinger, op. cit., p. 334. See also *TQ: Zürich*, No. 158, p. 164 (1526; a woman persuades her domestic to be baptized); *TQ: Baden-Pfalz*, p. 237 (1605; a miller with five sons, who seduce their employees to become Anabaptists).

37. Sinzinger, op. cit., pp. 534ff., 86f., 136. *TQ: Bayern, I*, No. 202, reports a similar case.

38. *TQ: Bayern, I*, p. 244 (1531). See Further Sinzinger, op. cit., pp. 204f. (1532); ibid., p. 498 (1579). Similar phenomena appear in Schwenckfelder circles *TQ: Württemberg, II*, section "Ulm" (Oct. 24, 1577).

39. *TQ: Bayern II*, No. 65. Further edicts; *TQ: Württemberg, II*, section "Reutlingen," Council edict of Feb. 8, 1528; section "Heilbronn," Apr. 26, 1534 (examination of citizens who were employing Anabaptist servants); Dec. 28, 1536 (warning by the Council to various citizens). *TQ: Baden-Pfalz*, No. 22 (Lahr and Mahlberg, 1543). Philipp of Hesse ordered (1537) that the craft masters should observe the religious attitude of their journeymen and report suspicious cases to the authorities. *TQ: Hessen*, p. 145. See also E. Widmoser, *Das Täufertum im Tiroler Unterland* (dissertation, Innsbruck, 1948), p. 114.

40. *TQ: Bayern, I*, p. 346. See also *TQ: Baden-Pfalz*, p. 444 (Anabaptist tailor, 1562); *TQ: Württemberg, I*, p. 399 (Anabaptist seamstress, 1574?).

41. *TQ: Baden-Pfalz*, p. 380 (1592). See also pp. 13 and 22 (Anabaptist straw-cutter, 1543) and "Vorwort," page XIV.

42. *TQ: Zürich*, p. 313 (examination of the Anabaptist leader Konrad Winkler, Canton Zürich, 1529); Roth, "Höhepunkt," p. 71 (Augsburg, 1528).

43. See *TQ: Württemberg, I*, p. 577 (1584).

44. See also Beatrice Jenny, op. cit., p. 34, note 46.

45. Roth, "Höhepunkt," pp. 39 and 17. Further, Sinzinger, op. cit., p. 159 (ca. 1531); Nicolandoni, op. cit., p. 194. The family problems which could arise when one of the spouses joined the Anabaptist movement are illustrated by the case of the above-named Elisabeth Sedlmair. Her husband did not agree with her, and visited her almost every week to try to get her to recant. Roth, "Höhepunkt," p. 40. See also Littell, op. cit., p. 91; *Mennonite Encyclopedia*, II (1956), pp. 75-76 (divorce from unbelievers); 502ff. (marriage).

46. Roth, "Höhepunkt," p. 37.

47. *TQ: Württemberg, I*, p. 473 (1576), 503, 508 (1577).

48. *TQ: Württemberg, I*, p. 1187 ("chaining Anabaptist women in their own homes," 1580-1615).

49. *TQ: Württemberg, I*, pp. 55, 23ff.; 439 (1575); 563 (1583); 687 (1596). According to Bullinger the common people judged the Anabaptists as follows: "Man sage gleich von den Täufern, was man wolle, wir sehen nichts an ihnen denn Ernst, und hören von ihnen nichts, den dass man nicht schwören und nicht unrecht, sondern jedermann recht tun soll." Josef v. Beck, "Georg Blaurock." *Comeniushefte, VII* (1898), p. 4. The Anabaptists had a good reputation among the nobility and the common people; *TQ: Württemberg, I*, Introduction, p. XII.

50. See Karl Müller, *Kirchengeschichte*, II, Section I (Tübingen, 1922), p. 226.

51. *TQ: Baden-Pfalz*, p. 68.

52. Fr. Hruby, "*Die Wiedertäufer in Mähren*," *Archiv für Reformationsgeschichte, XXXI* (1934), pp. 88, 91.

53. The Hutterite chronicle mentions (1545) a translator for the brotherhood who was present when houses were bought from the Slavic population. R. Wolkan, *Geschicht-Buch der Hutterischen Brüder* (Vienna, 1923), p. 205.

54. *TQ: Württemberg, I*, p. 341 (Paul Block, 1571).

55. Sinzinger, op. cit., pp. 299-300.

56. Wolkan, *Geschicht-Buch*, p. 334.

57. Wolkan, ibid., p. 199.

58. Wolkan, ibid., p. 330 (1569-71); p. 463 (1600).

59. Hruby, op. cit., *ARG* 30, 1933, p. 201 f.; See also E. Müller, *Die Geschichte der Bernischen Täufer* (Frauenfeld, 1895), p. 92.

60. Ulrich Stadler, "Eine liebe Unterrichtung," in Lydia Müller, *Glaubenszeugnisse oberdeutscher Taufgesinnter*, I (Leipzig, 1938), p. 224.

61. "Brüderliche Vereinigung zwischen uns und etlichen Schweizer Brüdern" (1556), *Glaubenszeugnisse*, p. 266.

62. Littell, op. cit., p. 127.

63. See G. Neumann, "Nach und von Mähren," *ARG*, XLVIII (1957), p. 83.

64. *TQ: Württemberg, II*, section "Esslingen," March 22, 1592.

65. *TQ: Württemberg, I*, p. 410 (1574); further letters reproduced, p. 1,111 (1593); 795 (1607), *TQ: Hessen*, No. 211 (1587), No. 216 (1597), No. 217 (ca. 1600). According to J. Loserth, "*Der Communismus der Mährischen Wiedertäufer*," *Archiv f. Oesterr, Gesch.* 81 (1895), p. 285, the Moravian Anabaptists used letter-carriers, at least later, for the letters in which they testified to their faith and invited their relatives and friends to come to Moravia.

66. See *TQ: Württemberg, I*, p. 712 (1598), 733 (1598); Loserth, *Communismus*, p. 208. The Hutterite missioner Werner Scheffer who was arrested in Hesse in 1587, had fourteen letters and notes for addresses in Hesse. Günther Franz, *TQ: Hessen* (Marburg, 1951), No. 211.

67. This happened mostly in connection with matters of inheritance. Neumann, "Nach und von Mähren," p. 85.

68. An enlightening example of this is found in *TQ: Württemberg, I*, p. 842 (Lienhard Kuonle, 1613). Kuonle joined the Swiss Brethren. Ibid., p. 841.

69. See *TQ: Württemberg, I*, Nos. 73 and 74 (1536): An Anabaptist couple who had returned from Moravia to live in Württemberg were examined about "such erroneous teachings." In Passau, about forty returning emigrants from Moravia were arrested in August and September 1535. According to the trial records they stemmed from Württemberg, Baden, and the Palatinate (*TQ: Württemberg, II*, section "Hohenlohe").

70. This was still the case at the beginning of the seventeenth century. For the empire, see *TQ: Württemberg, I*, p. 821 (1610); 828 (1611), 894 (1620). For Moravia, see footnote 83 in *TQ*, p. 794.

71. H. Urner, "Laiendienst," *RGG*, IV (3rd. ed.) col. 207.

72. W. P. Fuchs, *Das Zeitalter der Reformation*, in Bruno Gebhardt, *Handbuch der*

deutschen Geschichte, II (8th ed.), p. 77.

73. A. Lehmann, "Christentum," *RGG*, I (3rd ed.), col. 1705f.

74. H. H. Walz, "Laien," *Weltkirchen-Lexikon* (Stuttgart, 1960), col. 818ff.; "Laienbewegung," *RGG*, IV (3rd, ed.), col. 204.

Chapter 6

1. Wolfgang Schäufele, *Das missionarische Bewusstsein und Wirken der Täufer, dargestellt nach oberdeutschn Quellen*, Naukirchen-Vluyn 1966.

2. Schäufele, a.a.O., S. 15f.

3. Hans Hut, *Von dem Geheimnuss der Tauf, baide des Zaichens und des Wesens* in Lydia Müller, *Glaubenszeugnisse oberdeutscher Taufgesinnter, 1 Teil*, Leipzig 1938, S. 13.

4. Menno Simons, *Dat Fundament des christelycken Leers*, z.p., 1539, bl. A iijro.

5. Obbe Philips, *Bekentenisse* in *Bibliotheca Reformatoria Neerlandica, zevende deel*, 's Gravenhage 1910, bl. 124.

6. Melchior Hofmann, *Die ordonnantie Godts* in *Bibliotheca Reformatoria Neerlandica, vijfde deels*, 's Gravenhage 1909, bl. 133.

7. W. I. Leendertz, *Melchior Hofmann*, Haarlem 1883, bl. 184.

8. Menno Simons, *Van dat rechte christengheloove*, z.p., z.j., b.I.L vvo, C vijro.

9. Hofmann, *Ordonnantie*, blz. 164v.

10. Menno, *Christengheloove*, bl. K vrijro, vo.

11. *Het Offer des Heeren, de oudste verzameling Doopsgezinde Martelaarsbrieven en Offerliederen* in *Bibliotheca Reformatoria Neerlandica, tweede deel*, 's Gravenhage 1904, bl. 53v.

12. Michiel Satler, *Sendbrief uut zijn gevanckenis geschreven aen de Ghemeynte Gods tot Horb* in *BRN 5*, bl. 618.

13. Menno Simons, *Beantwoordinge over een schrift Gellii Fabri* in *Opera ofte Groot Sommarie*, z.p. (Haarlem) 1646, fol. 474b of in *Opera Omnia Theologica*, Amsterdam 1681, fol. 258a.

14. Menno, *Fundament*, bl. A vvo.

15. Hans Fischer, *Jakob Huter, Leben, Frömmigkeit, Briefe*, Newton 1856, Briefe, S. 62.

16. A. J. F. Zieglschmid, Die älteste Chronik der Hutterischen Brüder, New York w. y. (1943), p. 386f.

17. Obbe, *Bekentenisse*, bl. 130

18. Menno, *Fundament*, bl. J iiijvo.

19. Menno Simons, *Ein Fundament unde klare Anwisinge*, z.p., z.j (1558), bl. W iijvo.

20. G. Bossert, *Quellen zur Geschichte der Widertäufer, 1 Band, Herzogtum, Württemberg*, Leipzig 1930, s. 652.

21. Hofmann, *Ordonnantie*, bl. 152.

22. Menno, *Christengheloove*, bl. P. viijro.

23. Obbe, *Bekentenisse*, bl. 129.

24. Hofmann, *Ordonnantie*, bl. 150.

25. David Joris, *Een geestelijck Liedtboecxken*, z.p., z.j., bl. 53ro.

26. Menno Simons, *Van die gheestelicke verrysenisse*, z.p., z.j., bl. B iiijro.

27. Jörg Haug von Juchsen, *Ein christliche Ordnung eines Wahrhaftigen Christen zu verantworten die Ankunft seines Glaubens*, in *Glaubenszeugnisse*, S. 10.

28. Thomas Müntzer, *Protestation odder Empietung* in *Schriften und Briefe*, Gütersloh 1968, S. 233f.

29. Hans Denck, *Was geredt sey das die Schrift sagt*, in *Schriften, 2 Teil*, Gütersloh 1956m S. 45.

30. Hut, *Tauf*, S. 14.

Chapter 7

1. See George H. Williams, *The Radical Reformation* (Philadelphia: 1962). The designation "brotherhood" ("Brüderschaft") is a formal *terminus technicus* describing sixteenth-century Hutterian Anabaptism contextually.

2. See Ernst Troeltsch, *Die Soziallehren der christlichen Kirchen und Gruppen* (Tübingen, 1912; Eng., New York, 1931); and Johannes Kühn, *Toleranz und Offenbarung* (Leipzig, 1923).

3. A. J. F. Zieglschmid, ed., *Die älteste Chronik der Hutterischen Brüder* (Ithaca, N.Y.:1943), p. 436.

4. See Walter Klaassen, "The Nature of the Anabaptist Protest," *Mennonite Quarterly Review* 45:4, October 1971, pp. 291-311.

5. Zieglschmid, p. 433.

6. Ibid., pp. 458-59; Robert Friedmann, *Hutterite Studies* (Goshen, Ind., 1961), p. 73; Josef Beck, ed., *Die Geschichts-Bücher der Wiedertäufer in Oesterreich-Ungarn, 1526-1785* (Vienna, 1883), pp. 255-56 and passim.

7. Zieglschmid, p. 422; Gustav Bossert, ed., *Hertzogtum Württemberg, Quellen zur Geschichte der Wiedertäufer, Vol. I* (Leipzig, 1930), p. 367; "Steinabrunn," *Mennonite Encyclopedia* (Scottdale, Pa., 1959), Vol. IV, p. 624.

8. Christoph Erhard, *Gründliche kurz verfaste Historia* . . . (1588), fol. ciii^V -ciiii^r.

9. Cod. III-150 (Esztergom, Hungary), fol. 288r. Only in tolerant Moravia could meetings be held with tacit consent of the manorial lords, but here the services were generally closed to outsiders, in line with the Hutterian interpretation of Scripture.

10. See Herhard Neumann, "Nach und von Mähren. Aus der Täufergeschichte des 16. und 17. Jahrhunderts," *Archiv für Reformationsgeschichte* 48, 1957, pp. 89-90; Bossert, pp. 677, 874, 499, 179, 709; Wilhelm Wiswedel, *Bilder und Führergestalten aus dem Täufertum* (Kassel, 1928-52), Vol. III, p. 116; Wiswedel, "Die alten Täufergemeinden und ihr missionarischs Wesen," *ARG* 40, 1943, pp. 183-200; 41, 1948, pp. 115-32.

11. Zieglschmid, pp. 462-66.

12. Hans Joachim Hillerbrand, "Ein täuferisches Missionszeugnis aus dem 16. Jahrhundert," *Zeitschrift für Kirchengeschichte* 71, 1960, pp. 326-27.

13. Luke 18:18ff.

14. Hillerbrand, pp. 324-27. Hillerbrand states that "die Reformatoren an Mission gewiss nicht weniger interessiert waren als die Täufer." This is open to question, and is by no means the case, e.g., for the superintendent at Alzey, who questioned Leonhard Dax about the nature of mission. Also, as Hillerbrand implies, that a "martyr-theology" is more typical in later Anabaptism than earlier can hardly be maintained for Hutterian Anabaptism of the Walpot Era (1565-78, when Peter Walpot was head of the Hutterian Brotherhood) in light of the liturgy in the farewell service for missioners (see below): "So ist vnser begeeren / vnd biten auch gar schon, / das ir wolt got den herren / fier vns anrieffen thuen / vnd biten zu aller zeit, / das er vns wol behieten vor laidt / vnd vns mit seinem geiste / tröst, das wir werden erfreidt." Rudolf Wolkan, *Die Lieder der Wiedertäufer* (Berlin, 1903), p. 208. Of course, upon facing death, the clear note of victory was seen, where Hutterite martyrs continued to demonstrate the depth of their faith, even unto physical death. But the Hutterian will to live out a full life on earth dare not be minimized.

15. Bossert, p. 410.

16. Ibid., p. 411.

17. Ibid., p. 413.

18. The style of this document accords with Dax's "Refutation." Internal evidence points to Dax's authorship. A copy of this document is in Cod. III-107 (Alba Iulia, Rumania).

19. Ibid., fol. 57r.

20. Ibid., fol. 81v-94v.

21. The following is a summation and paraphrase, in prose, of the first part of the original document which is in verse. See Wolkan, pp. 206-9.

22. "Wie die brueder des worts / so in die Landt gezogen / vor der gemein vrlaub nemen," Cod. III-139 (Esztergom), fol. 125r-132v.

23. Ibid., fol. 126v.

24. Ibid., fol. 131r-132v. See also Loserth, pp. 228-31.

25. See Claus-Peter Clasen, *Die Wiedertäufer im Herzogtum Württemberg und in benachbarten Herrschaften* (Stuttgart, 1965), pp. 180-86.

26. Ibid., p. 184. See ibid., Chapter II and passim for an excellent analysis of Hutterian mission activity in and around Württemberg, with a detailed and solid sociological analysis of the social milieu of the Hutterian converts as contrasted to those of other Anabaptist groups.

27. Christoph Andreas Fischer, *Der Hutterischen Widertauffer Taubenkobel* . . . (1607), fol. B-i. See also Johann Loserth, *Der Communismus der Mährischen Wiedertäufer im 16. und 17. Jahrhundert* (Vienna, 1895), p. 229, n. 1.

28. Clasen, p. 61.

29. Neumann, pp. 89-90; Bossert, p. 511.

30. Cod. Hab. 5 (Bratislava), fol. 248r-315v.

31. Bossert, pp. 1089, 1093-94, 1098, 1050-52, 1054, 351-52; Cod. Hab. 17, fol. 314r-314v.

32. Cod. Hab. 5, fol. 233r-283v. See also Leonard Gross, "Leonhard Dax's Encounter with Calvinism, 1567/68," *Mennonite Quarterly Review* 49:4, October 1975, pp. 284-334.

33. Cod. III-150 (Esztergom), fol. 1r-237v. See also Friedmann, *Die Schriften der huterischen Täufergemeinschaften* . . . (Vienna, 1965), pp. 129-30, for a discussion of the problem of date and authorship. As with the Great Article Book, ca. 1577, it is possible that Peter Walpot wrote parts of the manuscript in 1576 or 1577, incorporating some materials from Dax's papers and some from other sources.

34. Cod. III-150, fol. 2v.

35. Ibid., fol. 145r-147r.

36. Ibid., fol. 147r.

37. Ibid., fol. 168r.

38. Ibid., fol. 209v-222v.

39. Ibid., fol. 222r-222v.

Chapter 9

1. *Time Magazine* ("Cope-and-Dagger Stories," *Time* 106 [August 11, 1975]:61-62) has shown the link between Vekemans and the CIA—from which he once received ten million dollars.

2. Cf., A. Manaranche, *Y a-t-il une éthique sociale chretienne?* (Paris: Cerf, 1969).

3. John Driver, "Paul and Mission," in *Mission Focus: Current Issues*, ed. Wilbert R. Shenk (Scottdale, Pa.: Herald Press, 1980), p. 63.

4. Wilbert R. Shenk, "Authoritarian Governments and Mission," in *Mission Focus: Current Issues* (Scottdale, Pa.: Herald Press, 1980), p. 297.

5. John Driver, op. cit., p. 56.

6. I agree with Jim Wallis that "the meaning of evangelism is the proclamation and demonstration of the 'good news' that a new order is upon us and calls us to change our former ways of thinking and living, to turn to Jesus Christ for a new way of life, to enter into the fellowship of a new community" (Jim Wallis, *Agenda for Biblical People* [New York: Harper and Row, 1976], p. 31). In that vein, Wilbert R. Shenk has written that "the purpose of mission is to lead in the formation of an alternative social order (not simply to deal with individual salvation)" (Wilbert R. Shenk, op. cit., p. 295).

7. Joachim Jeremías, *Palabras de Jesus (Die Bergpredigt)* (Madrid: Ediciones Fax, 1968), pp. 69-75.

8. Jim Wallis, op. cit., p. 23.

9. One should mention the great effort made today by Norwegian evangelist Aril Edvardsen (see his *Et faites des disciples* [France: Editions Vie Abondante, 1976]), whose Bible school takes seriously the demands of discipleship in the methods and message of today's mission.

10. Kenneth Scott Latourette, "A People in the World," in *The Concept of the Believers' Church*, ed. James Leo Garrett, Jr. (Scottdale, Pa.: Herald Press, 1969), p. 243.

11. Ibid., p. 244.

12. Ibid.

13. J. C. Wenger, *The Christian Faith* (Scottdale, Pa.: Herald Press, 1971), p. 91.

14. Cited in J. C. Wenger, ibid., p. 93.

15. J. C. Wenger, ed., *The Complete Writings of Menno Simons* (Scottdale, Pa.: Herald Press, 1956), p. 633.

16. Theron F. Schlabach, *Gospel Versus Gospel* (Scottdale, Pa.: Herald Press, 1980), p. 21.

17. Ibid., p. 22.

18. Robert L. Ramseyer, "Mennonite Missions and the Christian Peace Witness," in *Mission and the Peace Witness*, ed. Robert L. Ramseyer (Scottdale, Pa.: Herald Press, 1979), p. 115.

19. See Guy F. Hershberger, ed., *The Recovery of the Anabaptist Vision* (Scottdale, Pa.: Herald Press, 1957), and *Concern No. 18: Radical Reformation Reader* (Scottdale, Pa.: Herald Press, July 1971).

20. Ramseyer, ibid., p. 132.

21. Marlin E. Miller, "The Gospel of Peace," *Mission Focus* VI (September 1977), p. 5.

Chapter 10

1. Paul Peachey, "New Ethical Possibility: The Task of 'Post-Christendom' Ethics," *Interpretation*, 19:1 (Jan. 1965), p. 31. Reprinted in Martin E. Marty and Dean G. Peerman (eds.), *New Theology No. 3* (New York: Macmillan and Co., 1966), pp. 103-17.

2. Kenneth Scott Latourette gave currency to this characterization in his *History of the Expansion of Christianity* when he entitled volumes 4, 5, and 6 "The Great Century" (Grand Rapids: Zondervan, 1941-1944).

3. A critical minority has borne witness against this compromise from early times—a testimony which has continued into the modern period. Cf. Donald F. Durnbaugh's *The Believers' Church* (New York: Macmillan, 1968).

4. Ronald K. Orchard, "The Concept of Christendom and the Christian World Mission: A Question," in Jan Hermelink and Hans Jochen Margull (eds.), *Basileia* (Stuttgart: Evangelische Missionsverlag GMBH, 1959), p. 174.

5. Cf. Daniel Bell, *The Cultural Contradictions of Capitalism* (New York: Basic Books, 1976), pp. 155-58; and *The Winding Passage* (New York: Basic Books, 1980), pp. 334-37.

6. Walter Hobhouse, *The Church and the World in Idea and in History* (London: Macmillan and Co., 1911 [2nd ed.]), p. xix.

7. Ibid., p. 15 and p. 305ff.

8. R. Pierce Beaver, "Missionary Motivation Through Three Centuries," in Jerald C. Brauer (ed.), *Reinterpretation in Church History* (Chicago: University of Chicago Press, 1969), pp. 113-15.

9. Edwin Munsell Bliss, *The Missionary Enterprise* (New York: Fleming H. Revell and Co., 1908), p. 52.

10. Ibid., p. 67.

11. Eugene Stock, *History of the Church Missionary Society* (London: Church Missionary Society, 1899), Vol. 1, pp. 92-104.

12. Kenneth Scott Latourette, "Colonialism and Missions: Progressive Separation," *Journal of Church and State*, VII:3 (Autumn 1965), pp. 330-49.

13. Harold S. Bender, *The Anabaptists and Religious Liberty in the Sixteenth Century* (Philadelphia: Fortress Press, 1970) (Reprinted from *Archiv für Reformationsgeschichte*, 44 [1953], pp. 32-50).

14. M. Searle Bates, *Religious Liberty: An Inquiry* (New York: International Missionary Council, 1945), pp. 148-86.

15. Franklin Hamlin Littell, *From State Church to Pluralism* (New York: Anchor Books, 1962), pp. 1-29.

16. Stiv Jakobsson, *Am I Not a Man and a Brother? British Missions and the Abolition of the Slave Trade and Slavery in West Africa and the West Indies 1786-1838* (Uppsala: Gleerup, 1972).

17. Rufus Anderson, *Foreign Missions: Their Relations and Claims* (New York: Charles Scribners, 1869), p. 111.

18. Henry Venn, Letter to Rufus Anderson, September 4, 1854 (CMS file G/AC/17/2, 1838-53).

19. Henry Venn, "Instructions to Missionaries," *Church Missionary Intelligencer*, N.S. IV:10 (Oct. 1868), pp. 316-20.

20. Henry Venn, "Instructions to Missionaries," *Church Missionary Intelligencer*, XII:8 (Aug. 1861), pp. 183-88.

21. Henry Venn, *The Missionary Life and Labours of Francis Xavier* (London: Longman, Green, Roberts and Green, 1862).

22. Andrew Porter, "Cambridge, Keswick, and late-nineteenth-century Attitudes to Africa," *The Journal of Imperial and Commonwealth History*, V:1 (Oct., 1976), pp. 5-34; and "Evangelical Enthusiasm, Missionary Motivation and West Africa in the Late Nineteenth Century: The Career of G. W. Brooke," *The Journal of Imperial and Commonwealth History*, VI:1 (Oct. 1977), pp. 23-46.

23. E. A. Ayandele, *The Missionary Impact on Modern Nigeria, 1842-1914* (London: Longmans, 1966), p. 180.

24. Rufus Anderson, op. cit., p. 95f.

25. Ibid., p. 105.

26. John Robert Seeley, *The Expansion of England*, reprinted (Chicago: The University of Chicago Press, 1971). Introduction by John Gross. P. xxvi. Seeley was the product of a staunch Anglican Evangelical family. His father, a publisher, was a close friend of Lord Shaftesbury and Henry Venn. Like many other second and third generation Evangelicals, he had increasing intellectual difficulties with Evangelicalism and ultimately moved to the Broad Church position.

27. Alfred Barry, *The Ecclesiastical Expansion of England in the Growth of the Anglican Communion* (London: Macmillan and Co., 1895).

28. Albert J. Beveridge, "For the Greater Republic, Not for Imperialism," in Winthrop S. Hudson (ed.), *Nationalism and Religion in America* (New York: Harper and Row, 1970), p. 118.

29. A. T. Pierson, "Christian Missions as the Enterprise of the Church," *Missionary Review of the World*, N.S., II:1 (Jan. 1889), pp. 5-14. The foreign missions movement must be situated in the history of the church in the United States. Cf. Robert T. Handy, *A Christian America: Protestant Hopes and Historical Realities* (New York: Oxford University Press, 1971), especially chapter 5, "The Christian Conquest of the World (1890-1920)," pp. 117-54.

30. Robert E. Speer, *Missionary Principles and Practice* (New York: Fleming H. Re-

vell and Co., 1902), p. 415.

31. Robert E. Speer, *Christianity and the Nations* (New York: Fleming H. Revell and Co., 1910), p. 233.

32. Committee on the War and the Religious Outlook, *The Missionary Outlook in the Light of the War* (New York: Association Press, 1920), p. xv.

33. Ibid., p. xviii.

34. Ibid., p. 7.

35. Walter Marshall Horton, "Missionary Strategy Yesterday and Tomorrow," in William K. Anderson (ed.), *Christian World Mission* (Nashville: Commission on Ministerial Training, 1946), p. 177.

36. Cf. Harold W. Turner, "Religious Movements in Primal (or Tribal) Societies," *Mission Focus*, 9:3 (Sept. 1981), pp. 45-55; and Andrew F. Walls, "The Anabaptists of Africa? The Challenge of the African Independent Churches," *Occasional Bulletin of Missionary Research*, 3:2 (April 1979), pp. 48-51.

37. Hendrikus Berkhof, *The Christian Faith. An Introduction to the Study of the Faith* (Grand Rapids: Eerdmans, 1979), pp. 410-22.

38. Michael Webster, "Simeon's Doctrine of the Church," in Michael Hennell and Arthur Pollard (eds.), *Charles Simeon (1759-1836)* (London: SPCK, 1959), pp. 128f.

39. Ruth Rouse and Stephen Charles Neill (eds.), *A History of the Ecumenical Movement 1517-1948* (London: SPCK, 1967), p. 320, fn.

40. J. Edwin Orr, *The Second Evangelical Awakening in Britain* (London: Marshall, Morgan & Scott, 1949).

41. Stephen Neill, "The Church," in Stephen Neill, Gerald H. Anderson, and John Goodwin (eds.), *Concise Dictionary of the Christian World Mission* (London: Lutterworth Press, 1970), p.109.

42. Relatively little has been written on the problem of war and Christian mission. Cf. R. Pierce Beaver, *Envoys of Peace: The Peace Witness in Christian World Mission* (Grand Rapids: Eerdmans, 1964), chaps. 3-6; and, Charles W. Iglehart, "Modern War and the Christian Mission," in Rufus M. Jones (ed.), *The Church, the Gospel and War* (New York: Harper and Brothers, 1948), pp. 118-51.

Chapter 11

1. In what follows I am indebted to John H. Yoder, "Anabaptist Vision and Mennonite Reality," A. J. Klassen (ed.), *Consultation on Anabaptist-Mennonite Theology* (Fresno: Council of Mennonite Seminaries, 1970).

Chapter 13

1. Published as "The Anabaptist Theology of Mission" in *Mennonite Quarterly Review* (hereafter referred to as *MQR*) 41:1 (1947), pp. 5-17. Also chapter 1 of this book.

2. Franklin Hamlin Littell, *The Origins of Sectarian Protestantism. A Study of the Anabaptist View of the Church* (New York: Macmillan, rev. 1964). Originally published as *The Anabaptist View of the Church: An Introduction to Sectarian Protestantism* (Hartford ?: American Society of Church History, 1952).

3. George H. Williams, *The Radical Reformation* (Philadelphia: Westminster, 1962).

4. J. M. Stayer, *Anabaptists and the Sword* (Lawrence, Kan.: Coronado, 1972).

5. Cf. R. Pierce Beaver, "The apostolate of the church," in Gerald H. Anderson (ed.) *The Theology of the Christian Mission* (Nashville: Abingdon, 1961), p. 263f.

6. See John H. Yoder, "Reformation and Missions: a Literature Review," *Occasional Bulletin from the Missionary Research Library* 22:6 (June 1971). See also chapter 3 in this book.

7. "Proposal for an Anabaptist theology of mission," mimeographed paper of January 14, 1974.

8. C. J. Dyck, "Early Anabaptist *Sendungbewusstsein*," unpublished paper for a church history course at University of Chicago, 1957.

9. Cf. Andre Seumois, "The Evolution of Mission Theology among Roman Catholics" in Anderson, op. cit., p. 126.

10. See *Ad Gentes*, "Decree on the Missionary Activity of the Church," Walter M. Abbot (ed.), *The Documents of Vatican II* (New York: Guild Press, 1966), p. 589 (my emphasis).

11. See Lesslie Newbigin, *One Body, One Gospel, One World: The Christian Mission Today* (London: International Missionary Council, 1958), p. 29.

12. See William Richey Hogg, "The Rise of Protestant Missionary Concern, 1517-1914," in Anderson, op. cit., pp. 101, 109.

13. See Harry R. Boer, *Pentecost and Missions* (Grand Rapids: Eerdmans, 1964), p. 47.

14. On this, see my own little pamphlet, *His Spirit First* (Scottdale, Pa.: Herald Press, 1972).

15. Cf. Karl Barth, "An exegetical study of Matthew 28:16-20," in Anderson, op. cit., pp. 55-71.

16. See J. M. Stayer, op. cit.

17. From Leo Steinberg, "Michelangelo's 'Last Judgement' as Merciful Heresy," *Art in America* 63:6 (1975), p. 49.

18. Cf. Littell, 1964, pp. 109-113.

19. Wolfgang Schäufele, "The Missionary Vision and Activity of the Anabaptist Laity," *MQR* 36:2 (1962), p. 101. See also chapter 5 in this book.

20. Ibid., p. 208.

21. Ibid., p. 113.

22. Karl Barth, op. cit., p. 63.

23. See No. 42a, Leonhard von Muralt and Walter Schmid (eds.) *Zürich. Quellen zur Geschichte des Täufer in der Schweiz, I* (Zürich, 1952), p. 49.

24. Ibid., no. 29, p. 39.

25. Cited by Littell, 1964, p. 121 (note 60).

26. It is thus characterized strangely by Ekkehard Krajewski in "The Theology of Felix Manz," *MQR* 36:1 (1962), p. 85.

27. Fritz Blanke, *Brüder in Christo*, (Zürich, 1955). English translation by Joseph Nordenhaug (Scottdale, Pa.: Herald Press, 1961).

28. See W. Wiswedel, *Bilder und Führergestalten aus dem Täufertum II* (Kassel, 1930).

29. See Lydia Müller, *Glaubenzeugnisse ober Deutscher Taufgesinnten I* (Leipzig, 1938), pp. 67, 56.

30. Christian Hege, quoted by H. S. Bender in *Mennonite Encyclopedia III* (Scottdale, Pa.: Herald Press, 1957), p. 531.

31. See Walter Klaassen, "The Nature of the Anabaptist Protest," *MQR* 45:4 (1971). For Klaassen, the Anabaptists "raised questions about basic assumptions of European religion and culture."

32. The coins minted by the Münsterite kingdom had struck around their diameter the first letters of the Latin words in the text of the Great Commission.

33. C. J. Dyck, "Anabaptism and the Social Order," Gerald C. Brauer (ed.) *The Impact of the Church upon its Culture* (Chicago: University of Chicago Press, 1968).

34. Ernst Bloch, *Thomas Müntzer, Theologian of Revolution*, 1921.

35. Cited by George H. Williams, op. cit., p. 125.

36. See A. D. Nock, *Conversion* . . . (Oxford: Clarendon Press, 1933).

37. J. Lawrence Burkholder, "The Anabaptist Vision of Discipleship," in Guy Hershberger (ed.) *The Recovery of the Anabaptist Vision* (Scottdale, Pa.: Herald Press, 1957), p. 138.

38. Cf. John H. Yoder, "Die Sendung als Wesen der Gemeinde," *Täufertum und Reformation in der Schweiz* (Weierhof, 1962), pp. 178ff.

39. See Kenneth S. Latourette, *A History of the Expansion of Christianity: The Great Century in Europe and the United States of America A.D. 1800-A.D. 1914*, Vol. IV, (Grand Rapids: Zondervan, 1941), particularly, "The Process by which Christianity Spread," pp. 47-52.

40. Even H. S. Bender seemed to recognize the validity of this judgment which he felt was overplayed by the Marxist-socialist theoreticians. "Perhaps H. Richard Niebuhr is right in asserting in his book, *The Social Sources of Denominationalism*, that the Anabaptist movement was a movement of the socially and economically oppressed lower classes, but it is difficult to apply this theory to the founder of the movement." See "Conrad Grebel," *Mennonite Encyclopedia II* (Scottdale, Pa.: Herald Press, 1956), p. 567. Most of the class-theory protagonists recognize, of course, that usually the leadership for the lower classes does not come from those classes.

41. See Franklin Hamlin Littell, *From State Church to Pluralism: a Protestant Interpretation of Religion in American History* (Garden City, N.Y.: Anchor Books, 1962).

42. James Leo Garrett, Jr. (ed.), *The Concept of the Believers' Church* (Scottdale, Pa.: Herald Press, 1969).

43. Donald F. Durnbaugh, *The Believers' Church* (New York: Macmillan, 1968).

44. Garrett, op. cit., p. 5.

45. Ibid., p. 242.

46. Ibid., p. 318.

47. Ibid., p. 320.

48. See A. W. Eister, "Toward a radical criticism of church-sect typologyzing," *Journal for the Scientific Study of Religion* 6:2 (1967), pp. 85-90.

49. Henri Desroche, *Dieux d'Hommes* (Paris: Mouton, 1969), pp. 1-32; this was later expanded into his *Sociologie de l'Espérance* (Calmann-Lévy, 1973). Desroche defines messianism following Hans Kohn as "essentially the religious belief in the coming of a redeemer who will put an end to the present order of things either universally or for a particular group and will install a new order made of justice and happiness" ("Messianism," *Encyclopedia of Social Sciences* Vol. 9, [New York: Macmillan, 1933]).

50. Leonard Verduin, *The Reformers and their Stepchildren* (Grand Rapids: Eerdmans, 1964).

51. See John H. Yoder, "A People in the World: A theological Interpretation," Garrett, op. cit., pp. 250ff.

52. Ibid., p. 254.

53. John H. Yoder, *The Politics of Jesus* (Grand Rapids: Eerdmans, 1972).

54. Garrett, op. cit., p. 29.

55. Gottfried Oosterwal, *Modern Messianic Movements as a Theological and Missionary Challenge* (Elkhart, Ind.: Institute of Mennonite Studies, 1973).

56. Cf. M. M. Thomas, "Two kinds of messianism," *Ecumenical Review* 26:4 (1974). The statement is all the more remarkable because of the author's own roots in the sacral culture of India. In this connection, his concluding word should also be heeded. In writing of the spirituality of the conquering messiah, the superman who repudiates the suffering Messiah, which leads inevitably to aggressiveness, misuse of earth's natural resources, abuse of power, etc., Thomas concludes: "Modern History, with the inhumanities of Imperialism, Racism, Fascism, Stalinism, and Vietnam provides sufficient proof of this. Many moderns are therefore beginning to view the messianic consciousness itself as the source of dehumanization in the modern world, and to advocate a return of mankind to the spiritual

tranquility of some form of nature religion, or the unitive spiritual vision of the primal, monistic, and gnostic religions. This, however, would mean the repudiation of the whole experiment of modern history, of the search of men and women for adulthood and maturity in freedom; it would even halt the self-awakening of the two thirds world of Africa and Asia and the significant renaissance of their cultures and their religions taking place through the impact of modernity. Mankind can avoid the two alternatives, self-destruction in freedom and survival through a return to the womb of unfreedom, only through the messianism of the Suffering Servant."

Scripture Index

251

General Index

Persecution: Anabaptist reaction to,
59; avoidance of, 152; bearing of,
85; and church-world dualism, 31;
cost of, 20; crippler of missionary
impulse, 21, 195; driven by, 20;
Hutterian understanding of, 99,
104, 105, 115; inevitability of, 65,
184; in Moravia, 84-85; pressure of,
71, 81; result of, 86, 131; seeking
relief from, 55; steadfastness in, 23;
in Switzerland, 124; witness during,
57-58, 210
Philips, Dirk, 95, 121, 214; on
conversion, 30-31; on suffering, 33
Philips, Obbe, 91, 94-95, 121
Pietism, 40, 44, 46, 47-48, 87, 116, 158,
166, 236n.24; ecclesiology of, 174
Pilgrims, preaching, 55
Polish Brethren, 110
Politics, relationship to missions, 171
Post-Christian era, 194
Power, Anabaptist vision as antithesis
to domination by, 198
Powerlessness: willingness of believers
to accept, 33-34, 35, 38
Prayer, the need for, 156
Preaching the gospel, called to, 120
Preservation, concern for, 179-81
Priesthood of all believers: Anabaptist
principle of, 60, 85, 87; Luther's
principle of, 60, 71
Primitivism, Anabaptist emphasis on, 24
Proclamation: development of theory
and practice of, 48; oral, 73
Property, rejection of, as an end in
itself, 38-39
Prosperity, crippler of missionary
impulse, 21
Protestantism, diversity within, 208
Provincialism, 46-47
Psychology, use of, 145
Punishment, divine, 107

Quakers, 126, 133
"Quiet in the land," 152
Quietism, Anabaptism and, 31

Radical reformers: Anabaptists as,
151; witness of, 164
Reconciliation: calling to, 55; church
as a bridge for, 155; message of, 53,
117; work for, 185-86

Redemption of God, 105
Reformation and missions: believers'
church perspectives of the, 46-50;
Protestant interpretations of the, 40-
46
Regeneration, part of the Anabaptist
understanding of grace, 29
Regensburg, Decree of, 61
Religious liberty: a mark of a free
church, 24, 219; quest for, 164
Repentance: Anabaptist
understanding of, 29-30; calling to,
55, 128, 146; commitment to, 71;
evidence of, 53; hindrance of the
world to allow, 105
Restitution: of the early church, 17;
Party or Church of the, 15, 17, 64;
instead of reformation of the
church, 36
Resurrection, 144
Revivalistic influences, 135
"Right wing" of the Reformation, 24
Romanticism, 152
Roubli, Wilhelm, 66
Rule of Christ, 37

Sacramental signs, scriptural use of, 36
Salvation, 157; Anabaptist
understanding of, 29; the church as
a platform for, 155; Hutterian view
of, 106, 112; of the individual, 174;
message of, 140, 144-45, 155
Sanctification, 71
Sattler, Michael, 93, 239n.6
Schad, Jörg, 56, 66
Schiemer, Leonard, 66; on baptism,
37; on fellowship of believers, 212-13
Schleitheim Confession, 37, 62, 74,
213
Schmidt, Hans, mission vision of, 35
Schnabel, George, on economic
sharing, 34
Schwenckfeld, 224, 232n.32
Scientific rationalism, Anabaptism as a
judgment on, 194
Scientific technology, modern
promotion of, 197
Seclusion, Mennonite, 119-36
Sectarianism, characteristic of a
believers' church, 25
Secularism, post-Reformation term for
the irreligious, 26

Missionary Study Series

Published by Herald Press, Scottdale, Pennsylvania, in association with the Institute of Mennonite Studies, Elkhart, Indiana.

1. *The Challenge of Church Growth.* A symposium edited by Wilbert R. Shenk with contributions also from John H. Yoder, Allan H. Howe, Robert L. Ramseyer, and J. Stanley Friesen (1973).

2. *Modern Messianic Movements, As a Theological and Missionary Challenge* by Gottfried Oosterwal (1973).

3. *From Kuku Hill: Among Indigenous Churches in West Africa* by Edwin and Irene Weaver (1975).

4. *Bibliography of Henry Venn's Printed Writings with Index* by Wilbert R. Shenk (1975).

5. *Christian Mission and Social Justice* by Samuel Escobar and John Driver (1978).

6. *A Spirituality of the Road* by David J. Bosch (1979).

7. *Mission and the Peace Witness: The Gospel and Christian Discipleship.* A symposium edited by Robert L. Ramseyer with contributions also from James E. Metzler, Marlin E. Miller, Richard Showalter, Ronald J. Sider, Sjouke Voolstra, and John H. Yoder (1979).

8. *Letters Concerning the Spread of the Gospel in the Heathen World* by Samuel S. Haury (1981).

9. *Evangelizing Neopagan North America* by Alfred C. Krass (1982).

10. *Anabaptism and Mission* edited by Wilbert R. Shenk (1984) with chapters by Franklin H. Littell, Cornelius J. Dyck, John H. Yoder, Hans Kasdorf, Wolfgang Schäufele, H. W. Meihuizen, Leonard Gross, N. van der Zijpp, José Gallardo, Wilbert R. Shenk, Robert L. Ramseyer, Takashi Yamada, and David A. Shank.

The Missionary Study Series grows out of the Mennonite Missionary Study Fellowship (MMSF) program. The MMSF is an informal fellowship of persons interested in Christian mission, meeting annually for a three-day conference on issues central to their task. It includes missionaries, mission board administrators, theologians, sociologists, and others. It is sponsored by the Institute of Mennonite Studies (IMS), 3003 Benham Avenue, Elkhart, IN 46517. Books in the series may be ordered from Provident Bookstores, 616 Walnut Avenue, Scottdale, PA 15683.